Pvt. Ltd.

Panorama of Developing Countries

Editors
Virendra K. Goswami
&
J.N. Govil

2020

Studium Press (India) Pvt. Ltd.

Panorama of Developing Countries

ISBN: 978-93-85046-60-5

Published by:

Studium Press (India) Pvt. Ltd.
4735/22, 2nd Floor, Prakash Deep Building
(Near Delhi Medical Association)
Ansari Road, Darya Ganj, New Delhi-110 002
Tel.: + 91-11-43240200-15 (15 lines); Fax: 91-11-43240215
E-mail: pubdir@studiumpress.in

Printed at India

About the Editors

Prof. (Dr.) Virendra K. Goswami, Ph.D. (IIT), M.S. (USA), M.Sc; PDF (USA), LL.B 'Visiting Scientist': UNIDO, ICTP, ITALY, WMO, NOAA (NASA), NCAR (USA), UNV, ICAO & AIU, Former Vice Chancellor: Sangam & Sunrise University. Ex. Wing Commander (IAF), Prof. Emeritus & Member: AGU (American Geophysical Union), AMS & IMS. Founder President 'Environment & Peace Foundation (EPF)' & Advocate: Supreme Court of India. Vk_goswami1@rediffmail.com/ +919818731911.

Dr. Virendra Kumar Goswami, Ph.D. Indian Institute of Technology (IIT), Kharagpur, MS from the University of Wisconsin, USA. Post Doctorate Fellow(PDF) at the University of Illinois, Chicago, USA. 'Visiting Scientist' to United Nations Industrial Development Organization (UNIDO), ICTP, Italy. Expert Panelist International Civil Aviation Organization(ICAO), Canada and United Nations. Founder President 'Environment & Peace Foundation (EPF) & Ex. Wing Commander, IAF.

Dr. Virendra Goswami worked at Space Science Engineering Centre, NASA (National Aeronautics & Space Administration)/ NOAA (National Oceanic Atmospheric Administration) at University of Wisconsin, USA. Expert panelist of Association of Indian Universities (AIU), Vice Chancellor: Sangam & Sunrise Universities. Had been, Director General of Management Institutes & Director of Engineering Institutes as well as Vice-President Havells India Ltd. Ph.D & M. Tech Examiner at Centre of Energy

Studies at IIT Delhi. More than 44 years of teaching, research and administrative experience at Home and Abroad.

Presented Papers in the field of Chemical Technology, Atmospheric Sciences, Space Sciences, Satellite Application, Climate Variability & Control of Global Warming & Quality Higher Education at International and National Conferences held in India, USA, UK Latin America, South Africa, Canada and Europe (more than 32 countries of all the Continents). Besides, headed various delegations at National & International Levels.

Special Invitee by the World Meteorological Organization (WMO) of United Nations, Geneva in 2001. Special Invitee in Apr'15 at NPW: NCAR USA. Invited Speaker to the Coupled Data Assimilation Workshop, sponsored by Météo-France, WMO and US: CLIVAR, Toulouse, France October 2016 , IV Family Child Conference, Nigeria in Nov'16, 6th ICHVHE, IIT Kanpur, Feb'17 & got awarded for Human Value Education at RVIT by His Excellency Ram Nayak, Governor, Uttar Pradesh on 05 Jun'17. Invited Speaker at Lomonosov Moscow State University (MSU) during Sep17, Univ. of California, Berkley in Apr'18.

Also, Prof. Emeritus, Member: AGU (American Geophysical Union), AMS & IMS (American & Indian Meteorological Societies), Editor: Studium Publication, USA, Reviewer of US-Journal of Shipping and Ocean Engineering, Editor in Chief: Journal of Advanced Research in Alternative Energy, Environment and Ecology, Reviewer of US-Journal of Shipping and Ocean Engineering, JMEA (J. of Mechanical Engg. & Automation), JGRE (J. of Geological research Engg.) & Advocate: Supreme Court of India.

Chaired Sessions in Int. Natl. Conf. Metering, Brazil-2003, Invitee in Emergency Higher Education Conf. 2005, FEMA, Emmitsburg, MD, USA. Besides, headed various delegations at National & International Levels & Chaired session SSC-2006 (Int. Natl. Conf . on Solid State Chemistry), Pardubice, Czech Republic. Had been to Univ. of Limerick, Ireland in 2008. Presented Research

Paper on Control of Global Warming at ESF Conference, 6-11 Jun'09, Innsbruck, Austria & France 2010. I was invited by Cambridge University, UK to present research paper on Control of Global Warming during 13-17 Dec'10, again by Angila Ruskin Univ. Cambridge in Apr'17 & Boston Univ. Jun'2018.

I was invited in the Int. Natl. Conf. on Higher Education; held at Johannesburg (South Africa, during 3-4 May'13. Also, Chaired a Session in the 4th National Conf. on Climate Change held in New Delhi, on 18 Jun'15 & Solar Energy, 2017, under the aegis of ASSOCHAM & Dept. of Sc. & Technology (DST), Govt. of India. Invited Speakerat' AISSQ-15, Science & Spirituality at IIT Kharagpur 01 Nov'15 & Special Guest Speaker at SAARC: GWP-South Asia, New Delhi on 16 Jan'2015.

Dr. J.N. Govil *(b. 1945)*: Obtained his Master's and Doctorate degrees from Agra University, Agra, India. In his career span of 41+ years research experience at the Indian Agricultural Research Institute, New Delhi, Dr. Govil has been involved in the breeding of cross-pollinated, often cross-pollinated, and self-pollinated crops. His research was mainly focused on breeding for better quality, disease resistance, and for higher productivity in *Pennisetum, Sorghum,* maize, chickpea, and pigeonpea. During these years at IARI, he has released nine varieties of early pigeonpea in arhar-wheat rotation. Dr. Govil has been well exposed to the international scientific community through various programmes at UK, Denmark and Thailand. He also participated in various international seminars and conferences. Dr. Govil is credited with more than ninety research papers in various journals of national and international repute in various aspects of genetics, crop breeding, and topics on general agriculture. He has also guided more than a dozen post-graduate students. Dr. Govil is recipient of no. of Awards and Honor presented by ICAR and Agricultural Societies. He has written and edited a number of books on Medicinal Plants and other books with international authors. A new series **"Recent Progress in Medicinal Plants"** has been published by *Studium Press, LLC, USA* in 49 volumes under Dr. Govil's Chief Editorship. Dr. Govil has been the main resource person as Executive Editor in Execution, Co-ordination and Completion of Projects in bringing 12 Vols Set each on ***Nanotechnology, Biotechnology, Energy Science and Technology,*** and ***Environmental Science and Engineering***. Simultaneously, Dr. Govil has brought four volumes set of Chemical Technology Series comprising 2 vols each on ***Advances in Fertilizer Technology*** as well as on ***Petroleum Engineering*** under the capacity of Acquisition Editor of the Series. Besides, he has been Author/Editor of three Books in Social Sciences namely **Innovation & Education**, **Panorama of Developing Countries** and **Anti-ageing**. Dr. Govil retired from ICAR service during the year 2007. Presently, he is working as Publishing Director and Managing Editor with Studium Press LLC, USA (Camped at New Delhi, India) and has brought out nearly 340 scientific books publication during last eleven years. E-mail: jngovil@gmail.com; jngovil@hotmail.com

Preface

The omnipotent, omniscience, the great Almighty created this beautiful 'Cosmic Garden' of nature with full of energy comprising His the best creation: human embedded with humanity. The best creation(Children) toiled hard and acronym 'Global Panorama' of the 6- Inhabited Continents *viz. Africa, Asia, Europe, North & South America & Oceania (Australia & New Zealand)* consisting 126-Developing Countries out of total 232-Countries of with present population of more than 7.5 billion people. Based on Low & High Human Development Index (HDI) Statistics and the other criteria, it may be categorized into, 'Panorama of Developing Countries' & 'Panorama of Developed Countries' symbolizing as the 'Blooming Flowers' & 'Bloomed Flowers' respectively of the acronym 'Cosmic Garden'.

The present 'Panorama of Developing Countries' is a blooming flowery panorama of different colors of Human Development Index (HDI); picked up from the 'Cosmic Garden' by the different Gardeners of different blooming geographical regions of six pavilions *viz.* India, Bangladesh, Ethiopia, Malaysia, China & Russia exhibiting the beautiful innovative Indian flowers of Positive Child Parenting, Memorial Stones, Cultural Nationalism, District Planning, 'Panchayati Raj' Institutions, Sustainable Housing & Urban Development.

The next pavilion of Bangladesh exhibits fragrance of Socio-economic Status of Slum Dwellers, Human Rights, Acid Crime and Victimization followed by the Ethiopian flavor of Women and Ethnic Based Conflicts.

Table of Contents

1

Innovative Techniques of Positive Child Parenting in Global Perspective

PROF. (DR.) VIRENDRA GOSWAMI[1*]

ABSTRACT

The International Convention on the Rights of the Child (CRC) defines a "Child" as a person below the age of 18. In humans, a Parent is the caretaker of a child comprising mother & father. The efforts have been made to develop innovative techniques of child parenting with its Global perspective in order to increase the level of protection for all children under 18 regardless of their race, religion, or abilities. By positive parenting, it aims to create nurturing environment for children with the full realization of their rights and capabilities. Next, innovative technologies of positive parenting have been developed in adherence to the CRC's- 2030 Agenda for sustainable development, i.e. "all people, irrespective of sex, age, race, ethnicity, and persons with disabilities, migrants, indigenous peoples, children and youth, especially those in vulnerable situations, should have access to life-long learning opportunities that help them to acquire the knowledge and skills needed to exploit opportunities and to participate fully in

[1] Founder President, Environment & Peace Foundation (EPF) & Former Vice Chancellor, Sangam University & Sunrise University

**Corresponding author:* E-mail: vk_goswami1@rediffmail.com

society." Keeping in view the above; an innovative spectra of Positive Child Parenting (PCP) has been devised comprising of child parenting, morphology of Positive Child Parenting & demographic factors in Global perspective viz. Indian Perspective, Western Perspective (European & American), Asian Perspective & African Perspective. Also, Hub-Spoke and Parenting-Hint based Positive Child Parenting (PCP) Models have been developed. Lastly, the Scope of Positive Child Parenting (PCP) in prevention of children drug abuse & criminal activity involving juvenile inmates has been discussed.

***Key words*:** Hub-Spoke, Parenting-Hint, Positive Child Parenting (PCP), Models, Spectra, Morphology, Environment, Peace, VG (Virendra Goswami).

---

1. INTRODUCTION

The International Convention on the Rights of the Child (CRC) [1] defines a "Child" as a person below the age of 18. In humans, a Parent is the caretaker of a child comprising mother & father. When God was creating this universe and when the turn came to create a human; He called the child and told him to go to the Earth Planet and live there. The child was also told that for his survival; he'll be given all the amenities and two people who shall give him a life first followed by nurturing, protecting, keeping him healthy and guiding all the time. These two people He acronym Mother & Father or simply Parents. Child Parenting is a tact to nurture, secure, care & teach the child the traits needed for his all round development to make him self- reliant, disciplined and an ideal human being. Parents are the first & persistent Teachers. Therefore, Parents ought to be embedded with 5 Cs:

- ***Character***
- ***Conviction***
- ***Courage***
- ***Commitment***
- ***Courtesy***

In my view, Parenting, is the sum of Nurturing (N), Security (S), Teaching (T) & Health (H). Mathematically,

$$P = (N+S+T+H) \quad \ldots \text{Eqn. (1)}$$

i.e. 'VG: Parenting Equation'

As per the Indian mythology parents are worshipped as Gods and children are taught to respect Mother, Father & Teacher by reciting the couplets "Matra Deva Bhav, Pitra Deva Bhav & Gurudevo Bhav" meaning that "Be devotee to Mother, Be devotee to Father & Be devotee to Teacher". In most of the Indian families, people first in the morning touch the feet of their parents as a salutation to their Parenting. The children are taught by the Parents by reciting verses out of the epic 'Ramayana' wherein; God Rama touches first the feet of His Mother, Father & Teacher to pay respect for their parenting & teachings.

1. Convention on the Rights of the Child, article 3.

2. STAGES OF CHILD'S LIFE

From the time of birth child till the age of a teens and attaining maturity; the child passes gradually through many stages with different spectra of activities comprising anatomical cum biological changes *e.g*. Infant, Toddler, Pre- Schoolar, Younghood & Teens.

Stages of child's life are as below:

Infant: 0-1 Year	Toddlers: 1-2 Years
Senior Toddlers: 2-3 Years	Pre-Schoolars: 3-5 Years
Middle Childhood: 6-8 Years	Upper Middle Childhood: 9-11 Years
Young Teens: 12-14 Years	Teenagers: 15-17 Years

STAGES OF CHILD'S LIFE

INFANT (0-1)

TODDLERS (1-2)

Toddlers (2-3)

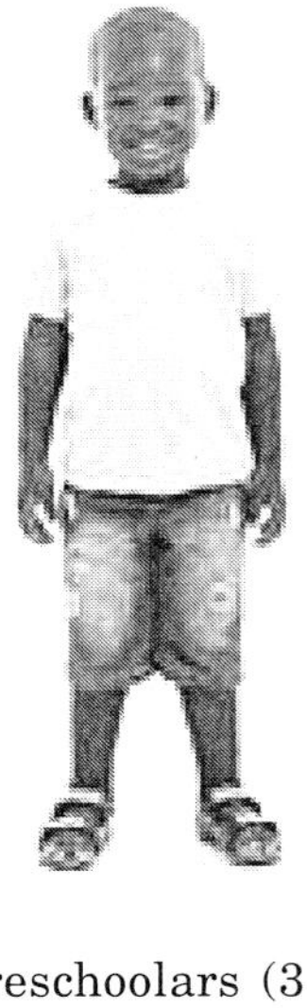

Preschoolars (3-5)

Middle Childhood (6-8)

Middle Childhood (9-11)

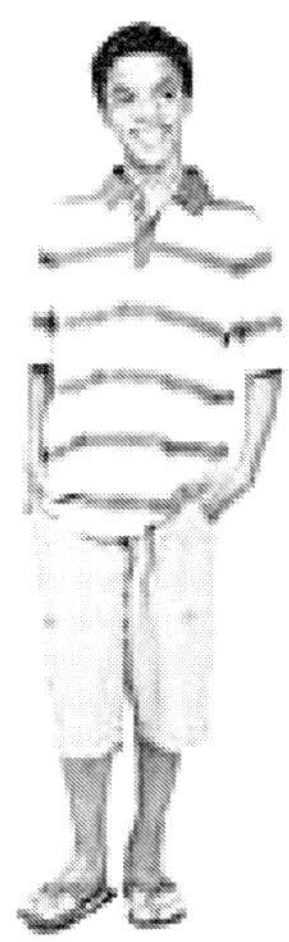

Young Teens (12-14)

Teenagers (15-17)

Innovation

@ ***Innovation*:** means (Lat. innovare: "to change") *i.e.* doing something different or doing in different ways. Innovation refers to the use of a better and, as a result, novel idea or method. (Innovation) VG is directly proportional to (Curiosity)

3. POSITIVE CHILD PARENTING (PCP) & POSITIVE PARENTS (PP)

In my view, Positive Child Parenting (PCP) can be simply defined as the parenting of child with positivity (p). The parents ought to have totally positive attitude while nurturing[2], securing & teaching their children for their bright future. They must be optimistic all the time and bring their children up with Smile & Love (L). No doubt I would like to acronym 'Parenting With Love' is a 'Positive Parenting'. When you love your child, you get rid of automatically from three viruses *viz.* Anxiety, Anguish & Anger (3A's). These are the natural barriers to the Positive Child Parenting[3] (PCP) as they all lead to negativity followed by the destruction. If, one does not control these three A's then it leads to loss of wisdom leading to loss of peace of.

PCP has to be embedded with Forgiveness (F). As a Positive Parent (PP); you cannot be harsh to your children. Love (L) them, meet all their demands with best of your capability. Nurture them well, give them protection, Security (S) of all kind (Health & Wealth) but, be strict Disciplinarian (D) and friendly while teaching them to become a leading professional and human being of a strong character embedded with Values (V) & respect for Nature's free gifts (*i.e.* water, air, time) by providing them good Environment of Peace & Positivity (Ep).

i.e. Positive Child Parenting is directly proportional to Love,

Positive Child Parenting is directly proportional to Forgiveness,

Positive Child Parenting is directly proportional to Security (Health & Wealth)

Positive Child Parenting is directly proportional to Values (V)

---

[2] 'The Whole-Brain Child': 12 Revolutionary Strategies to Nurture Your Child's Developing Mind, Daniel J. Siegel, Tina Payne Bryson

[3] Simplicity Parenting: Using the Extraordinary Power of Less to Raise Calmer, Happier, and More Secure Kids by Kim John Payne.

Positive Child Parenting is directly proportional to Discipline

Positive Child Parenting is inversely proportional to Anxiety, Anguish & Anger (3A's)

Mathematically,

PCP = K. (LFSVD/3A's) ....Eqn. (2)

i.e. 'VG: Positive Child Parenting Equation'

Where, K ('Karma') *i.e.* Action is Constant.

This Eqn. (2) holds when the Positive Peaceful Environment (Ep) prevails. Remember 'Charity begins at home' ; that as Parents the way you cuddle, hold, and play with your child, in the same manner the child is going to interact with other children. In PCP, one has to be a role model to their children and one has to perform *i.e.* to do 'Karma' (Act/Action).

Examples of Positive Child Parenting

Well, I was not lucky to have a full Parental love as I lost my father at the age of one during Indo-Pak partition but, lucky to have a great Goddess teacher mother whose penances, struggles amalgamated with love and discipline, always led me to the righteous path with total realization that whole world is one family of single God ('Vasudev Kutmbhkam'). Being only son, I had to be involved in the household jobs apart from studying.

I was 9 years young and was asked to buy wheat from the Government Ration shop, standing in the long queue along with other customers. By the time my turn comes, I find my purse missing as somebody pick pocketed me. Without buying the wheat I reached home quite scared of mother's scolding. Surprised, she did not scold me on losing the money but, definitely took me on task that how did I become so careless that somebody got smarter to take away my wallet without my knowledge. With love and positivity, she taught me that:

"Never be careless, be hard & smart worker that you may not get cheated by anybody but, not be that smart ever that you start teaching others". Please give "Values" (V) to your children & be positive child parent. Infuse good habits into them, emphasize on good character & inculcate watch through the recitation of the few couplets* and quotes** as they ever remain in memory whatever a child is taught during childhood through the art of PCP. It's an old saying that:

"Wealth is loss, nothing is lost,

Health is lost, something is lost,

When character (ethics, action etc.) is lost,

Everything is lost."

Also, as a Positive Parent (PP), always infuse into your child this very Urdu couplet which says:

"O my child, remember the time of your birth,

When all were smiling and you only were crying,

You must live your life in such a way,

That at the time of your death

You remain smiling and all others cry for you"

As a positive parents you have to remember that the Childhood Memory is very strong. Whatever, you teach the child and the way you train them, they always remember throughout their life. When child is growing you have to decide the Tact, Technology of Teaching/Training to the child by deciding your role commensurate with the Age/Stage of Child's Life stated above. In other words the PCP (Positive Child Parenting) role is highly dependent on the Age (Stage) of your child. PCP is dependent on the Age/Stage of Child's Life. Mathematically,

$$PCP = f(AGE) \qquad \text{...... Eqn. (3)}$$

VG: Hypothesis of Positive Child Parenting.

PCP is a function of Child's Age

Substituting from Eqn. (1) into Eqn. (3), we get under Ep

$$P = (N+S+T+H) = f(AGE) \quad \text{... Eqn. (4)}$$

i.e. VG: Functional Hypothesis of Positive Child Parenting

It means that under the peaceful positive environment, all the three Positive constituents *viz.* Nurturing, Security & Teaching/Teaching/Tact change with the AGE or Stage of Child's Life. You can not adopt the same technology of all these Skills/Tact to all the children of different Age. It would differ for Infant-Toddler-Pre-Schoolers-Middle Young-Teenagers; resulting the change in Morphology of Positive Child Parenting (PCP) and hence, computing the VG: PCP-Eqn. for the each and every aforesaid stage of child Life is essential.

Positive Parents (PP) always teach 'Success Mantra (formula) to their child by adopting the different role of a Teacher as per the Age/Stage of Life of their children.

'Success Mantra' *i.e.* the elements of success are:

- WATCH (*i.e.* Watch your: Words, Action, Thought, Character & Health)
- Clear purpose
- Team attribute
- Strong relationships
- Communication
- Trust & Confidence
- Accountability. Leadership

Einstein Success Equation: $S = X+Y+Z$

S - Success, X - Think (Dream), Y - Hardwork & Z - Rest (Quiet)

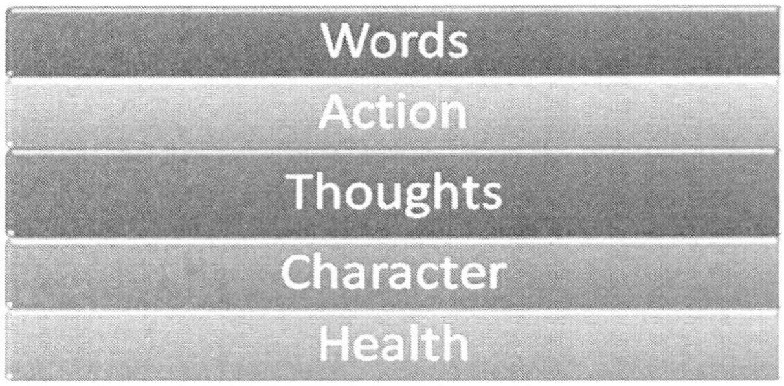

I strongly feel that Positive Child Parenting (PCP) is nothing but, WATCH *i.e.* inculcating the WATCH or keeping WATCH on child & teaching WATCH (*i.e.* Watch your: Words, Action, Thought, Character & Health.

4. MORPHOLOGY OF POSITIVE CHILD PARENTING (PCP) & SPECTRA OF POSITIVE CHILD PARENTING (PCP)

Further, from the above discussion, the other mathematical analogies can be derived to understand the morphology of Positive Child Parenting. Let us devise the Carriers (Cr) & Barriers (Br) of Positive Child Parenting to understand its morphology. The Carriers (Cr) are the elements to carry the vehicle of the Positive Child Parenting and the Barriers (Br) are the so called obstructions on the road of the Positive Child Parenting. Obviously, the Carriers are directly proportional and Barriers are inversely proportional to the Positive Child Parenting (PCP). Mathematically, the PCP-Carriers (Cr) & Barriers (Br) may be defined

PCP-Carriers (Cr)

PCP is Directly Proportional to Love (L) .... (a) Eqn.

PCP is Directly Proportional to Forgiveness (F)............. (b) Eqn.

PCP is Directly Proportional to Discipline (D) ....(c) Eqn.

PCP is Directly Proportional to Character (C)................. (d) Eqn.

PCP is Directly Proportional to Teaching (T) .... (e) Eqn.

PCP is Directly Proportional to Belief (B)/Trust .... (f) Eqn.

PCP is Directly Proportional to WATCH (W) .... (g) Eqn.

PCP-Barriers (Br)

PCP is Inversely Proportional to Negativity (N) .... (h) Eqn.

PCP is Inversely Proportional to 3A (Anxiety, Anguish, Anger) .... (i) Eqn.

PCP is Inversely Proportional to Harshness/ Rudeness (R) .... (j) Eqn.

From the above traits it can be categorized that the directly proportional trades (a) to (g) as CARRIERS (Cr) & Inversely Proportional traits (j) to (j) as BARRIERS (Br) of the PCP.

Adding the above (a) to (j) Eqns.

PCP is Proportional to (LFD.CTBW/NAAAR)

$$PCP = K.(LFD.CTBW/ NAAAR) \quad \ldots Eqn. (5)$$

Under Environment of Peace (Ep) & where, K ('Karma' *i.e.* Action) is Constant.

i.e. VG; Positive Child Parenting Guide Equation

In terms of Carriers (Cr) & Barriers (Br), the Eqn. (5) can be written as:

$$PCP = K (Cr/ Br) \quad \ldots Eqn. (6), under (Ep)$$

i.e. VG; Positive Child Parenting Guide Equation

Also, from the above Eqn. (6), its evident that:

PCP is Directly Proportional to magnitude or number of Carriers (Crs) & PCP is Inversely Proportional to magnitude or number of Barriers (Brs) *i.e.* Under Ep, PCP = K (Crs) ....Eqn. (6) a. & PCP=K / (Brs) ....Eqn. (6) b.

Adding Eqns. (6) a & (6) b; we may get the VG: Eqn. for innovative Spectra of Positive Child Parenting (PCP).

PCP = K (Crs/Brs) .... (7) Eqn.

i.e. VG: Eqn. for Positive Child Parenting (PCP) Spectra.

VG: Eqn (7) interprets the Positive Child Parenting (PCP) Spectra that the PCP shall depend how strong are (Cr) than (Br). Higher the (Cr) better is the PCP & Lesser the (Br) would enhance PCP. This Eqn. would also guide to parents to achieve PCP, provided 'Karma' *i.e.* efforts (Acts) are done (K is Constant) and Peace prevails at home.

Where, (Ep) is Conditional Constant (Cc) & K means ACTION/ ACT ('Karma')/Duty is a Constant *i.e.* Without working hard or without Action/Act ('Karma') /Duty, the Positive Child Parenting (PCP) cannot be achieved.

The importance of Action/Duty has been chanted by Lord Krishna (an incarnation of God) in the holy book 'The Geeta' (Essence of all the Vedas & Epics)[4] that:

"Its better to do your Duty than
to remain without doing anything
Action is important because we
Cannot even maintain our
Own body without it."

—The Geeta (Chap. 3.8)

The same has been narrated by our Late President of India, Dr. A.P.J. Kalam

[4] 'The Geeta' (Essence of all the Vedas & Epics), Chap 3

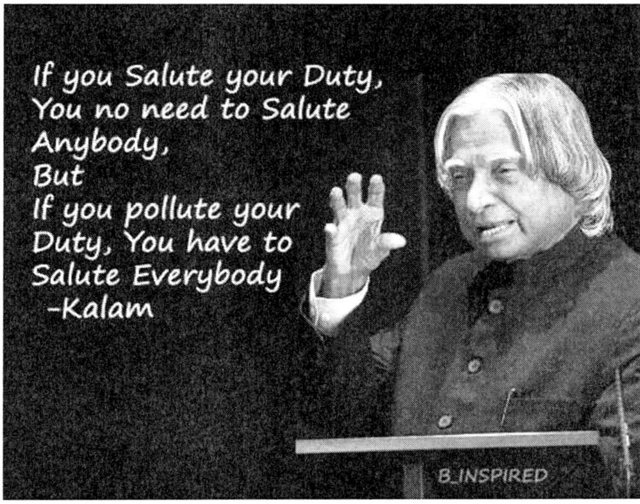

Hence, my advice to the Parents for PCP is: Do Your DUTY (ACTION) honestly, sincerely, Smilingly with priority as its leads to PEACE (MENTAL).

Next, its evident from the above VG-PCP Eqn. (6); that under peaceful Environment (Ep) & unquestioned Belief (B)/Trust in parents by the child & *vice-versa*. Positive Child Parenting increases if, the parents give more and more love to children, forgive their mistakes but, remain strict disciplinarian in handling the child, build up their good character, give them good training/ teaching & keep close watch on their WATCH *i.e.* their Words (Language/Good Communication), Actions, Thoughts (positive), Character & last but, not least is their Health.

On the other hand, Positive Child Parenting decreases due to negativity & rudeness of parents. More and more you are negative and harsh to your children the lesser is your parenting.

Next, PCP decreases with 3A *i.e.* moment you step into unwarranted Anxiety, become Anguish and loose temper (Angry), you loose parental love and regard from the child and your emotional bond between parents & child gets highly affected (weakens).

5. COMPUTATION OF CHILD 'S ENVIRONMENT PEACE EQUATION

For the Positive Child Parenting (PCP), it has been observed in the aforesaid discussion that it needs the conditional Constant of (Ep) *i.e.* Environment of peace and positivity or simply Environment of peace (Ep). How to develop such an environment wherein, the positive parenting be given to the children. In order to develop Ep, the below mathematical approach has been made by developing the Child's Environment Peace (CEp) Equation.

Child's Peace (P) is Inversely Proportional to
Entropy (Disorderliness) *i.e.* E ... (8) Eqn.

Child's Peace (P) is directly proportional
to Satisfaction (S) ... (9) Eqn.

Child's Peace (P) is directly
proportional to Positivity (P) ...(10) Eqn.

Adding the (8-10) Eqns., Child's Environment Peace (CEp) Equation can be deduced as:

$$(CEp) = A\,(SP/E) \qquad \text{.... (11) Eqn}$$

i.e. VG: Child Environment Peace Equation.

It means that lesser the Entropy (Disorderliness) in the environment, more healthier and Peaceful is the environment with increased orderliness.

$$\text{Or, } (CEp) = A.SP\,E^{-1} \qquad \text{... (12) Eqn.}$$

i.e. VG: Child Environment Peace Equation.

i.e. Peace is directly proportional to Orderliness (Negative Entropy)

Entropy (ds=dq/t) of Environment can be computed through standard chemical thermodynamic calculations.

6. CORRELATION OF PCP & STAGES OF CHILD'S LIFE

From PCP = f (AGE) ...... Eqn. (3) VG: Hypothesis of Positive Child Parenting, its seen that as the child grows in the Stages *i.e.* from Infant-Toddler-Pre-Schoolers-Middle Young-Teenagers by attaining the above defined Age-Bracket, one cannot adopt the same technology to all the children of different Age to compute equation of Positive Child Parenting (PCP), since the deduced morphology of Positive Child Parenting (PCP) changes. All children are different due to their age factor as PCP = f (AGE). Hence, the variables like Carriers (Cr) & Barriers (Br) have to undergo change in their magnitude (number & types leading to the computing of VG: PCP-Eqn. for the each and every aforesaid stage of child's Life.

Next, there is a strong relation between PCP & Teaching Methodology or in the modes operandi of training to a child when he/she is passing through different stages of life by attaining the age brackets *e.g.* Infant-Toddler-Pre-Schoolers-Middle Young-Teenagers. As the child steps into the different stages of life, so the parents do change their role of teaching with change of teaching methodology.

There is a composite Correlation of Age with Carriers *viz.* Love (L), Forgiveness (F) Discipline (D), Character (C), Teaching/ Training (T), Belief (B) & WATCH (W) & Barriers (Negativity, 3As)

All these above mentioned Carriers (Crs) & Barriers (Brs) are intrinsic, qualitative in nature and are beyond quantitative estimation till now. These are variables and can be added and subtracted with respect to the age of child with a little variation in degree. Carriers & Barriers may be either Relevant & Irrelevant as per the Age/Stage of the child. These all Carriers & Barriers are the morphological properties of Positive Child Parenting (PCP). How are these to be applied by the Parents for the PCP (*i.e.* Nurturing, Security, Training, Health) in order to help the child growing through stepping into the different aforesaid Stages of Child's Life till the baby attains the manhood *i.e.* becomes major.

This is the threshold of PCP perhaps, from there onward child's dependency on PCP vis-à-vis Parents start reducing gradually due to sharing, change of proportionality, ratio variation and get regenerated when the same child attains to maturity and attains parenthood.

Thus, VG: PCP-Cycle *i.e.* cycle of Positive Child Parenting follows on from generation to generation all over the Globe. To understand this very VG: PCP-CYCLE; its imperative to innovate dynamical Properties of PCP with respect to the Stages of Child's Life.

In order to innovate dynamical properties of Positive Child Parenting (PCP) & VG: PCP-Cycle; as well as to evolve innovative technologies of Positive Child Parenting, one has to innovate models of Positive Child Parenting by taking into account the above investigations.

7. VG: DYNAMICAL PROPERTIES OF POSITIVE CHILD PARENTING (PCP), PCP-CYCLE & PCP- 'HUB & SPOKE' MODELS (PARENT HINTS) [5 & 6]

To develop these models, the authors have used contrast to globally 'Hub & Spoke' spatial model wherein; the organized retailers have primarily focused on the front-end ('Spoke'), hence enhanced the possibility of disinvestment resulting the make-over, inefficiency in the distribution system due to the loss incurred by the organized retailers.

The above resulting concept of superimposing of 'Hub & Spoke' on the existing built-in environment *i.e.* Carriers *viz.* Love (L), Forgiveness (F) Discipline (D), Character (C), Teaching/Training (T), Belief (B) & WATCH (W) & Barriers (Negativity, 3As) concept has been used to develop 'Hub & Spoke' model of Positive Child

[5] 'Child well-being in rich countries A comparative overview', Innocent Report Card 11 (UNICEF Office of Research, 2014.

[6] CDC: (Centers For Disease Control & Prevention) Website.

Parenting to run different Stages of Child's Life Cycle by making use of, the innovated mathematical equations (2) & (4) to bring objectivity in the PCP- Models for the different ages of children.

Let us, add VG-Eqns.*viz*. PCP = (Np+Sp+Tp+Hp), under (Ep) & . (Np+Sp+Tp+Hp), under (Ep) = f (AGE), it can be deduced that under (Ep),

PCP = A (Np+Sp+Tp) = f (AGE) > ...VG-Eqn. (13)

Next, adding VG: Eqn *i.e.* PCP = A (Cr/Br), under (Ep) to VG-Eqn. (13), we get, under (Ep)

PCP = A (Cr/Br) = A (Np+Sp+Tp+Hp) = f (AGE)

...VG- Eqn. (14) say.

Applying 'Hub & Spoke' Model Concept: Assume Under (Ep) & (A) Constant, (Np+Sp+Tp+Hp) are, Hubs' & (Cr/Br) are 'Spokes' & all these are f (AGE), hence, conceptual 'Hub & Spoke' Model Models of PCP are to be developed as per the Age or Stages of Child's Life *i.e.* by designating the 'Hub & Spoke' for each and every stage, based on the AGE of the children.

In these models the Basic needs of the child like Nurturing, Health, Security, Teaching/Training; which are to be provided solely by Parents have been designated as Hub & SKILLS which pertains mainly the child *i.e.* activities of the Child (*e.g* taking a first step, Smiling first time, crawling, walking, jumping) have been designated as Spokes. These skills are also known as Developmental Milestones (DM) since these are things most children can do by a certain age.

The innovated 'CARRIERS' & 'BARRIERS' have been superimposed on the 'HUB' as a part of PARENT's responsibility & on 'SPOKES' as a CHILD'S duty/reciprocity towards parents during different stages of child's life, since PCP is f (Age).

In brief, Basic Needs (Nurturing, Security, Teaching, Health) of the Child fulfilled by Parents are' Hubs' & the Child's Activities/ Skills are 'Spokes' with superimposition of innovated CARRIERS

& BARRIERS on HUB & SPOKES would reveal the Structural 'Hub & Spoke' Model Of PCP. Efforts have been made to devise Parent Hints (PH) to run these probable 'Hub & Spoke' PCP-Models.

Parent Hints (PH) [5 & 6]

The gist of Parent Hint (PH) is to take care of 'SPOKES' to maintain the 'HUB' and help the child to grow through all the Stages of Child's Life successfully by running the life-cycle of 'Hub & Spoke'

Infant (0-1)

Hubs' (Basic Needs)	:	Spokes (Skills/ Child Activities/DM)
(Np+Sp+Hp)	:	(a) taking a first step, @ smiling for the first time
Nurturing (N)	:	(b) playing, learning, speaking and waving "bye-bye"
Security (S)	:	(c) behaving and moving (crawling, walking, Jumping)
Health (H)	:	(d) focus their vision, reach out, explore & learn about
	:	things that are around them. Listening, Understanding.
	:	(e) learning Language *i.e.* making sounds ("babble"), or
	:	(f) saying "ma-ma", "pa-pa"". knowing the names.
	:	(g) develop bonds of love and trust with their parents &
	:	(h) others as part of social and emotional development

On Superimposition of the few Carriers *viz*. Love (L), Forgiveness (F) Discipline (D), Character (C), Teaching/Training (T), Belief (B) & WATCH (W) & Barriers (Negativity, 3As) over 'Hub' & 'Spokes' in case of INFANT (0-1):

INFANT (0-1) Structural 'Hub & Spoke' Model of PCP

LOVE (L), BELIEF (B)

|3rd Circle|: (Reciprocity) (CHILD) Superimposed with CARRIERS & BARRIERS

INFANT (a) to (h)

|2nd Circle|: SPOKES- (Skills) (CHILD)

LOVE (L)), BELIEF (B)

|1st Circle|: SPOKES (PARENTS) - Superimposed with CARRIERS & BARRIERS

Nutrition (N), Security (S), Health (H)

| Nucleus | :   HUBS (Basic Needs) (PARENTS)

From VG - Eqns. under (Ep), PCP = A (Cr/Br) = A (Np+Sp+Tp+Hp) = f (AGE)

We can deduce the PCP-INFANT (0-1) Eqn. (15) as: Under (Ep),

PCP = A(L+B)+A(Np+Sp+Hp)+INFANT(a-h) = f (AGE). Eqn. (15), VG- INFANT

Parent Hints (PH)-INFANT

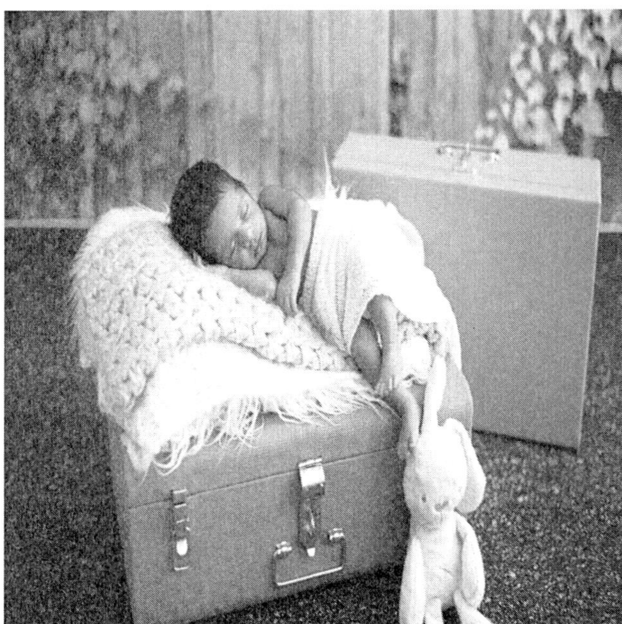

\# This is the first stage where parents have to play major role as the child does not know anything and even does not recognize parents. One has to devote almost 24 hours in nurturing, taking care of health, securing and watching your child. At this stage there is hardly any training involved.

Follow the Child Specialist's (Pediatrician) advice and learn from the experienced parents. Follow the vaccination schedule for the baby

Respond to your baby all the time. Keep watching, reading your baby, playing, talking, singing, laughing, enjoying, playing music, cuddling, holding your baby.

Baby hygiene, your hygiene & the persons who come in his/ her contact is paramount as the child is very tender and sensitive to catch infection. Though not very practical and feasible as the child is so loving, still avoid excessive kissing specially mouth and cheeks.

Give lot of soft toys and move him to safe areas when he starts moving and touching things that he shouldn't touch.

Security of the baby is paramount so do not leave the baby alone at this stage. Must have safe, secure, clean well ventilated room where baby to be housed.

Beyond doubt it has to be Smokeless environment *e.g.* No Smoking Zone. Take care of yourself physically, mentally, and emotionally as you are healthy so is your baby.

Do take care of your diet too as your diet matters for breast feeding to baby. Breast milk is baby's needs for about the first 6 months of life. Between 6 and 12 months of age, baby be given healthy solid food, but breast is the best.

Handling baby is an art.one has to trained to hold very small babies. Never shake your baby¯ever! Babies have very weak neck muscles that are not yet able to support their heads. Shaking your baby, can damage his/her brain.

Always put your baby to sleep on her back and don't leave the baby in swings, strollers, bouncer seats, and exercise saucers for too long.

Ensure that during Car-ride, baby in a rear-facing car seat in the back seat.

Ensure your child is active. Let him/her keep little arms and legs moving.

TODDLERS (1-2)

Hubs' (Basic Needs)	:	Spokes (Skills/Child Activities/DM)	
(Np+Sp+Hp)	:	(a)	Moving (crawling, walking, Jumping) Increases
Nurturing (N)	:	(b)	Awareness about themselves and surroundings sets in
Security (S)	:	(c)	Child shows independence & increase in reach out
Health (H)	:	(d)	increased focus in their vision, explore more & learn
	:		more about things that are around them.
	:	(e)	begin to show defiant behavior.
	:	(f)	recognize themselves in pictures or a mirror;
	:	(g)	Copy the older and imitate the behavior of elders.
	:	(h)	Start following Directions and recognizing objects.

Its observed that except the changes in Skills (Child)/Spokes (a)-(h) & enhancement in Security/Safety of the child due to his/her increased movements, there is no change in case of TODDLERS (1-2) *i.e.*

On Superimposition of the few 'Carriers' like LOVE (L), FORGIVENESS (F) DISCIPLINE (D), CHARACTER (C), TEACHING BELIEF (B) & WATCH (W) & Barriers (Negativity, 3As) over 'Hub' & 'Spokes' in case of TODDLERS (1-2)

TODDLERS (1-2): Structural 'Hub & Spoke' Model Of PCP

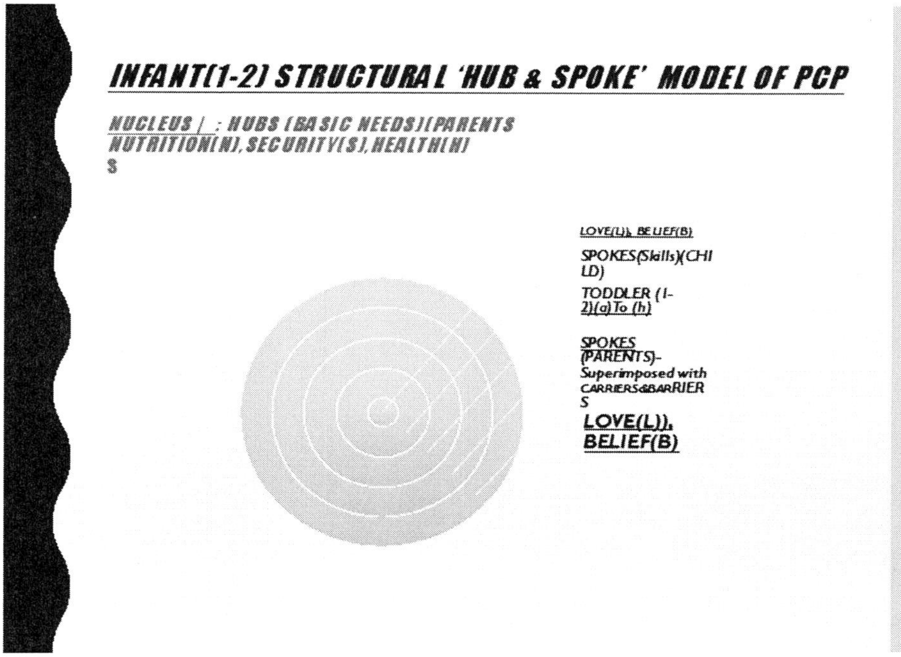

LOVE (L), BELIEF (B)

| 3rd Circle | : (Reciprocity) (CHILD) Superimposed with CARRIERS & BARRIERS

Toddler (1-2): (a) to (h)

| 2nd Circle | : SPOKES- (Skills) (CHILD)

LOVE (L), BELIEF (B)

| 1st Circle | : SPOKES (PARENTS) - Superimposed with CARRIERS & BARRIERS

Nutrition (N), Security (S), Health (H)

| Nucleus | : HUBS (Basic Needs) (PARENTS)

From VG- Eqns. under (Ep), PCP = A(Cr/Br) = A(Np+Sp+Tp+Hp) = f (AGE)

We can deduce the PCP-TODDLER (1-2) Eqn. (16) as: Under (Ep),

PCP = A(L+B)+A (Np+Sp+Hp)+Toddler1-2: (a-h) = f (AGE). VG-Eqn. (16) Toddlers (1-2)

Parent Hints (PH) -TODDLER 1-2:

- # In addition to all the Hints given to parents in case of INFANT (0-1) above are applicable with the enhancement of the activities and
- # Read to your Child, Play with him, tell him to recognize body parts, TV, Moon, Son, Stars, toys, relatives, friends and help him to learn language by responding and encouraging your child.
- # After one year add the element of helping your child in dressing, playing.

Since, the movements of the Child increases and so the curiosity of child, hence be careful that your child does not go to dangerous places *e.g*. Water places (Swimming pools, ponds, river bank), Sharp edges, kitchen appliances, Electrical switches, fire appliances (Burner etc.) & staircases etc.

Ensure about manicure and pedicure of your child so that he/she does not get hurt by nails.

At this stage the child becomes erratic eater so don't insist him for particular food but, avoid sugary drinks. Give him water, milk, solid food with the guidance of Doctor and dietician. Of course massage to your child is the best for baby's health right from the Infant age onward.

TODDLER (2-3)

As the child grows so the skills. More and more new skill starts either replacing the earlier Infant skills, Toddler (1-2) skills or elevating and adding of more.

Hubs' (Basic Needs)	:	Spokes (Skills/Child Activities/DM)
(Np+Sp+Hp+Tp)	:	(a) Taking turns, Walking, Jumping, playing Increases
Nurturing (N),	:	(b) DM (playing make believe, and kicking a ball, added
Security (S),	:	(c) Child shows more independence & increase in reach out
Health (H),	:	& hence, this stage is often called the "terrible twos.
Teaching (T)	:	(d) Child experience huge thinking & emotional changes
	:	(e) Starts going to Play Schools between 2-3 yrs
	:	(f) Start playing, talking, mixing, eating in absence of Parents

: (g) Start exploring new world, imitating & accommodating.

: (h) Start following two- or three-step directions, sorting objects by shape and color & recites Nursery rhymes, feel lie dressing etc.

Its observed that except the changes in Skills (Child) /Spokes (a) - (h), Addition in Hub of TEACHING/TRAINING (T) & enhancement in Security/Safety of the child due to his/her increased movements, there is no change in case of TODDLERS (2-3) *i.e.*

On Superimposition of the few 'Carriers' like LOVE (L), FORGIVENESS (F) DISCIPLINE (D), CHARACTER (C), TEACHING (T), BELIEF (B) & WATCH (W) & Barriers (Negativity, 3As) over 'Hub' & ' Spokes' in case of TODDLERS (2-3):

TODDLERS (2-3): Structural 'Hub & Spoke' Model of PCP

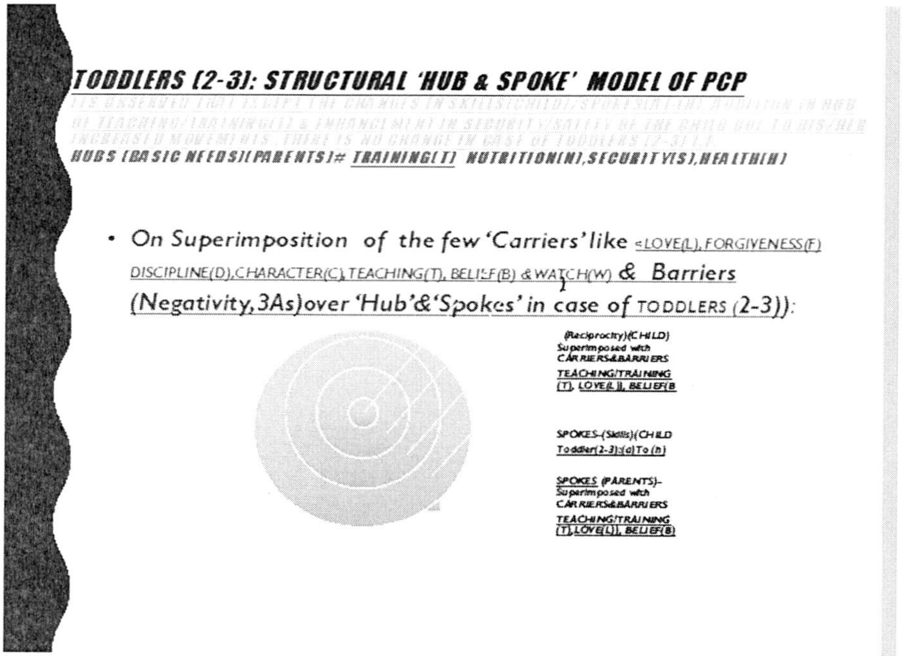

TEACHING / TRAINING (T), LOVE (L), BELIEF (B)

| 3rd Circle | : (Reciprocity) (CHILD) Superimposed with CARRIERS & BARRIERS

Toddler (2-3): (a) To (h)

| 2nd Circle | : SPOKES- (Skills) (CHILD)

TEACHING / TRAINING (T), LOVE (L), BELIEF (B)

| 1st Circle | : SPOKES (PARENTS) -Superimposed with CARRIERS & BARRIERS

Teaching/Training (T) Nutrition (N), Security (S), Health (H)

| Nucleus | : HUBS (Basic Needs) (PARENTS)

From VG - Eqns. under (Ep), PCP = A (Cr/Br) = A (Np+Sp+Tp+Hp) = f (AGE)

We can deduce the PCP-TODDLER (2-3) Eqn. (17) as: Under (Ep),

PCP = A(L+Bs+T)+A(Np+Sp+Hp+Tp)+Toddler 2-3: (a-h) = f (AGE) ....Eqn. (17), VG: TODDLERS (2-3) Eqn.

Parent Hints (PH)-TODDLER 2-3

- # In addition to all the hints given to parents in case of INFANT (0-1 & TODDLER (1-2)) above are applicable with the enhancement of the activities *e.g.* make a habit to read the books, play music, sing song, play games, encourage him to participate in play school activities & encourage him to recite poetry and start participating outside games by the time the child touches the age of 3 years.
- # Take him along to malls, garden and teach about plants, flowers, birds, pats, kids parties, morning, evening walk in pram, places like Disney land for his enjoyment, eating joints and family gathering with kids etc.
- # Start teaching basic Maths, vocabulary, painting, through toys and play games as well as play videos. Encourage him to learn & tell names of his/her teacher, friends, relatives and own name as well as home address & name of kindergarten school.
- # Praise the child always. Be Positive, Never scold or punish and make afraid
- # Remember child has grown with enhanced movements not at home but, outside too. Be very careful about his safety and follow all the precautions discussed earlier with more care and attention.
- # Teach your child eating manners gradually and try to eat with him and encourage your child to sit on baby chair to eat and also to sit on baby study table to read for some times. Let your child develops healthy habits under your loving parental guidance. Take him away from hot and very cold things. Take expert advice of trained Dietician as regards to your child's diet.
- # Play with your child as his/her friend of his/her age play. Take your child on shoulder, head, play mock games like you become horse and your child rides on you.

PRESCHOOLARS (3-5)

As the child grows so the Skills. More and more new skills start either replacing the earlier Toddler (1-2) & Toddler (2-3) skills, elevating or adding of more 'Carriers' *e.g* FORGIVENESS (F), DISCIPLINE (D) & CHARACTER (C) & element of Barriers.

Hubs' (Basic Needs)	:	Spokes (Skills/Child Activities/DM)
(Np+Sp+Hp+Tp)	:	(a) They start showing love and also getting anxious.
Nurturing (N),	:	(b) Get demanding, irritant, riled, anguish & angry slightly when their demands not met specially when they see their peers and during play in schools hours.
Security (S),	:	(c) Start hopping on one foot, tricycling, using scissors,
Health (H),	:	dressing-undressing themselves, videogames, TV, mobiles
Teaching (T)	:	(d) Child experience huge thinking & emotional changes
	:	(e) Starts going from Play Schools to School.
	:	(f) Start talking, mixing, outing & eating in absence of Parents.
	:	(g) Start exploring more new world, imitating & accommodating.
	:	(h) Start making boy and girl friends, sings songs & gets naughty

Its observed that except the changes in Skills (Child)/Spokes (a) - (h), Addition in Hub of TEACHING/TRAINING (T) & enhancement in Security/Safety of the child due to his/her increased movements (outside like Schools, Parks & inside the home), there are changes in case of PRESCHOOLAIRS (3-5) as regards CARRIERS & BARRIERS, This is the stage wherein, ANXIETY (A1),

ANGUISH (A2) & to some extent ANGER (A3) steps in PRESCHOOLARS & also in PARENTS in responsive manner *i.e.* (RESPONSIVE) 3A's; which are not good at all.

On Superimposition of the few 'Carriers' like LOVE (L), FORGIVENESS (F) DISCIPLINE (D), CHARACTER (C), TEACHING (T), BELIEF (B) & WATCH (W) & Barriers (Negativity, 3As) over 'Hub' & 'Spokes' in case of PRESCHOOLARS (3-5):

Preschoolars (3-5): Structural 'Hub & Spoke' Model of PCP

FORGIVENESS (F), DISCIPLINE (D) & CHARACTER (C) TEACHING/TRAINING (T), LOVE (L), BELIEF (B) ANXIETY (A1), ANGUISH (A2) & to some extent ANGER (A3)

| 3rd Circle |: (Reciprocity) (CHILD) Superimposed with CARRIERS & BARRIERS

PRESCHOOLARS (3-5): (a) To (h)

| 2nd Circle | : SPOKES- (Skills) (CHILD)

FORGIVENESS (F), DISCIPLINE (D) & CHARACTER (C)
TEACHING/TRAINING (T), LOVE (L)), BELIEF (B) &
ANXIETY (A1), ANGUISH (A2) & to some extent ANGER (A3) of
Responsive nature (Not Good)

| 1st Circle | : SPOKES (PARENTS)-Superimposed with CARRIERS & BARRIERS

Teaching/Training (T) Nutrition (N), Security (S), Health (H)

| Nucleus | : HUBS (Basic Needs) (PARENTS).

From VG - Eqns. under (Ep), PCP = A (Cr/ Br) = A (Np+Sp+Tp+ Hp) = f (AGE),

We can deduce the PCP-PRESCHOOLAR (3-5) Eqn. (18) as: Under (Ep),

PCP=A(L+B+T+F+B+C/3A)+A (Np+Sp+Hp+Tp) + PRESCHOO LARS (3-5): (a-h) = f (AGE) ....Eqn. (18) VG: PRESCHOOLARS (3-5) Eqn.

Parent Hints (PH) -PRESCHOOLARS:

This is a very fascinating stage and the Parents get enormous pleasure in seeing off the kids to School. Specially, Mother is excited to make tiffin packed with delicious eatable of the child's taste to keep in his/her School-bag.

This the stage when the child requires a Baby-Sitter if, both parents are working and elderly people (grand-parents) are not at home. Barring the few families *viz*. Indian, Asian & perhaps African; its mandatory to have Baby-Sitters or Baby-Care Takers to look after the children in absence of parents while away for short time and crutches for children are not available.

Remember the Security of your child is paramount so ensure the Baby-Sitter/Caretaker of the baby is most reliable, known, from the registered organization amalgamated with police clearance and if, trained the nothing like that.

Be careful from the kidnapping menace of child which is very common in Asian, African & Middle-East countries. Use modern digital technology (CCTV) ; to monitor your child on your mobile/laptop while away from your child.

As a Parent not only close watch to your child is needed but, also a very comprehensive reading of your child by you is the must to help him for all round development. Try to understand your child and his/her aptitude to learn.

Adopt a collaborating approach with total positivity, smile mixed with discipline to your child. Be part and parcel of each and every activity of your child and be available to guide him, hold his/her hand at each and every step of life.

Never impose your will or anything on your child. Explain him logically with lot of love, preferably with practical examples, live demonstrations and with reasoning why and how this should be done and not to be done.

Help your child in completing homework at the age of 4-5 years. Teach language speaking in correct pronunciation by talking with your child and teach writing in beautiful hand writing. I think, GOOD COOMUNICATION (VERBAL & WRITNG) IS POWERFUL TOOL FOR SUCCESS.

Arose curiosity in your child by asking questions *e.g.* What is this, What is that and give him convincing answers with explanation if, he/she is not able to answer. Remember you are a great lovable immediate and the first Teacher to your child. Just for you a quote:

> "The mediocre teacher tells.
>
> The good teacher explains.
>
> The Superior teacher demonstrates.
>
> The great teacher inspires."
>
> William Arthur Ward

So, PLEASE INSPIRE YOUR CHILD.

MIDDLE CHILDHOOD (6-8)

As evident from the above derived mathematical equations; the growth of child is directly proportional to skills. As the child grows so the skills. More and more new skills start elevating or adding more' Carriers' & 'Barrier' elements.

Hubs' (Basic Needs)	:	Spokes (Skills/ Child Activities/DM)
(Np+Sp+Hp+Tp)	:	(a) Start showing love & also getting anxious for others.
Nurturing (N),	:	(b) Get more demanding, irritant, riled, anguish & angry when their demands not met, specially when they see their peers are getting more. Competition/ envy sets in.
Security (S),	:	(c) Start hopping on one foot, bicycling, using scissors to cut paper for drawing, knives to cut the fruits & salad.
Health (H),	:	Teaching (T): (d) Child experience peers pressure & emotional changes

: (e) more independent to dress and versed with electronic & home appliances operations and even sitting in car & belting.

: (f) Start teaming, mixing, outing & eating, playing with outsiders.

: (g) Start loving excursions, celebrations, exploring & innovating.

: (h) Start Physical, Social, Learning and mental skills development.

Again, it's observed that except the changes in Skills (Child) / Spokes (a) - (h), addition in Hub of TEACHING/TRAINING (T) & enhancement in Independence of the child due to his/her increased outside interactions (Schools, Parks, excursions), there are changes in case of MIDDLE CHILDHOOD (6-8) as regards CARRIERS & BARRIRS,

This is the stage wherein, ANXIETY (A1), ANGUISH (A2) & ANGER (A3) step in MIDDLE CHILDHOOD (6-8) & also in PARENTS in responsive manner *i.e.* (RESPONSIVE) 3A's; which are not good at all.

MIDDLE CHILDHOOD (6-8): Structural 'Hub & Spoke' Model of PCP

On Superimposition of the few 'Carriers' like LOVE (L), FORGIVENESS (F) DISCIPLINE (D), CHARACTER (C), TEACHING (T), BELIEF (B) & WATCH (W) & Barriers (Negativity, 3As) over 'Hub' & ' Spokes' in case of MIDDLE CHILDHOOD (6-8):

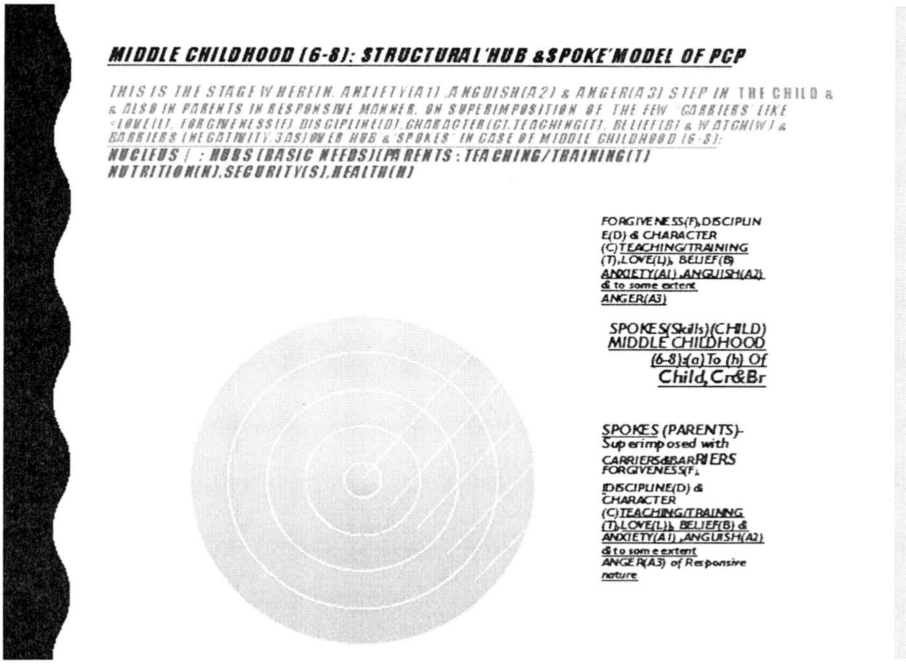

FORGIVENESS (F), DISCIPLINE (D) & CHARACTER (C) TEACHING/TRAINING (T), LOVE (L)), BELIEF (B) ANXIETY (A1), ANGUISH (A2) & ANGER (A3)

| 3rd Circle |: (Reciprocity) (CHILD) Superimposed with CARRIERS & BARRIERS

MIDDLE CHILDHOOD (6-8): (a) To (h)

| 2nd Circle |: SPOKES- (Skills) (CHILD)

FORGIVENESS (F), DISCIPLINE (D) & CHARACTER (C) TEACHING/TRAINING (T), LOVE (L)), BELIEF (B) & ANXIETY (A1), ANGUISH (A2) & ANGER (A3) of Responsive nature (Not Good)

| 1st Circle |: SPOKES (PARENTS)-Superimposed with CARRIERS & BARRIERS Teaching/Training (T) Nutrition (N), Security (S), Health (H)

| Nucleus |: HUBS (Basic Needs) (PARENTS)

From VG- Eqns. under (Ep), PCP = A (Cr/ Br) = A (Np+Sp+Tp+Hp) = f (AGE)

We can deduce the MIDDLE CHILDHOOD (6-8) Eqn. (19) as: Under (Ep),

PCP = A (L+B+T+F+B+C/3A)+A (Np+Sp+Hp+Tp)+MIDDLE CHILDHOOD (6-8): (a-h) = f (AGE) .... Eqn. (19) VG: MIDDLE CHILDHOOD (6-8) Eqn.

Parents Hints (PH) - MIDDLE CHILDHOOD (6-8)

- # In addition to the above mentioned Parent Hints in case of Pre-schoolars (3-5), the few PH are added with a caution that as a Parents you must remember that your child is out of the home and start living in the challenging world with due adjustment with home (internal) and external environment with the confidence in himself/herself and that too with Independence.
- # At this stage you are to be very collaborative, encouraging, appreciating the child's activities and learnings with the instinct of friendliness, love and affection. Direct pointing out mistakes and scolding is never appreciated by the child and hardly fruitful. So be judicious and careful.
- # Teach manners, etiquettes, patience, sharing to your child. Help your child in planning, completing school home-work & discuss about his/her goals, schools, friends and things of his/her interest with inherent solutions intrinsically and playfully.
- # Make you child aware of safety & traffic regulations *i.e.* safety from accidents, pollution and unwarranted elements of society (kidnappers, thieves etc.)
- # Let your child know that 'HEALTH IS WEALTH'. Inculcate habit of light exercise, jogging, teach Swimming in child's pool and eating habits of nutritious and healthy food. My

advice is: "NEVER MAKE YOUR & YOUR CHILD's BELLY A DUSTBIN & NEVER BE OBESE"

MIDDLE CHILDHOOD (9-11)

This is the first transition stage from Childhood to Adolescence. During this stage not only biological and anatomical change take place but, child gets more oriented towards his/her friends *i.e.* like to be more in friends company and less under Parent's guidance, more in schools, outside and less at home.

As the anatomical changes are obvious towards the end of this child's stage, specially in case of girl's child undergoing hormonal changes in comparison to boy child, so the parents and mother in particular must create awareness of the cause and effect of the body to the child, so that they are not caught unaware. During this phase growth is fast & so is the increments in above devised Skills/ Spokes/DM with the addition of a 'WATCH' (Word, Action, Thought, Character & Health). This is the stage where one has to watch the 'WATCH' as your child starts getting attracted towards opposite sex between 10–11 years.

Hubs' (Basic Needs)	:	Spokes (Skills/ Child Activities/DM)
(Np+Sp+Hp+Tp)	:	(a) Start showing love & also getting anxious for others.
Nurturing (N),	:	(b) Get more demanding, negative, riled, anguish & angry when their demands not met, specially when they see their peers are getting more. Competition/ envy sets in.
Security (S),	:	(c) It is first transition stage; Childhood to Adolescence
Health (H),	:	when hormonal & anatomical change take place
Teaching (T)	:	(d) Child experience more peers pressure & emotional changes

: (e) Radical changes in WATCH' (Language, Action, Thoughts, Character, Health) & gets attracted towards opposite sex.

: (f) Start teaming, viewing classified content on Internet, outing

: playing with friends. Loves to play outside games and to be on Top

: (g) Love loud music, dancing, kid parties, cakes & junk food.

: (h) Academics, Learning talent, Thoughts (Dreams), health Pressure

Its observed that except the changes in Skills (Child) /Spokes (a) - (h) & more enhanced independence of the child due to his/her increased outside interactions with friends, there are changes in case of MIDDLE CHILDHOOD (9-11) as regards CARRIERS & BARRIRS.

This is the stage wherein, ANXIETY (A1), ANGUISH (A2) ANGER (A3) & 'WATCH' (WORD, ACTION, THOUGHT, CHARACTER, HEALTH) significantly, steps in MIDDLE CHILDHOOD (9-11) & also in PARENTS in responsive manner *i.e.* (RESPONSIVE) 3A's; with the addition of watch for child's' WATCH'.

On Superimposition of the few 'Carriers' like LOVE (L), FORGIVENESS (F) DISCIPLINE (D), CHARACTER (C), TEACHING (T), BELIEF (B) & WATCH (W) & Barriers (Negativity, 3As) over Hub' & 'Spokes' in case of MIDDLE CHILDHOOD (9-11):

MIDDLE CHILDHOOD (9-11): Structural 'Hub & Spoke' Model of PCP

FORGIVENESS (F), DISCIPLINE (D) & CHARACTER (C) TEACHING/TRAINING (T), LOVE (L)), & The 'WATCH (W)', BELIEF (B) ANXIETY (A1), ANGUISH (A2), ANGER (A3) & NEGATIVITY.

| 3rd Circle | : (Reciprocity) (CHILD) Superimposed with CARRIERS & BARRIERS

MIDDLE CHILDHOOD (9-11): (a) To (h)

| 2nd Circle | : SPOKES- (Skills) (CHILD) FORGIVENESS (F), DISCIPLINE (D) & CHARACTER (C) TEACHING/ TRAINING (T), LOVE (L)), BELIEF (B) & The 'WATCH (W) ', & ANXIETY (A1), ANGUISH (A2), ANGER (A3) & NEGATIVITY.

| 1st Circle | : SPOKES (PARENTS) -Superimposed with CARRIERS & BARRIERS

Teaching/Training (T) Nutrition (N), Security (S), Health (H)

| Nucleus | : HUBS (Basic Needs) (PARENTS)

From VG- Eqns. under (Ep), PCP = A (Cr/ Br) = A (Np+Sp+Tp+ Hp) = f (AGE)

We can deduce the MIDDL CHILDHOOD (9-11) Eqn. (20) as: Under (Ep),

PCP = A (L+B+T+F+B+C+W)/(3A+N)+A(Np+Sp+Hp+Tp)+ MIDDLE CHILDHOOD (9-11): (a-h) = f (AGE) .... (20) Eqn. VG: MIDDLE CHILDHOOD (9-11)

Parents Hints (PH) - MIDDLE CHILDHOOD (9-11)

In addition to the above mentioned Parent Hints in case of MIDDLE CHILDHOOD (6-8), the few PH are added with a caution that as Parents you must remember that your child is out of your lap & home. Your child is in transition stage of

first order inherited with hormonal changes cum anatomical changes and lives in the challenging world with due adjustment and natural stress at home (internal) and in external environment with the confidence in himself/herself and that too with much more Independence & confidence..

Lot of collaborative guidance with encouragement is needed to you child from you specially during the stage of hormonal change. More time with friendly mode to be spent with your child.

You must visit your child's School and never miss Parent-Teacher Meeting (PTM) & monitoring the child's progress in academics and extra curricular activities.

Due to adolescence keep close but, indirect, implicit watch on your Child's WATCH (WORDS, ACTION, THOUGHT, CHARACTER & HEALTH).

Inculcate Leadership qualities in your child from this stage onward:

"I always Create, never Destroy

I always Believe, never Doubt

I am a Successful person, not a Victim

I have the Capacity & Knowledge to help People

I am a Leader"

William A. Foster

YOUNG TEENS (12-14)

This is the actual transition stage from MIDDLE CHILDHOOD (9-11) to YOUNG TEENS (12-14) wherein, word 'YTEEN' is added to the Stage of Child's Life.

This is very challenging, competitive & sensitive stage of your child where he/she has to experience the phenomenal changes in body, mind, soul and environment at home and outside of the home and even may consist of regional and continental changes.

Hubs' (Basic Needs)	:	Spokes (Skills/ Child Activities/DM)
(Np+Sp+Hp+Tp)	: (a)	Start loving & attracted towards opposite sex..
Nurturing (N),	: (b)	Get stressed with hormonal changes (puberty) & hair
Security (S),	: (c)	It is transition stage from CHILDHOOD (9-11) - YTEENS (12-14) when
	:	Health (H) change occur in body, mind, with day-dreaming.
Teaching (T)	: (d)	Girls grow pubic hair and breasts & period begins
	: (e)	Boys grow facial and pubic hair & gets voices heavier.
	: (f)	Changes in WATCH' (Language, Action, Thoughts, Character, Health). Monitor through PTM (Parent-Teacher Meet).
	: (g)	Urge for alcohol, tobacco, drugs, and to have sex.
	: (h)	Academics, depression, peers and family problems

Its observed that except the changes in Skills (Child)/Spokes (a) - (h) & transitional changes (hormonal, puberty & family problems), there are changes in case of YOUNG TEENS (12-14) as regards CARRIERS & BARRIRS, This is the stage wherein, ANXIETY (A1) -ANGER (A3) & 'WATCH' (WORD, ACTION, THOUGHT, CHARACTER, HEALTH) significantly, steps in YOUNG TEENS (12-14) & also in Parents in responsive manner *i.e.* (RESPONSIVE) 3A's; with the addition of watch for child's 'WATCH' & the rider of 'teen' with 'HEALTH' of 'WATCH' depicting pubic changes. *i.e.* (H teen) or simply ' (W) y teen', differentiating with Middle Young (9-11).

On Superimposition of the few 'Carriers' like LOVE (L), FORGIVENESS (F) DISCIPLINE (D), CHARACTER (C),

TEACHING (T), BELIEF (B) & WATCH (W) & Barriers (Negativity, 3As) over Hub' & 'Spokes' in case of YOUNG TEENS (12-14):

YOUNG TEENS (12-14): Structural 'Hub & Spoke' Model of PCP

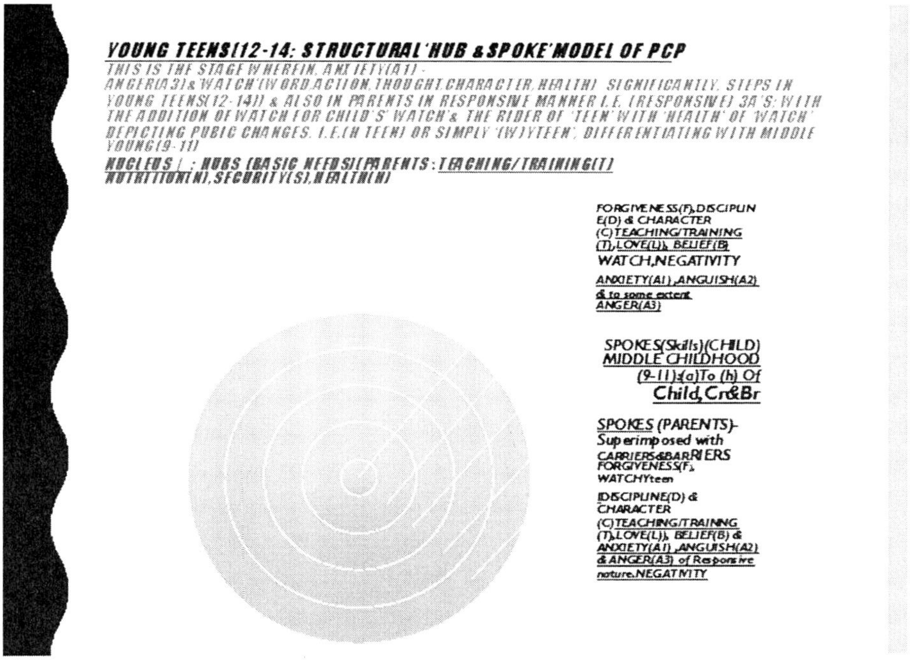

FORGIVENESS (F), DISCIPLINE (D) & CHARACTER (C) TEACHING/TRAINING (T), LOVE (L)), & The 'WATCH (W) teen', BELIEF (B) ANXIETY (A1), ANGUISH (A2), ANGER (A3) & NEGATIVITY.

| 3rd Circle | : (Reciprocity) (CHILD) Superimposed with CARRIERS & BARRIERS

YOUNG TEENS (12-14): (a) To (h)

| 2nd Circle | : SPOKES- (Skills) (CHILD): FORGIVENESS (F), DISCIPLINE (D) & CHARACTER (C) TEACHING/ TRAINING (T), LOVE (L)), BELIEF (B) & The

'WATCH (W)' yteen, & ANXIETY (A1), ANGUISH (A2), ANGER (A3) & NEGATIVITY.

| 1st Circle |: SPOKES (PARENTS) -Superimposed with CARRIERS & BARRIERS

Teaching/Training (T) Nutrition (N), Security (S), Health (H)

| Nucleus |: HUBS (Basic Needs) (PARENTS)

From VG- Eqns. under (Ep), PCP = A(Cr/ Br) = A(Np+Sp+Tp+Hp) = f (AGE)

We can deduce the YOUNG TEENS (12-14) Eqn. (21) as: Under (Ep),

PCP = A (L+B+T+F+B+C+Wyteen)/(3A+N)+A(Np+Sp+Hp+Tp)+ YOUNG TEENS (12-14): (a-h) = f (AGE) ..... (18.) Eqn. VG: YOUNG TEENS (12-14) Eqn.

Parent Hints: YOUNG TEENS (12-14)

In addition to the above mentioned Parent Hints in case of MIDDLE CHILDHOOD (9-11), the few PH are added with a caution that as Parents you must remember that your child has entered into young Teens which may be termed as transition from Young to Teens with Pubic Changes in case of both Boy & Girl child. Your child is in pure transition stage of fist young Teenager inherited with pubic changes cum other anatomical changes (*e.g.* mensuration/period in case of girl child and appearing of facial hair in case of Boy child with commonality of pubic hair.

Obviously these changes result increased stress, depressions and family problems acts as catalyst and living in the challenging they do develop different urges like addiction to alcohol, drugs, smoking resulting total disaster to health. Please take care your child intelligently and lovingly with full confidence and trust.

This is the stage you have to protect your child from rapist and bad elements of the Society if, any. Periodical visits to Gynecologist is recommended particularly, in case of girl child.

Be broadminded, liberal but strict disciplinarian. Keep watch on the friends of your children. Do discuss Sex as a parent teacher so that they are not entrapped by the bad element of society. Self Defense courses are recommended. Draw a line of decency between your Child-Friend relations.

TEENAGERS (15-17)

Well, this is the last stage of Child's Life after which no longer your child remains child but, becomes major after having crossing the thresh-hold of minor. Obviously, the role of parents stars getting gradually reducing with the growth of your child as his/her dependency on parents gets receding. This is the actual transition stage from YOUNG TEENS (12-14) to TEENS (15-17) wherein, word 'TEEN' is added to the Stage of Child's Life.

This is very challenging, competitive & sensitive stage of your child where he/she has to experience pubic changes & enhanced phenomenal changes in body, mind, soul and environment at home and outside of the home and even may consist of regional and continental changes.

Hubs (Basic Needs)	:	Spokes (Skills/ Child Activities/DM)
(Np+Sp+Hp+Tp)	:	(a) Start loving & attracted to opposite sex as Teenager
Nurturing (N),	:	(b) Get stressed with hormonal changes (puberty) & hair
Security (S),	:	(c) It is transition stage from YOUNGTEEN (12-14) - TEENS (15-17) when
	:	Health (H) more visual changes occur in body, mind, with day-dreaming.

Teaching (T)	: (d)	Girls grow pubic hair and breasts & period begins.
	:	Become conscious and possessive, shy, in nature & mature.
	: (e)	Boys grow bearded and pubic hair & get mature.
	: (f)	Changes in WATCH' (Language, Action, Thoughts,
	:	Character, Health) to be less monitored by parents & be left on child.
	: (g)	increase in urge for alcohol, tobacco, drugs, and to have sex.
	: (h)	Increased Stress, Academic, depression, peers and family problems

Its observed that except the changes in Skills (Child) /Spokes (a) - (h) & enhanced visible transitional changes (hormonal, puberty & family problems), there are changes in case of TEENAGERS (15-17) as regards CARRIERS & BARRIRS, This is the stage wherein, ANXIETY (A1) - ANGER (A3) & 'WATCH' (WORD, ACTION, THOUGHT, CHARACTER, HEALTH) significantly, step into TEENAGER (15-17)) & also in PARENTS in less responsive manner *i.e.* (RESPONSIVE) 3A's; with the addition of watch for child's' WATCH' & the rider of 'teen' with 'HEALTH' of 'WATCH' depicting pubic changes. *i.e.* (H teen) or simply ' (W) teen', differentiating with Young Teen (12-14).

On Superimposition of the few 'Carriers' like LOVE (L), FORGIVENESS (F) DISCIPLINE (D), CHARACTER (C), TEACHING (T), BELIEF (B) & WATCH (W) & Barriers (Negativity, 3As) over Hub' & 'Spokes' in case of YOUNG TEENS (12-14):

TEENAGERS (15-17): Structural 'Hub & Spoke' Model of PCP

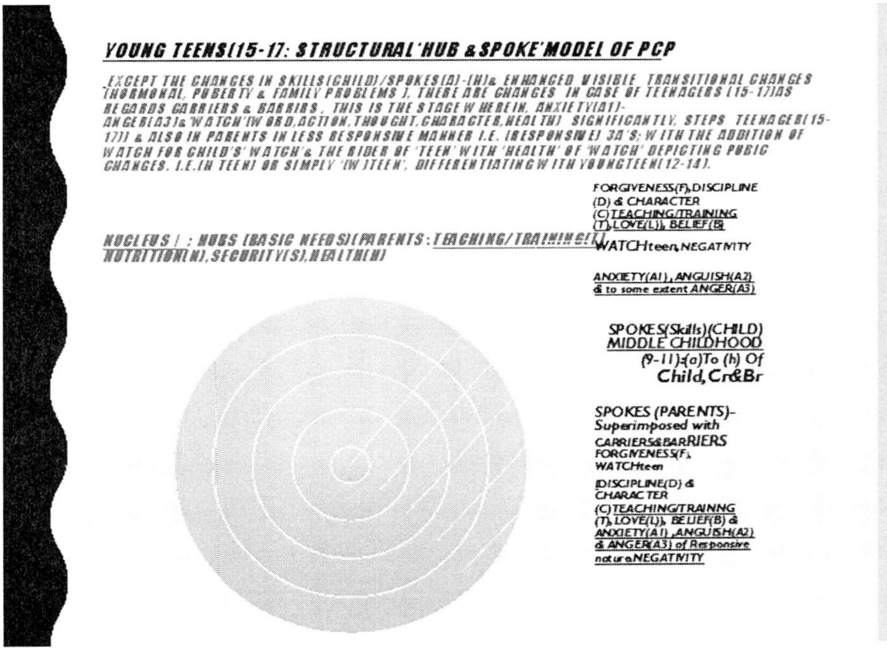

FORGIVENESS (F), DISCIPLINE (D) & CHARACTER (C) TEACHING/TRAINING (T), LOVE (L)), & The 'WATCH (W) teen', BELIEF (B) ANXIETY (A1), ANGUISH (A2), ANGER (A3) & NEGATIVITY.

| 3rd Circle | : (Reciprocity) (CHILD) Superimposed with CARRIERS & BARRIERS

YOUNG TEENS (12-14): (a) To (h)

| 2nd Circle | : SPOKES- (Skills) (CHILD)

FORGIVENESS (F), DISCIPLINE (D) & CHARACTER (C) TEACHING/TRAINING (T), LOVE (L)), BELIEF (B) & The 'WATCH (W) 'teen, & ANXIETY (A1), ANGUISH (A2), ANGER (A3) & NEGATIVITY.

| 1st Circle |: SPOKES (PARENTS) -Superimposed with CARRIERS & BARRIERS

Teaching/Training (T) Nutrition (N), Security (S), Health (H)

| Nucleus |: HUBS (Basic Needs) (PARENTS)

From VG- Eqns. under (Ep), PCP = A (Cr/ Br) = A (Np+Sp+Tp+ Hp) = f (AGE)

We can deduce the TEENAGERS Eqn. (22) as: Under (Ep),

PCP = A (L+B+T+F+B+C+Wteen)/(3A+N)+A (Np+Sp+Hp+Tp) + YOUNG TEENS (12-14): (a-h) = f (AGE) .... Eqn. (22). VG: TEENAGERS (15-17) Eqn.

Parent Hints (PH): TEENAGERS (15-17)

\# At this stage the parents and child both get seasoned and mature to deal with the day today problem of their child as well as guide them properly for their future careers, goals and missions independently on their own.

\# Let me add the few hints in addition to above mentioned Parent Hints in case of Young Teens (12-14), with a rider that as Parents you must not forget that your child has entered into Teens and he/she is no more minors. They are mature and going to be a majors just after this phase and would attain all the legal rights of the land/Country where they have born. They are just like you with lesser experience of life but, with fully developed body & mind with the capabilities to become parents like you. No doubt, they love you, regard you and do have right on you to have their blessing which may be termed as transition. They require your blessings and time to time parental guidance but, definitely not an INTERFERENCE in their way of life. Advice is welcome but, not the imposition. You have to be persuasive parents, democratic parents, friendly parents and not at all an autocratic.

8. SCOPE OF POSITIVE CHILD PARENTING: GLOBAL PERSPECTIVE

Well, children are same all over the world. Child is child whether he/she is Indian, Asian, African, American, European. God has not created child country wise and faith wise.Its we who created the faith (religion) and political boundaries for obvious reasons which should only be used as means of identification of demography. Therefore, the innovative technologies of Positive Parenting (PCP) and the models developed by the authors and acronym as VG: Hub & Spoke Models of PCP for all stages of Child's life are meant for each and every child crated by the great Almighty on this mother Earth. The technology may take variation for differently abled, single parent child and an orphan for the sake of accommodation but, PCP is right of every child of this Universe and its righteous duty of all parents to do their righteous duties of PCP and Positive parents with thanks and gratitude to great God that they are gifted with happy parenthood.

However, parents remain parent to their children at all the stages of his/her life and keep on showering their love on them irrespective of their age and achievements and so for so the children become parents and some type children children's too become parents. The chain goes on but, the role changes from Parent-Grant parents-Grant Grant parent from generation to generation -because of PARENTAL LOVE & PARENT_ EMOTIONAL BOND which had been

developed through innovative techniques of each and every Parent in their own way for their own child through Positive Child Parenting (PCP)

LOVE OF PARENTS~GRANDPARENTS LIVE EVER: GOD BLESS.

2

Memorial Stones of Sangam Age

S. CHANDNI BI[1*]

ABSTRACT

The first phase of historical period of South India referred as Sangam Age, extended from 300B.C to 300 A.D. could be found with ample reference of memorial stones better known as Veerakal and Nadukal. This article looks into the existence of them through the Sangam age literary sources. The size, strength, process of growth of these stones has been traced. The content of the stones such as the picture, inscription containing the name, fame genealogy and the feud have been studied. The practice of worship, ceremonies and the prayers that followed were also looked in to. Finally there has been an attempt to analyze the need and circumstances that led to the construction of these memorial stones has also been carried out.

***Key words*:** Memorial stones, Sangam age, Nadukal, Veerakal.

[1] Centre of Advanced Study, Dept. of History, Aligarh Muslim University, Aligarh, Uttar Pradesh.

* *Corresponding author:* E-mail: chandnibi@gmail.com

Sangam age is the earliest phase of historical South India, called so, basing upon the literature produced of the time. It is generally accepted by the historians in the present scenario, as the period supposed to have existed from Third Century B.C. to Third Century A.D. it is believed that there functioned an association of prominent literary persons under the lofty patronization of the Pandyan dynasty rulers. The usual procedure to introduce a new literary work required the accreditation of the association which was obtained after thorough thread bare discussion. It is needless to state that this fact has been supported by many literature of the time.

This long phase of six hundred years over which the available literature is spread serves as a mirror of socio-economic and cultural life of the Tamils besides the political history. This particular time period is more known for hospitality, love and valour. The enigmatic concept of willingness for war and loose life was much portrayed in the poems. A mother deeply sorrowed after losing her husband and only son could be a natural feeling. But she was sad for not missing them but for having no more sons to be sent to the battle field was the way the poems praise love for motherland overcoming the very love of a mother and a wife. It is very practical for the Sangam age trio monarchs, the Chera, Chola and Pandya, who had engaged in feuds very often to promote, praise and celebrate the love for valour so as to maintain continuous supply of human power to take battles. In course of time it was assumed that very purpose of being born was to sacrifice life in fighting.

In such circumstances it is evident that the dire need of a ruler was to glorify in all possible means, the death of a martyr. One such means of glorification that could be found in the Sangam works is the cult of remembering the dead by erecting a memorial stone that are usually referred as *Nadukal* and *Veerakal.*

Here it is attempted to trace the prevalence and growth of this practice of remembering the dead and understand the different dynamic dimensions it obtained in the Sangam age through its literature. It has been already mentioned that literature of this period spreads over a span of six hundred years which is too long a time period. Above this so far neither historians nor the Tamil linguistic scholars tried to make any time denoting classification of the available literature. Hence one cannot categorically fix the literature with time specification within these six hundred years. So with this difficulty the growth is not assessed on time frame but from the additions and modifications that were observed in the practice of revering, respecting and paying homage to the dead so called heroes.

Again, we will be making definitely a major mistake if we suppose that the men who fought battles in saving mother country by giving their precious lives alone were considered as heroes to be remembered. There was another major act of heroism that was saving the cattle from the hands of cattle lifters. The enigmatic problem here is that it is also conceived that the first step of a battle was the cattle lifting. So one side cattle being backbone of the agricultural economy and secondly the cattle lifting was either theoretically or practically associated with a feud or battle in a smaller or bigger level. Thus it appears saving the cattle was a multipurpose activity where men sacrificed their lives. It can also be in the other way that since cattle lifting was seen as a precedent to war, later every cattle saver was equated with a warrior. But the underlying fact is that loosing life for the public cause either saving cattle or saving motherland was regarded as an act of heroism and revered and remembered. That may be the reason for the literature of the time to speak so loudly about this cult or practice.

Aga nanuru, Purananuru, Pattinap-palai and Malaipadu-kadam are the four Sangam literatures that provide us ample information about the cult of memorial stones.

The Agam literature mentions that the people who were dead in the battle field due to the hit of the arrows were given memorial stones[1].

[1] Agananuru-231

கடும்போரில்வில்பட்டுஇறந்தவர்களை

இட்டுமூடியமயிரைமேலுடையகற்குவியல்கள்

கள்ளிக்காட்டுஇடங்கள்தோறும்கூட்டமாகக்கிடந்து

நினைப்பவர்க்குஅச்சம்தரும்.

The dead bodies of those who died fighting in the battle field were buried and covered by heaps of stones. These heaps of stones could be found in the regions which are manifested with cactus grown like forests. The very thought of such numerous burials in crowds would terrorize anyone was the description of the memorials of the warriors. From the above description we can infer two things one is that the burials of the fighters were marked by covering with huge heaps of stones which was not an ordinary way of a burial but specially marked for further remembrance. Secondly such burials were in large numbers good enough to terrorize anyone who could recollect the scene.

Still the same idea is supported by a song in Purananura also[2].

...பிழையாததறுகண்மைஉடையமறவர்தாம்

அம்புவிடவீழ்ந்தோர்உடல்மூடியபுதியகற்குவியல்

The bodies of the soldiers who died of the arrow shot by the men of flawless valour was covered by stones and that was the new head's of stones was the message we derive from the above mentioned lines of Purananuru poem. Here also it is stated that the dead soldier's body was covered by stockpile of stones. Thus we may find that the both the literatures support the same idea that the body of the soldiers dead in the battle field were identifiable by the presence of mound of stones placed over their burials. There are many other Agananuru poems telling us the

[2] Purananuru–3

same custom of burying the dead soldiers, especially of those who fall due to the hit of arrows and covering the burial site with hill of stones[3].

The *Nadukal* as referred in the Tamil Sangam age literature had the name of the hero died written on it. A poem from Agananuru goes to the extent of detailing how the messages were written on the hero stones[4]. It says that the letters were chiseled with the help of sharp chisels and the letters were bent and curved. It also mentions the message was written on the other side of the stone that was left unwashed. It could be inferred that the obverse side of the stone perhaps the picture of the hero was engraved and on the reverse side perhaps contained the name and deeds of the concerned person. The reason for such a conclusion is that since it is mentioned in the above quoted poem it has been specifically stated that one side of the stone was left unwashed it automatically means that the other side was washed. As the *nadukal* were under worship in general and the family in particular it is supposed that the side which was washed and ceremonially cleaned and decorated for worship must contain the picture of the person, as idol worship was in vogue. Apart from all these issues only these two aspects are noted as far as these memorial stones are concerned. One is about the picture of the hero and the second is the message of his heroic deeds, nativity and genealogy. Hence as per the Agananuru poem the picture was on one side while the written content was on the other side of the stone and the first side was taken care, washed and maintained while the second side lacked the same.

Anyway we, at present cannot generalize both the practice of writing on one side and the picture on the other as well as the custom of washing and unwashing. It will not be a theory deviated from truth to assume that so far no such hero stone has come to the notice of our knowledge.

---

[3] Agananuru–109,157, 215, Purananuru–264
[4] Agananuru– 343

Malaipadukadam in another Sangam literature which also refer to the availability of numerous *veerakal* in a territorial division called Pal Kunrak Kottam. This is one among the 24 kottams of Tondainadu, a bigger division. This particular literature when it describes about the topography of the Pal Kunrak Kottam to the bards who use to wander in search of patrons who could praise their poems/songs and support their materialistic needs of life. The poet cautions them that on their way they would with all certainty encounter with a large number of *Nadukals* while crossing the forest to meet Nannan, the ruler of the region. In this context the poem reveals that the memorial stones were dedicated to the warriors who fell in the battle fields and these stones contained the great deeds of them which gained fame to them[5].

When two *panans* met and got engaged in a formal enquiry of wellbeing and purpose of movement from home, one informs the other that his purpose was to meet the leader of the area to gain some gifts. Then the other bard who sympathizes with him and informs the patron had died when he fought and got back the cattle from the cattle lifters. Further he advises him that he could never ever meet him as he has become nadukal. Hence he could find the *nadukal* as his name has been written on it and offer worship. Such is the vivid description of a Purananuru song which makes it very clear to us that the hero stones bore the cause of the death as well as the name of the person on whose memory that has been established there[6]. This poem too support the fact that the details like name and the heroic deeds were inscribed on the hero stones that helped for their identity by others.

The *nadukals* were sometimes referred as defensive fort of the concerned regions[7] makes us to wonder how big and huge these stones would have been. We get adequate references to imagine the size of the then existed hero stones. One other poem from Agananuru goes in a very imaginary way that gives us an idea of

[5] Malaipadukadam–ll 388–396.
[6] Puranaru–260.
[7] PattinaPalai–l 79

the size of the *nadukals*. It says that when an elephant was passing through the area where a number of hero stones stood, the elephant suspecting one such *nadukal* for a human and perhaps thinking as a hindrance it kicked the hero stone. As a result the wild elephant got its big nail broken. The simile that shown is still more supportive of the huge size and strong nature of the stone. The nail of the wild elephant got broke so easily like a thorn of a palm tree[8]. The ferocious red dogs that wander aimlessly in the arid and forest regions used to take shelter under the shadow of these *nadukals* to escape from the hot sun, is another *Agam* poem, describing the topography of arid region through the lady in love, who exclaims the hard and terrific way through which her hero had to pass[9].

The *nadukals* are mentioned mostly in *Palai* region which means a dry land filled with thorny bushes and infested with robbers and thieves. In certain instances the huge *nadukals* have served as a resting place with its own shadow. At the same time the *nadukals* were planted under the shade of trees that grow in the region. One such reference comes from a Agananuru poem which tells us that a tree called *kongai* tree stood near the *nadukal*[10]. The *veerakals* were planted under the shades of trees after inscribing many messages on them. The poem from Malaipadukadam enlists the content that these *veerakals* contained. They said about the battle in which the person fought and fall and his personal name so that the world should know about the heroic deeds and persons responsible for the same. After describing the content it tells that such stones were planted under the shadow of the trees[11].

The *nadukals* were worshiped by the relatives and other common public together. We could not say clearly in the present situation if these memorial symbols were worshiped from the

---

[8] Agananuru-365
[9] Ibid–53
[10] Ibid–157
[11] Malaipadukadam–ll–388–396

beginning or since when. We have more than adequate source in the Sangam age. The literature of this period throws a flood of information on the different customs that were followed in the whole custom of worship. We have already seen how one bard was informing the other; about their patron had become a *nadukal* and asking him to offer his worship to him.

The way the sources speak about the process of worship, it gives a picture that it was not a simple one but more complicated. The open space around the *nadukals* was first cleaned in a very proper way. First the space was swept with brooms and then smeared with cow dung[12]. The hero stones were washed with fresh water, sometimes fresh water associated with paddy seeds[13], decorated with peacock feathers, it was garlanded with a flower garland[14], instruments like small and big musical drums[15] (*thodi, parai*) and string instruments like *Yaal*[16] were sounded. There were many things like the toddy made of paddy[17], honey[18], and animals like goat and sheep were also sacrificed[19].

The worship was conducted in a same way as it was to gods and they believed that the heroes had become gods and so considered as same as gods only and referred as God[20]. The worship time was considered as a very precious and holly time. Hospitality was a much revered and celebrated characteristic aspect of Sangam age people. But the guests who arrived at the time of *nadukal* worship were looked like enemies by the king and people alike, informs a Sangam literature[21].

---

[12] Purananuru–249
[13] Agananuru–343
[14] Purananuru–264, Agananuru–67
[15] Agananuru–35
[16] Malaipadukadam–388–396
[17] Agananuru–35
[18] Ku.Ve. Balasubramaniyan, *Sanga Ilakiyathil Puraporul*, Ch–4, p.158
[19] Agananuru–35
[20] Ibid
[21] Purananuru–306

The offerings to these *nadukals* were also assumed as holly and special. We hear about a chieftain Pari who ruled over Parambumalai region was a well-known large hearted leader and his charity of his own royal chariot to a jasmine creeper which hanged loose in the breeze as it could not get a pole or a tree to spread. When this ruler happened to see the hanging jasmine he left his chariot for the creeper to climb was an incident that has passed since Sangam age to the present generation of Tamils. Such a celebrated chieftain would not accept any large kingdom offered freely but would receive with much reverence the little honey that was offered to the *nadukals* says a poem, indicating the amount of respect attached to the offerings and finally the *nadukals*[22].

When worship was conducted, we understand from our sources that people prayed for many of their needs and wants with a belief they will benefit surely. A lady prayed for certain peculiar things like that she should be blessed with guests every day, her husband should win in the wars he fights and also requests that she should be blessed with enemy rulers to fight[23]. She prayed Every day to her forefathers who had become *nadukals*. Prayers were offered for wellbeing, prosperity and betterment of life[24].

There are two different issues on which the *nadukals* were erected that we have seen so far. One is the heroes who last life in saving the cattle and the other is all those who lost their life in fighting against the enemies to save their mother land rather in support of their particular ruler of the land. Hence we understand that every normal death did not associate with erection of a *nadukal*.

Still there is one more interesting and a very different issue where a *nadukal* was established to a Sangam age king. A Chola king by name Kopperuncholan was mentioned in the Sangam literature Purananuru[25]. There was an unpleasant event in his

---

[22] Ku.Ve. Balasubramaniyan,*Sanga Ilakiyathil Puraporul,* Ch–4, p.158

[23] Purananuru–306

[24] Ibid–263

[25] Purananuru–212–223

life. His two princes due to their association with certain people they revolted against their father. Kopperuncholan and his sons got ready to fight with each other. But the well versed poets with good intention wanted to avoid the feud. This king was also known for his association with many well versed scholars. In the midst of his way to fight he was stopped by a poet of his region and advised to avoid the battle as neither the victory nor the loss would give him happiness and the poet suggested him to retire from worldly life.

The king took to his advice and the battle was averted. As a next step the king decided to starve and die facing north direction. This has been referred as *vadakkiruthal* in Tamil language. The whole process has been well defined in the Purananuru poems. A lonely place just on the outskirts of the region was chosen and the place was cleaned and good amount of fresh green grass was spread over. The king who renounced worldly life would sit facing northern direction and would start meditating. He will starve but was associated with a number of intellectuals and at times spoke to them too. This would continue until his death. In this case we find a number of poets also renounced their life along with him. But one poet namely Pottiyar was advised by the king not to follow him as the wife of the poet was in the family way. The king and all his associates were given the privilege of memorial stones. The king's best friend a poet namely Pisiranthaiyar native of Pandyan kingdom happened to arrive after his death and renounced his life too. The best part of their life is that both the king and his poet friend had never met in their life but had great respect and friendship for each other.

When the king had passed away *nadukal* was established for him and the poems further specify the reason behind the construction of a *nadukal* for him. As the king was able to withhold the good name, fame and prestige of the royal family and also for renouncing this worldly life by *vadakkiruthal* he was bestowed with a memorial stone.

This is a single and specifically different issue where the king was given a hero stone by the intellectuals of his own domain. But still we are yet to find such stones through excavation or exploration. This instance also reveals the fact the practice of others accompanying the ruler and sacrificing their life by themselves without an iota of compulsion in it had existed in that land.

The exhaustive references of the memorial stones, particularly of this period of study do definitely make us to think that what may be the reasons, circumstances and rather compulsions that would have necessitated for such a cult of establishing and worshiping the dead.

One must be the frequent wars fought by the three crowned monarchs and his subordinates of this time the Cheras, Cholas and Pandyas. This was also revered by the kings too for one obvious reason practically speaking to keep the flow of human resource in the form of soldiers eternal in which their personal interest also rests. From the side of the family members of the person who met with untimely death that would have been a great loss or even greatest. So, as a source of consolation this practice of memorial stones would have begun. We could see people, even today going to the graveyards of their beloved ones. The practice of inscribing the details of the incident and heroic deeds of the concerned person and family genealogy besides the use of long lasting stone would have provided a chance to be remembered for a very long time. This would have served the purpose of remembering the particular soldier by many generations. The ideology of believing the dead as an eternal in the form of a superior sprit and equal to God would have provided a sense of pride and dignity to the grieved family members and their progeny. In one instance we have already seen the purpose of the inscription was for the world to know about as contested by the poet himself. So this appears to be an effort to convert the dead as an eternal and immortal. The customs followed by them in conducting the worship of these memorial stones do deliver us the meticulous efforts by the family and the society in rewarding and recognizing the service of the person with public interest. It will not be far from truth if we consider this act of our forefathers as a means of preserving and passing the facts of history from generation to generation. In true sense, these are the historical records which they have left for us to know and understand their pattern of lifestyle and the amount of greatness attached to selflessness during this period of study.

3

Cultural Nationalism in Indian Perspective

D.D. Pattanaik[1]*

ABSTRACT

Indian variant of nationalism needs to be differentiated from the rest of the world. Indian nationalism is essentially cultural rather than political. It is nation-based state rather than state-based nation. Indian nationalism could be crystally expressed in term of indigeneous language 'Rashtra' which encompasses entire spectrum of 'Dharma', philosophy, literature, culture, heritage and ethos. The substratum of Indian nationalism is essentially Hindu. The nomenclature Hindu refers to nationality rather than religion. Religion is a Semitic concept. Hinduism is neither institutionalized nor proselytizing. It is catholic and inclusive. The term Hindu though used by the foreigners by first millennia the community, i.e., the people of this land, said to have internalized the entirety of this 'rashtra' since five millennia earlier if Saraswati River civilization is the genesis. Hindu identity of India could hardly be jettisoned since a few foreigners walked over it. Interpretation of Indian society and culture was basically done by the colonial super-structure as a matter of conspiracy syndrome, and the Indian intellectuals who emerged out of it wholly emulated it, and hence the subterfuge. The nomenclatures pluralism, composite culture, multi-culture, multi-nation are all employed to marginalize Indian national identity.

[1] Indian Council of Social Science Research, Aruna Asaf Ali Marg, New Delhi 110067.
**Corresponding author:* E-mail: ddpatnaik1952@gmail.com

Indian society is not a manufactured one. Its totality since inception of its civilizational chord must be studied in entirety. Its fall out was peculiar breed of secularism compounded with minrtyism – an aberration indeed. Indian nationalism is humanistic and universalistic; and it would not be assessed from western prism. Cultural nationalism glorifies the India, i.e., 'Bharat Varsh', but hardly there is any iota of chauvinism. The concept of Motherland is very well there; but elevates one to the entirety of humanity and the universe. So the peculiarity and distinction of Indian nationalism is to be probed, of course with critical reasoning, but without bias. It is ironical that the oldest possible civilization, i.e., India is struggling to gain identity in the comity of nations. There are nations like Great Britain and a dozen others who have certain parity when we analyze Indian nationalism. Could anyone contemplate to present an idea on Great Britain without Anglo-Saxon, English and Protestant Christianity? These need detailed study. Finally India surfaces with its Hindu cultural identity as a nation.

***Key words*:** Western thinking, Rashtra, Vedic nationalism, Organic idealistic elements, Universalistic nationalism, Integral Humanism, Inclusive assimilative feature.

CLARIFICATION

To initiate the discourse on the aforementioned subject it would be imperative to spell out the narrative of cultural nationalism itself so much so that this phrase is being employed in manifold nations variously to suit their mindset and environment[1]. It is relevant to notice cultural revolution of China in the year 1948 which was a crystal political acrobatic from Indian parlance since the revolution catapulted then the established political status quo. Of course this conforms the western authors, to whom culture seems to be natural repository of political legitimacy. To the Indian nationalists it constitutes the sum-total of virtues which govern the individual as well as the society[2]. Culture as a whole is necessary minimum for integration and in-built system of beliefs, customs, traditions, attributes and values[3]. Thus, the adjective culture here connotes the cumulative effect of a people's reservoir and provides a collective life in a given land.

Further, while plunging into the ocean of Indian nationalism it would be pertinent to delve upon the western paradigm since there is no parallel on this dimension under the driving force of history. A given people has its own backdrop, inclination, way of life, aspiration and language to express its own mind and feeling. But the Indian intellectuals have become prisoners of their imagined 'el dorado' emulating the colonial super-structure since late 18th century and thus vainly endeavour to map and measure Indian ideals and phenomena from western prism, and hence the subterfuge occurs giving rise to utter confusion and aberration. Therefore little space may be spared to western nationalism preceding the polemic of Indian variant as a matter of perusal.

As such the sketch of this paper is essentially analytical with certain dose of comparative-contrasting bid for increasing clarity and intellectual dispension.

WESTERN TERRITORIAL POLITICAL NATIONALISM

The western world, precisely Europe, made its debut as political organization reciping with Greek city states. From mere city states the political edifice reached its zenith to the leviathan power structure of Holy Roman Empire within a span of one millennium. With the emergence of renaissance and reformation the secular world-view sought to insulate the state from the ambit of church, and to some this is the genesis of western nationalism[4], whereas Nocolo Machiavellie was the principal architect who articulated the nation (state) as embodiment of territorial, secular and political ingredients. Some others, again, hold that the Treaty of Westphalia, 1948 followed by Thirty Years of War, delineating the territories of Europe was the harbinger of nationalism. The given populations within a definite territory were constrained to share the nationalism of the same land[5].

Composition of the United States of America (1776–89) and the occurance of the French Revolution (1789) almost synchronized together which spelt out tangible nationalistic outburst equating the nation with the entailing people. Nineteenth century, further, accentuated the popular imagination passing through unification of Italy and integration of Germany. Mazinni surfaced as the spiritual protagonist of European nationalism who hastened to empirically believe that common memory of pain of a given people acts as the cementing force to reckon with.

The fall out of the First World War marginalized the notion of nation as regimented, jingoistic, chauvinist compounded with narrowness and competitiveness. Thus an idea cropped out that nationalism is essentially detrimental to global peace and human progress. Same thing was repeated during the course of Second World War. Following both the Wars the League of Nations and the United Nations came into vogue with a kind of aspiration to mitigate the hate hysteria and usher into a just world order.

In this march of history nationalism in Europe primarily became a political device; and the nomenclature nation-state came into fore universally. From Bluntschlie down to Heric J. Hobbesworm and Gellner all have well founded basis to conclude nationalism precisely with European experience and this is supposed to be the standard bearer for the intellectuals world over. But the critical side rests with the Indian variant exlporing indigenous genius.

NATIONALISM IN INDIAN CONTEXT

Indian experience of nationalism is somewhat markedly different and distinct in consonance with the underlying historical and sociological development of the Indian people. So when the term nationalism is portrayed in Indian context it is constraint to be confused and felt obscure. Therefore principal authorities on Indian nationalism like B.C. Pal, during the heydays of Indian renaissance, used the veritable Indian expression 'Rashtra', not nation, in order to get rid of confusion and exhibit clarity of thought[6]. Rashtra implies geo-cultural dimension whereas 'nation' rests with the territorial-political-secular elements. The former upholds nation-based state, whereas the later conforms state-based nation[7] exhibiting cognizance to political spectrum. Western nationalism ended with self, *i.e.,* inherent national interest, whereas Indian nationalism aims at securing universalism. These differences would appear crystally in the course of the present analysis.

Nationalism in India dates back to the Vedic epoch cropping up during 5000 B.C., while Saraswati River civilization gained ground. Rig Veda, the earliest Vedas and also the earliest literature of humanity, defined the geographical existence of Bharat varsh' as 'Sapt Sindhu', a land encompassing seven principal rivers. 'Vishnu Purana' deciphers the geographical existence of 'Bharat varsh' thus:

"Uttaram yat samudrasya Himachaleshaiva Dakshinam
Varsham tad Bharata nama Bharati yatra santati"

It means the land lies north of the ocean and the south of the snowy mountains is called Bharata, and there dwell the progenies of Bharata". This Purana was composed during second century A.C., and interestingly Arnold Toynbee deciphered India's ancient geographical landscape exactly same way. It is also relevant here to recall Meghasthese, the Great ambassador to the court of Chandragupta Maurya in third century B.C., who observed that India was a vast land and yet the remotest people had precise idea regarding the geography of the country. Its reason may be that the religio-cultural sentiment of the people all across this landscape ruled the roost. It is testified when Kautilya during the same period raised the banner of 'Rashtra' from North West of India preceding the establishment of Mauryan empire[8].

Vincent Smith sketches out the factor of Indian nationalism in most glowing terms, thus: "The political unity of India, although never attained perfectly in fact, always was the idea of the people through centuries..... The conception of universal sovereign as the

Chakraborty Raja through Sanskrit literature and is emphasized in score of literatures to the battlefield of Kurukshetra, as told in the Mahabharata, implies the belief that all the Indian peoples including those of the extreme south, were united by real bonds and concerned in interests common to all. European writers, as a rule, have been more conscious of the diversity rather than unity of India. Joseph Cunningham, author of universally independent spirit, is an exception. When describing the Sikh fears of British aggression in 1885, he recorded the acute and true observation that Hindustan, from Cabut to the valley of Assam, was one country and domination on it is associated to the minds of the people with the dominance of one monarch or one race. India, therefore, possesses and always has possessed for considerably........ (thousands) years of ideal political unity......India offers a unity in diversity. The underlying unity being less obvious than the superficial diversity, its nature and limitations merit exposition in spite of several kingdoms, and so on.......India beyond all doubt possesses deep underlying fundamental unity far more than that produced either by geographical isolation or by political suzerainty. That unity transcends the innumerable diversities of blood, colour, language, dress, manners and sect[9].

It is further evident that with the turn of the first millennia, Kharabela, the emperor of Kalinga (present Odisha) sent a garrison to north India to thwart the forces of the Greek Demetrians who had surrounded Magadh and Ayodhya. When the Greek General Minander attacked north India, the Vedic kings of the same region being inspired by Kharabel counter-attacked the Greeks[10].

While the age-old Indianness continued to flow unabated as a living force notwithstanding manifold foreign aggressions and consequent rule, the same became oblivious in ancient civilizations like Greek, Roman, Baylonean and Egyptian. The Britishers in mid nineteenth century got amazed as how could the ancient Indianness was till then "alive inspite of eight centuries of Islamic rule"! "The Indian 'Rashtra' is not merely a geographical concept. It is some kind of thought which mystically keeps a patriot in a frame of mind to transcend all material and immediate interests and protect the motherland from all odds, calamities, aggressions and evils. The love for the country is not the same way as striving for nationhood, self-determination, sovereignty of a composite culture. 'Rashtra bhakti' (veneration to the Nation) is erroneously meant loyalty to the nation rather than patriotism, Patriotism is subconscious feeling or state of mind of being Indian whose hearts beat with the same intensity. Patriotism in this context is a civilizational concern. In this sense the Indian patriotism involves a greater emotional attachment to the motherland than nationalism can ever do. Rashtra unlike nation involves unflinching dedication to the land"[11]. It expects disinterested performance of duty rather than obtaining rights, a unique feature of Indian national life.

Hindu Substratum of Indian Nationalism

While the entirety of Indian history is discerned closely or from distance, it is evident that it smacks of Hindu make up in its complexion. Conceptually and behaviourally cultural nationalism in Indian perspective surfaces as Hindu nationalism.

The term Hindu again creates a kind of ambivalence, much of which are manufactured by the critics by fusing with traditional mind set concoted under colonial education. Well, Hindu here is meant to a way of life which cropped up in this land since millennia encompassing the entire wavelength of history, and it is not to be fused with Semitic religions which appear as creeds[12]. It is true that the term Hindu owes its etymological genesis to the use of the foreigners who envisioned the land of mighty river Sindhu as Hindu as a matter of phonetical jugglery; and it became a common stock in the lexicon to hold the Indians as Hindus. So, empirically and epistemologically those who carried aloft the long cherished cultural legacy of this land were made known as Hindus[13], and this geographical entity becomes a 'rashtra' by its cultural unity[14]. So Hindu refers much to nationality encompassing the entire panorama of India's civilizational concerns such as its literature, philosophy, heritage and ethos[15].

With this kind of backdrop the Hindus were given to learn the phenomenon 'Rashtra' from Rig Vedas. It is naïve to expect a kind of blossomed nation at the dawn of human civilization which is a growing concept with the vicissitude of history, but the components of a Rashtra was obviously, albeit elusively, found space. Striking feature here is that first the civil society came into the cradle of civilization, and then the state occupied space. It implies that the political organization came up as a matter of expedience, an contrivance to fulfil human needs. So while the state as a political tool in a necessary concommitment it does not constitute the nucleus of the Rashtra.

However, Yajurveda defined 'Rashtra' in somewhat modern vocabulary. To it, Rashtra constitutes "a people living in a definite territory who accept the pre-eminence of God or nature as the determining force, accept the pre-eminence of knowledge and respect the man learning and are well equipped to protect their country from foreign invasion and internal or national or natural calamities". Atharva Veda also incorporated the word 'Rashtra' and endowed upon it as almost tantamount to present day Directive Principles of State Policy.

Atharva Veda evoked phenomenally on patriotism which was the adequate ode of expression of Nationhood. It held: "Mata bhumi putroham prutivya"(12/1/12). It means, "May the land be my mother and I am the son of the motherland". So the concept of motherland is latent and inherent in India since the Vedic period to acknowledge the Nation.

Encyclopedia of Hinduism, from this perspective, defines 'Rashtra' as "a community that forms a cultural unity. It may not necessarily connote a single political unity......(it) the entire 'Bharat Varsh is a given geographical entity inhabitated by diverse people, who are however, bound together in a cultural unity and a sense of oneness". This vindicates and conforms the relationship of India and Hindu as inextricably interwoven and mutually comprehensible.

One devout Hindu recalls Ganga, Yamuna, Saraswati, Narmada, Sindhu, Kaveri and Godavari at the time of bath even in the remotest countryside and wishes all these water to mingle with his water in hand. He also recalls Ayodhya, Mathura, Maya, Kashi, Kanchi and Avantika though he might not have moved out of his village or region. He recalls seven sacred mountains and feels the Himalayas as divine abode. All these chantings contain 90% patriotism and 10% metaphysics. When he goes through Ramayana and Mahabharata, different places of the country and its historical episodes move like a film before his eyes so much so that the characters and places are so familiar to him that he finds them in his surrounding. Moreover, he learns entire fabric of ethics and metaphysics out of the vast mores of these epics. It is evident that all the vernaculars of this country made debut after translating these epics. Out of these classics that myriads of legends, myths and fables were popularised in the entire land in consonance with local cultures and usages. Thus inspite of micro differences there is a kind macro unity, and to an Indian the whole of Bharat Varsh is 'poonya bhoomi' (sacred land) and 'karma bhoomi' (land for activism) and not 'bhog bhoomi' (land for enjoyment) as one alien is likely to treat.

Then there are 4 'Dhamas' (holy shrines) located in four directions of the country, 51 'shakti pithas' (holy places embodied with Mother Power), 12 'Jyotirlingas' (Lord Shiva), 12 Sun temples, 12 Ganesh temples and innumerable Vishnu temples all across the country; and a Hindu is epected to move for pilgrimages to all these places in order to attain self-realisation. Adi Shankaracharya who was instrumental to institute those four 'Dhamas' also organized Kumbh Mela at Prayag Raj in every twelve years, which is supposed to be largest human gathering. Thus Indian religion, in crude language, and patriotism merge together which neither assiduously manufactured nor it is the offshoot of deliberate institutionalization. In fact, Hinduism is neither institutionalized nor proselytizing.

Six fold of Indian metaphysics constitute Indian philosophy, *viz.*, Vedanta, Sankhya, Nyaya Vaisheshika, Purva Mimamsa and

Uttar Mimansa. It was later added with Jainism and Buddhism. To add more, the classical dances of India, namely, Bharatanatyam, Kathakali, Odissi, Kuchipudi and Manipuri, are all dedicated to Hindu pantheons. Similar is the case with the indigenous songs and music. Nausad, a Hindi music director, once conceded that Shiva is the pioneer of Indian music[15].

Sanskrit language, considered as divine language of the Hindus, serves as the mother of all Indian vernaculars including Tamil whose 40% vocabulary owe to Sanskrit. Sanskrit gains primacy since it is the original language which provided shape to Indian literature and philosophy. It may be added with the fact that all the ancient literatures were scribed in Sanskrit for which it is contemplated as sublime. It followed that all the religious 'slokas' (recitations) were composed in Sanskrit all over the country.

M.S. Golwalkar, one foremost cultural nationalist, clamours, "We (the Hindus) existed when there was no necessity for any name"[16] – and that too in the form of a Nation. Nationhood, to Hindus, is not a matter of letter, but of spirit. The Hindus inherit everthing, in this land in term of language, history, religion, common attitude regarding national icons compounded with identical historical loss and gain and claim to have a religion which corroborates the national stock[17]. Therefore Aurobindo Ghose hastened to believe that nationalism in India is 'Sanatana Dharma'[18] - implying Hinduism.

It must be borne in mind that when we talk of sublime culture of this land it is in fact referred to Hindu culture so much so that Bhagvat Geeta represents Indian metaphysics and culture though other religious texts are not to be undermined. Dr. Karan Singh beautifully pens it thus:"It is true that throughout her (India's) long history it is Hinduism that set the term of national culture in India, that acted as the great creative force behind most of her varied achievements, that provided the ethos, the cultural milieu, the great backdrop, as it were against which the drama of her history was played out"[19]. In similar strain another critic observes thus: since the Hindus are the creators, historical careers and enjoy an overwhelming numerical predominance, they are to constitute the cultural basis of Indian nation. "India can only be and ought to aspire to become a nation-state in the sense of the Hindu nation"[20]. If certain foreigners walk over a nation as matter of political expedition, it in no way compromises the long cherished way of life of the land.

British Premier (of hundred years back) rightly observed that it was amazing to find the Hindus who contemplate the whole of India as "temple goddess" and concluded that India was akin to body and Hindu as the soul[21]. Indian turned Irish savant Annie Besant stated in her Banaras Hindu University Convocation in 1917 thus:".....Christians came to India and may go away, but India would remain the same. Islam came to India and might go way without affecting the Indian nation, similar is with Zoroastrians......but if Hinduism goes out of this land, then India would remain as a corpse". This spells volumes on the ingredients of Indian nationalism, and the imposition of pluralism and such others factors in subsequent years does not mitigate the identity of the nation. After all a nation is studied from its origin and not to be carved out from the midst to suit predilection of a colonial outfit.

Lord Meston observes forcefully, thus:"Amid all chaos and conflicts of India's history, Hinduism has been the constant force in the country's life and cultural vicissitude. Its power has lain, not in political organization, nor even a religious organization, but in building men's daily lives and giving them a standard authority which is important of temporal changes[22]. To recall Vincent Smith again, "The most fundamental unity of India lies with Hinduism"[23]. Sir Robert Risley, "the great divider" (of Indian society) also believed that in spite of thousands of ethnic divisions in this country, Hindusim serves as the basic common ground"[24]. Jawaharlal Nehru, a protagonist of secularism pertinently probed Indian nationalism and felt that this is the land of pilgrimages (in his Madurai address to the All India Congress Committee in 1961). So it is pilgrimage to whom? This vindicates cultural nationalism as well as the Hindu foundation of India.

Insights of Indian Cultural Nationalism

The second half of nineteenth century is characterized with emergence of neo nationalistic fervor which was essentially Hindu in tone and temper. It made its debut with the 'Swadeshi Mela' organized by Raj Narain Bose and Nabagopal Mitra in Bengal in the year 1867. Since it used to meet in the month of 'Chaitra', it was also called 'Chaita Mela', and even 'Hindu Mela'. It continued till 1880. Bose was the first to coin the expression Hindu Rashtra. Swami Vivekananda, Bal Gangadhar Tilak, Bipin Chandra Pal, Aurobindo Ghose, Annie Besant all employed the expression 'Hindu Nation'. Though Dayananda Saraswati did not use it his expression 'Vedic Swaraj' recalling the glories of prestine past was rather more vigorous. A point must be noted here is that during those days the term Hindu was not being viewed communally.

Bankim Chandra Chattopadhyay used by means of his superb literary works – 'Vande Mataram' (Salutation to Motherland) being the song celestial in finest possible texture.

Role and contributions of Swami Vivekananda in the firmament of igniting nationalism and religious fervor accentuated the underlying concept of 'Bharat Mata' – a kind of syncretic manifestation of Indianness, which may be otherwise called Hinduness. In his words, "Right from Kashmir to Kanyakumari this Bharat Mata is exact incarnation of Jagadamba". Aurobindo equated the Indian nation with the sum-total of 'Sanatana Dharma'. Swami Shraddhanand urged the people to erect 'Bharat Mata' temples all across the country.

The last decade of nineteenth century witnessed waxing up the nationalist forces within the Congress fold through Lal-Bal-Pal (Lala Lajpat Rai, Bal Gangadhar Tilak, Bipin Chandra Pal respectively), triumvirate and save the national organization which was steadily drifting towards westernization.

This stream of thought-structure Vedic culture may be summed up a Cultural Nationalism in Indian perspective. One may also name it "neo nationalism" in India. By whatever nomenclature it might be known, it is no display of any kind of racist arrogance nor any jingoistic narrow creed as the world has experienced in Europe then. This kind of nationalism in India has been the natural offshoot of self expression of the nation in entirety. This nationalism gives rise the following outcome and sidelines as a matter of perusal:

(1) Synthesis of religion and nationalism, in broader sense Hinduism and India, as a matter of natural corollary in Indian context. This is not all manufactured to meet certain end, but based on self-evident cultural inputs since the inception of its collective life. It accrues out of the fact that the terminology 'Bharat vrash' or 'Bharat khand', as found in ancient literature, epistemologically has cultural connotation rather than any political signification. So, albeit, we use the term religion here for the sake of understanding in contemporary sense, it must be taken crudely.

(2) It follows that Hindu foundation of Indian nationalism is self-evident. It is testified that the very idea of Bharat, *i.e.,* India, is a cultural one, and Hindu refers to nationality compounded with culture. It must be distinguished from religion, as commonly found in semitic sense.

(3) Laying emphasis on 'Dharma', culture, language, tradition, point of honour, ethos and whatever which buttress all these components. Dharma has wider connotation than relgion as narrated in the *Encyclopedia of Religions* (Vol. IV).

(4) Cherishing the underlying chain of India's past, present and future. Bankim Chandra articulated it as Jagaddhatri, Kali and Durga symbolizing the prosperous past of India, devastating present and resurgent future respectively.

(5) It follows that this approach pushes one to study Indian history from the Saraswati-Vedic epoch dating back to seven millennia and not from the midst, which is fallacious. But the critics adhering to critical reasoning escape from serious debate and do not bother for ancient India rediculing it as figment of imagination.

(6) Eulogizing the glorious achievements of India casting glance to the ancient and medieval period which have remained elusive as part of colonial conspiracy agenda.

(7) Jettisoning the Aryan invasion theory and upholding the Saraswati river civilization dating back to 7000 years as per recent researches[25]. In fact this singular formulation questioned the legitimacy of the Aryans, say the Hindus, as the career of national stock. This became popularized only during the colonial rule and that too without evidence – rightly challenged by Dr. B. R. Ambedkar, the architect of Indian Constitution, in his work "Who are the Shudras? How the Fourth Varna Came?"

(8) Envisions India as "one nation, one people, one culture". While it gives due cognizance to the myriad varying sub-cultures and traditions it is not oblivious of the macro synonymity. It is well comparable to differentiation and integration.

(9) Critical to western culture and civilization to be infused in India which is crept with materialism under manifold 'isms' to illustrate its civilizational chord.

(10) Last but not the least is "adhering to nation-based state in sharpt contrast to state-based nation of the West. In other words, Indian nationalism is prone to be identified with culture rather than political edifice.

Further, Cultural Nationalism broadly upholds the following theories with adequate reservations and variations from western standpoint.

(1) Organic Theory of the Nation (not of the state).

(2) Idealistic Theory of the Nation (not of the state).

(3) Universalistic Nationalism.

(4) Integral Humanism.

Cultural Nationalism presupposes nationalism as one layer, not an end in itself or final culmination as the western Idealism upholds, though conspicuous of course under the present circumstance; but simply as one phase in the process of evolution of humanism and universalism. Hindu worldview is dominantly inclusive and universalist. It is, further, humanistic, but is critical to the western variant of humanism which are crept with utter materialism and cynicism under concoted existentialism, utilitarianism etc. Indian thinking views man integrally and not as part. Accordingly body, mind, intellect and soul must be knit together and placed in the entire wavelength of family, society, nation, the world and universe giving credence to individuality. It means, while the west crave much for material aspect as humanism, Indian side lay adequate emphasis to matter, intellect and spirit in order to address human need.

Concerns of Indian Cultural Nationalists

Every philosophy, ideology must have some careers, may be indefined. It is no monopoly of any organization or party or individual. But every thought-structure is obviously carried aloft by certain sections – at least they lead and highlight though it is everybody's domain. There is no scope here to deliberate on the careers or the points at stake here. But those who claim to be the protagonists of veritable nationalism in Indian lay absolute stress on nation and nationalism. To them "Nation First" stands at the apex whenever they are to determine any point and address any problem. National integration occupies the focal point to them. Here then crops of myriad burning tangible issues and problems. But the nationalist agenda is to see the nation in highest esteem and consider all other points subservient to it.

It is a historical question as how to look India and for that matter Hinduism from the nationalist angle so much so that without Hinduism India can hardly sustain and *vice versa*. This conceptual and empirical fact is overlooked by the Macaulayen-Liberal or say Nehruvian school along with the Marxists. The question at stake is to interpret the very idea of India, its society and culture in proper perspective. The cultural nationalists pose counter challenge to the well in-built intellectual edifice of the said domain shaped under the cloak of super colonial approach to Indian problems.

CRITICAL APPRAISAL

Fed with western intellectual diet compounded with colonial conspiracy syndrome the neo Indian intelligentia in nineteenth century were enamoured with western assessment of India, its view on Indian culture and society. This school got associated with twentieth century Indian Marxists and jettisoned whatever cultural nationalists evoked, and rather ridiculed the nationalist aspiration as primordial, narrow, communal and even fascist. Following achievement of independence it was expected to plunge into introspection; but the colonial intellectual burden was increasingly boosted by these two schools who ruled the roost.

Right from Sir William Jones down to Max Muller a kind of mind set was engineered to alienate the Indians themselves from the fundamentals of their nationhood. As a sequel they were given to understand that the so-called original Aryans were migrants from Eurosia marginalizing the Indian aborigines. This theory was out and out based on figment of imagination deficient of evidence; yet this acted as a singular hard assault to disfigure the composition of Indian society giving rise to the peculiar idea of "India: A Nation in Making" tinged with composite culture theory and social pluralism. It's another fall out was import of the maxim of minority syndrome to prove its secular credential, an aberration indeed!

Cultural nationalism rejects the minority syndrome which is eating into the vitals of India's soul. It generates fissiparous tendencies as evident from dismemberment of India in 1947. Cultural nationalism takes serious exception to it since political division does not affect nationality which owes its existence to time immorial. Aberration of secularism reduced it to mere minority privilege and treated it as necessary concomitant to secularism while heeding credence to it (secularism) as the soul of this nation. But secularism has nothing to do with Indian nationalism. The very concept of secularism cropped up in European soil in order to insulate the Church from the State which has no relevance in India. Secularism in its distorted form may best be applied to as a principle of the government to checkmate theocracy as the rest of Afro-Asian countries upheld, and can hardly be treated as foundation of Indian nation. Cultural nationalism carries aloft the age old Indian tradition of paying honour to all beliefs and spur discrimination against the citizens on the ground of religion. It is the broader Hindu ethos which safeguards the interests of all; but when this Hindu phenomenon is being jeopardized the notion of religious equality would be at stake. This catholicy is often considered as a weak point if we look at the successive demands on minority privileges. So in spite of incorporating the basic secular values the substratum of Indian nationalism remains unaffected, and it must be realized in proper perspective[26]. Unfortunately religious toleration has swerved India to pursue the course of appeasement policy unabated, and electoral politics is being falsely masquerading as torch bearer of Indian nationalism.

To conclude, cultural nationalism in Indian conext is only a civilizational assessment. It is neither a blue-print nor a political creed. It sketches out the basic appearance of taking into consideration its entire gamut of history and way of life of the entailing society. It is not intended to institutionalize any doctrine nor to formalise any imposition. The natural course of history is only probed and acknowledged and that too appended by the great savants after due introspection. Those who champion the course of critical reasoning seem to have swayed with imported text book maxims and marginalizing indigenous scrutiny. Could any one ponder over Great Britain without Anglo-Saxon, Protestant Christianity and English? The same is the case with India while contemplating its national identity. There are about a dozen nations where geo-cultural factors rule the roost to shape the nation as we deliberate here in Indian context. Unfortunately certain expressions such as secularism, pluralism, composite culture and the like are put before the (nation) cart which pushes

Indian nationalism without direction. The Gandhian era during the freedom struggle could not carry the spiritual fruits of renaissance and rather bore the burden of extra-national imbroglio of Khilafat. Thus the final phase of freedom struggle and post independence restructuring failed to unleash the identity of India. This ideology of cultural nationalism is a sincere bid to exhibit the national identity of India, which may be called Hindutva. But this term is at the receiving end in contemporary electoral politics without perusal. No intellectual attempt to debate or study is undertaken on it, but to generate popular euphoria has been the singular agenda of the competitive political parties, and the media, academica, and intelligentia are all engaged in popular, passionate debate rooms. Under the backdrop of Partition in the name of religion, it is the Hindu leaders in the Constituent Assembly who inserted secularism in the Constitution. The Hindu worldview is catholic and inclusive. Rig Veda says "Let noble thoughts come to us from all sides". Bhagvat Gita says "I (Lord Krishna) could be reached in any way one offers". Upanishad says "Truth is one and wise men call it in many ways".

Arguably could Great Britain's national identity be questioned there by any rival political party or critics? If the British nationalistic features seem justifiable, at what point the India side suffers fallacy? It is deplorable that whenever the discourse on national identity of India is resorted the bogey of minoritism is posed. When the Swadeshi Movement in India was undertaken by the Cultural Nationalists, *viz*, Aurobindo, Bal Gangadhar Tilak and Bipin Chandra Pal, Jawaharlal Nehru quipped in 1907 when he was studying in Cambridge, "....so what would happen to the the Muslims, who constituted one third of the population (exaggerated figure) who have lived here since generations?" If some new community crops up within the Indian society under the driving force of history it would endeavour to internalize the indigeneous coulture flowing down since ages and certainly not scuttle it to pieces.

In fact manifold Indian problems such as sub-nationalism, regionalism, linguism, fissiparous tendencies, foreign policy imperatives, multiple domestic policies suffer due to ambiguity of its own nationalism. It is mystically limited only to defence service and security concerns. But nationalism is much higher and nobler. It permeats the entire life span of the Indian society. If Indian society is not one, then only disaster awaits the country. An individual enriches himself with fullness which he inherits from the broader framework of the Nation. It is during the course of partition that Rajani Palme Dutt authored "India Today" in London, where he articulated India as conglomeration of several nationalities, and the Communist Party ventured to claim 15 Constituent Assemblies for 15 Provinces! We have witnessed so many up and down in the course of the history of last several decades following independence, but there has been no open intellectual, academic discourse lest it would be pulled down with pejorative adjectives! With this kind of intellectual shyness could a nation thrive? Objective of this paper is to roll a ball in intellectual firmament to unfold the identity of India in proper perspective, which is yet lacking till this day, and this is ironical that a nation with longest possible civilizational history is clamouring for identity crisis. While the local differences are being highlights so much by the so called post-modernists of India under the cloak of subaltern empowerment and micro ethnic, behavioural study, why they do not look into the macro integrating factors? What is their objective. Erstwhile Soviet Union is no parallel to India. An individual or a microspscopic or marginalized ethnic community enriches himself with fullness which he inherits from the macro frameworks of this country. Indian problems could hardly be addressed mapping it with other visible society. Typical Indian problems could be addressed in Indian way. Illustratively, caste system. The divisionists attribute it to hate hysteria. But Mahatma Gandhi looked into it a horizontally existing in the society in oceanic circle model[27]. Critics' interpretation of vertical existence of the castes splits the society while the horizontal existence integrates the society. Cultural nationalism is assimilative, cohesive and integrative. Why the unique features of Indian society and culture is not being taken up for serious study? This would not only serve the amaciating Indian nationhood, but would contribute phenomenally to the cause of humanity and kindle universalism which is ultimate goal of Indian nationalism.

NOTES AND REFERENCES

[1] Kosaku Yashino, Cultural Nationalism in Japan, 1992; Rag Starrs, Japanese Cultural Nationalism At Home and in the Asia Pacific, 2004; Guo Yingjie, Cultural Nationalism in China: The Search for National Identity under Reform, 2004; Gainor J. Allen, Performing America; Cultural American Theater, 2001; A Study on The Twilight of Britain Multiculturalism and the Politics of Toleration; etc.

[2] Gellner Ernest (1983). *Nations and Nationalism*, Basil Blacwill; Oxford, p. 55.

[3] Khan Basiruddin (*ed.*) (1987). *Composite Culture of India and National Integration*, Indian Institute of Advanced Study, Shimla, in Editorial, p. 30.

[4] Kohn Hans (1951). *The Idea of Nationalism*, The Macmillan Co., New York, pp. 119–120. For more details on European nationalism – Hayes, C.J.H. (1959). The Historical Evolution of Modern Nationalism, Macmillan Co., New York.

[5] Pattanaik, D.D. (2016). *Cultural Nationalism in Indian Perspective*, Serials Publication, New Delhi, presents in detailed in Chapter 1.

[6] Pal, B.C. (1958). *Writings and Speeches*, Vol. 1, Yugantari, Calcutta, p. 199.

[7] Bhishikar, C.P. and Upadhyay Pandit Deendayal (1988). *Concept of Rashtra*, Suruchi Prakashan, New Delhi, p. 66. Upadhyay formulated these words.

[8] Nehru Jawaharlal (1956). *The Discovery of India,* Meridian Boulds Ltd., pp. 122–123.

[9] Smith, Vincent A. Ancient and Hindu India, Oxford, London (Year of Publication not mentioned -National Library, Kolkata), pp. xviii–ix.

[10] Savarkar, V.D. (2008). *Six Golden Epoch of India (Hindi)*, Prabhat Prakashan, Delhi, pp. 59–60.

[11] Sankhdher, M.M. (1993). "Rashtra vs. Nation", Organiser (English Weekly), New Delhi, p. 2.

[12] Radhakrishnan, S. (1933). *Hindu View of Life*, London, p. 7. To him, the term Hindu is not employed in creedal sense, but it carries geo-cultural signification.

[13] Seshagiri Rao, K.L. (2011). *Encyclopedia of Hinduism*, Rupa & Co., New Delhi, IV: 513.

[14] Seshagiri, Ibid., p. 551.

[15] Nausad is a Muslim he opined so describing Hindu god Shiv as Nataraj. Doordardshan, National, Interview, 12 December 1987.

[16] Golwalkar, M.S. (1996). *Bunch of Thoughts*, Jagran Prakashan, Bangalore, p. 23.
[17] Another Hindu Nationalist, RSS ideologue, Dani Bhayaji, Organiser, 20 October 1952.
[18] Ghose Aurobindo (1965). Famous Uttarpara address, 1908, Ed., His Life and Teachings, Pondicherry Ashram, Popular Prakashan, Bombay.
[19] Singh Karan (1990). *Essays on Hinduism*, Ratna Sagar (P) Ltd., New Delhi, p. 15.
[20] Parekh Bhiku (1989). *Colonialism, Tradition and Reform*, Sage Publication, New Delhi, p. 66.
[21] Mukherjee Radhakumud (1960). *Fundamental Unity of India*, Bharatiya Vidya Bhavan, Bombay, Forewird, p. ii.
[22] Meston Lord (1931). Nationhood for India, Oxford Press, London, p. 46. Also Gilchrist, R.N. (1981). Indian Nationality, arrived at the conclusion that provides the primary base of Indian nationalism, Usha Publications, New Delhi.
[23] Smith, Vincent, Ibid, p. x.
[24] Risley Sir Robert (1965). *The People of India*, Oriental Books, Reprint Corporations, Delhi, Preface.
[25] Massive research work have been undertaken of late. Two international conclaves have been organized – one at Atlanta (1977) and another at Los Angeles (2008) in the United States where two hundred in each, historians, archeologists, sociologists and philologists met. In India there had been such Conventions at Bangaluru in 1992, at Kurukshetra in 2000 and another in 2008. Michale Dadino, David Frawley, Rajaram, S.R. Rao beside others have worked a lot on the same. Three books as illustration: Telagiri, Srikant, Aryan Invasion Theory and Indian Nationalism, Voice of India, New Delhi, 1993; Malhotra, Raajiv, Neelkandan, Aurobindon, Breaking India, Amryllies, New Delhi, 2011; Ed., Raman, S. Kalyan, *Vedic River Saraswati and Hindu Civilization*, Aryan Book International, New Delhi, 2008. A.P.
[26] Sir Syed Ahmed, the Aligarh Muslim University, state so in 1987 at a Muslim congregation in Punjab thus:"All of us are Hindus by nationality though religiously Muslim". Mahammed Bukhari of Jama Masjid visited Mecca in 1976 and had faced a situation when he was reminded by an Arabian that they (the Indian Muslims) were Hindus by nationality.
[27] Hazary Narayan and Sanghamitra Buddhapriya (*ed.*) (2007). *Immortal Sarvoday*, Publishing Corporation, New Delhi, p. 179.

4

District Planning in India

R. ARUNA JAYAMANI[1*] AND R. CHINNADURAI[2]

ABSTRACT

Ideas of "planning from below" or "grass roots planning" have been stated time and again since the inception of planning process in India. Planning at the district and lower levels has been seen as an input to the process of strengthening democracy in a country. The 73rd and 74th Constitutional Amendments (Articles 243G, 243W) envisage planning for economic development and social justice by PRIs and Municipalities respectively. In order to take the process of participative district planning forward, the foremost necessity is to set up District Planning Committee (DPCs) on the lines of Article 243ZD and has mandated to prepare District Development Plan. The district planning is to arrive at an integrated, participatory, coordinated idea of development of a region. An essential step in this direction is to ensure that each Panchayat at any level or Municipality is treated as a planning unit and the 'district plan' is prepared through consolidation and integration of these plans as well as by considering the development of the district as a whole. Reinforcing Administration and Planning through delegation of powers, setting up an effective grievance redressal

[1] Centre for Good Governance and Policy Analysis, National Institute of Rural Development and Panchayati Raj, Rajendranagar, Hyderabad-500030.

[2] Centre for Decentralized Planning, National Institute of Rural Development and Panchayati Raj, Rajendranagar, Hyderabad–500030.

**Corresponding author:* E-mail: arunajayamani.nird@gov.in

system, and creation of necessary infrastructure, service conditions, and facilities for all personnel working in these areas would also need to be specifically addressed in the District Plan. This chapter deals on the origin, conceptual clarity, mechanism in place for planning at the various levels of governance, status of planning, problems and suggestions to strengthen the district planning. This paper drawn its discussion based on an elaborative field study conducted in 10 states from India.

Key words: Decentralization, Decentralized planning, District planning Participation.

BACKGROUND

India being the largest democratic country in the world, decentralization of planning and development administration becomes mandatory to ensure effective delivery system and good governance. Decentralized planning as an approach to balanced development and reduction of regional disparities emerged well before Independence. The 73rd and 74th Constitutional Amendments (Articles 243G, 243W) envisage planning for economic development and social justice by PRIs and Municipalities respectively, and their consolidation (Article 243ZD) into District Development Plans by the District Planning Committee (DPCs), after consideration of matters of common interest between the Panchayats and the Municipalities including: spatial planning, sharing of water and other physical and natural resources, integrated development of infrastructure, environmental conservation, the extent and type of resources available whether financial or otherwise. The initial attempts towards decentralized planning however began from the second five year plan onwards. The Eleventh Plan further envisaged participatory district planning process as an integral part of the preparation of State Five Year Plans and Annual Plans. The Planning Commission and MoPR, Govt. of India jointly prepared a Manual for Integrated District Planning to guide the stats and districts in the context of preparation of district planning. Based on the manual, each district should prepare an integrated vision for development (for both urban and rural areas) over 10 to 15 years, and a perspective plan of 5 years, not constrained or conditioned by the existing schemes and programmes. In order to take the process of participative district planning forward, the foremost necessity is to set up District Planning Committee (DPCs) on the lines of Article 243 ZD. The District Planning Committee (DPC) has powerful mandate of aggregating village level plans prepared through active participation of Gram Sabha and citizen-centric urban plans.

Need for District Planning

The Constitution of India provides for the distribution of legislative and financial power between the Centre and the States. Further, the Constitution does not specify any political authority for the districts. Thus, this raises the important issue of the possibility of district planning. However, the Constitution can be amended given the necessary will. The case for district planning arises from the fact that a coordinated inter-departmental effort is likely to give greater benefits from the same outlay. At the sub-state levels, usually the development activities are handled by various departments with specific organizational structures. The non-departmental public agencies such as commercial banks, input corporations, market agencies, etc., also operate at the district and sub-district levels with separate plan of action. Thus, development functions get highly fragmented among numerous departments and agencies. Immense benefits can be reaped by integrating and coordinating these individual efforts into a consistent regional plan framework. This requires setting up of planning agency which can benefit from the fact that most departments and agencies. Therefore, coordinated, consistent and integrated district planning is crucial for development and social justice. Thus, it is desirable that planning is decentralized atleast up to the district level so that effective use can be made of local resources after identifying local needs and problems. To plan at a centralized level would mean either the neglect of diversity or would involve costly collection of data and information from a large area and the processing of such voluminous amount of information to evolve a consistent and integrated plan. Therefore, decentralized planning to be of manageable size while at the same time accounting for regional needs and resources.

The emphasis on sub-state level planning in India has primarily been the outcome of political values. The influence of Gandhian ideals of self-reliance of small communities is viable only through decentralized planning. Ideas of "planning from below" or "grass roots planning" have been stated time and again since the inception of planning process in India. Planning at the district and lower levels has been seen as an input to the process of strengthening democracy in a country. The political ideals of democracy and socialism have been the concepts underlying whatever efforts that have been made to decentralize the planning process.

Concept of District Planning

The district planning is to arrive at an integrated, participatory, coordinated idea of development of a region. An essential step in this direction is to ensure that each panchayat at any level or municipality is treated as a planning unit and the 'district plan' is prepared through consolidation and integration of these plans as well as by considering the development of the district as a whole.

As of now, the concept of district planning is considerably diluted by the fact that most department schemes envisage in their guidelines, separate and self-contained 'planning' processes. In other words, district level planning implies evolving a developmental scenario at district level focus with specific need of people, growth potentials of region and with resources available. Though, the district plan must be specific to its agro-climate and socio-economic conditions and with the national goal focus of increasing production, reducing employment and poverty alleviation.

Decentralized Planning Initiatives

The idea of District Planning was advocated even at the time of the formulation of the First Five Year Plan which had mooted a village production council for agricultural planning, village, block and district plans were required to be prepared on the eve of the formulation of the Second Five Year Plan. Following the report of the Balwantrai Mehta, the Third Plan laid emphasis on the role of people's participation in local level planning under the framework the Panchayati Raj. The Third Plan described the methodology for preparing state plans for rural development by consolidating the district and block plans.

A decade after the Balwantrai Mehta Committee's recommendations, the Administrative Reforms Commission noted that the attempts at district planning have not been effective due to lack of clear guidelines and lack of specific resources at the district. The Commission therefore recommended to create appropriate planning mechanism for formulation of plans at district level.

Later based on the recommendations of Administrative Reforms Commission, the Planning Commission issued guidelines in the year 1969. These guidelines were worked out so as to encourage the formulation of district plans. The guidelines stressed the need for decentralized planning and suggested the involvement of local self-governments through participation of local people including progressive farmers and entrepreneurs for assessment of existing problems, needs and matching with the available resources for addressing the priority issues. This was the first major document giving comprehensive outline on the methodology of district planning. Followed on the planning commission's guideline some states were attempted preparation of district plans but did not made any dent on the realistic process of decentralization. In the Fourth Plan, a central scheme was initiated to assist the States strengthening their planning mechanism and it was extended to the district.

In its approach to the Fifth Five Year Plan, the Planning Commission has stressed the importance of District Planning for effective use of funds and local resources for the cause of reduction of inequalities among the states and for better coordination of planning and implementation with the prime role of PRIs. Some states were able to formulate district schemes during the Fifth Plan. But not much development took due to administrative reluctance and non-cooperation of various line departments. The states felt lack of freedom and flexibility to frame their own schemes of priority.

District Planning Board (DPB)

There was an approach to establish a three-tier planning machinery at district level with the adequate powers of decision making on local matters of administration and development by establishing a planning cell. This unit is called District Planning Board (DPB) comprises both officials and non-officials. The District Collector and some development officers at the district level are usually associated with the DPB along with the representation from sectoral departments. In few states the board was headed by the State's Minister and some other states the district collector work as Chairman of the Board. The Collector occupied a key role in the board even in those states where he was not the Chairman. The control of the Collector over the district planning process was further exercised through the District Planning Officer who works under him and who is the member secretary of DPB.

The DPB, could not become effective instrument for performing detailed planning functions such as analysis of data and formulation of schemes. Thus, in many states a small sub-committee or executive committees of the DPB were constituted. Those committees were designated in different names in different states. The committee assisted the district planning board in the field of identifying the problems, suggesting targets, proposing inter-sectoral or intra-sectoral transfers when necessary and supervising budgetary allocations and expenditure. These committees meet once in a month or two months. Since the officers of the smaller committee of the DPB have their own other responsibilities to attend, they were not in a position to spare time for the preparation of district plan. Thus, very few states have attempted to provide for full-time staff. According to the information obtained by the Planning Commission's Working Group on District Planning, the number of purely technical personnel available in the states ranged from 2 to 6 officers in 1984. They have usually been seconded from other departments and do not seem to possess any particular planning experience.

In 1982 the Planning Commission set up a working group on district planning and it submitted its report in 1984 under the Chairman of Shri C.H. Hanumantha Rao. This Group suggested setting up of a broad-based District Planning Body compromising of representatives from the Zilla Panchayat, Panchayat Samitis, Municipalities and Corporations, MLAs and MPs from the district, prominent personalities, workers and entrepreneurs representatives, back representatives etc. The working group further recommended that to aid the District Planning Cell in Technical matters, there could be a District Planning office headed by a Chief Planning Officer with a status next to that of the District Collector. The Group also suggested the strengthening of the Collector's role and clear definition of financial and administrative powers for the district level government and adequate disaggregation of outlay according to districts. Thus the Working Group made far reaching recommendations on the technical and administrative aspects of district planning. It is clear that the organization support for planning rural development programme, whether at the block or the district level, is inadequate and weak. Therefore, there is a need to review the entire setup for planning at the grass-roots.

The G.V.K. Rao Committee, which was set up to review the administrative arrangement for rural development and poverty alleviation also stressed the need for decentralized planning at the district and block level. More specifically, it endorsed the Working Group's recommendation for setting up district planning bodies and the suggestions for decentralization of financial and administrative powers.

L.M. Singhvi Committee (1986) on revitalization of Panchayati Raj institution has also emphasized the concept of District Planning for constructive rural development and nation-building.

To streamline and radically change the entire process of planning, the importance of micro-planning and people's active participation at lower cannot be denied. Since district planning is a vital part of the process of decentralization, the Planning Commission was directed to readjust its priorities so as to serve this aim and thus ensure considerable gain to the economy and promote human resource development. Under this directive, considerable importance is henceforth to be given to development in blocks and districts in the Eighth Plan.

A good planning organization at the grassroots is necessary for the success of planning at these levels. Realization of this need has led several state governments to establish planning boards at the district level, while the launching of the Integrated Rural Development Programme (IRDP) and National Rural Employment Programme (NREP) has also created a new organization, known as the District Rural Development Agency, for their planning and implementation. Both these agencies are interesting and important experiments.

The Constitution (64th Amendment) Bill was followed in July 1989 with the Constitution (65th Amendment) Bill that sought to endow urban local bodies – from town Panchayats and Municipalities to Metropolitan Councils – with powers similar to those that were sought to be devolved to the rural panchayats. A particularly significant provision was for buckling the development of the rural hinterland in every district to the neighbouring urban centres through the mechanism of a District Planning Committee (DPC) jointly elected by, from and amongst the members of the Panchayats at all three levels and the Municipalities within the district. The DPCs so constituted were to be entrusted with the task of consolidating' the plans prepared at lower levels into a draft district development plan' which would then be forwarded to the State Government.

The 73rd and 74th Constitutional Amendments (Articles 243G, 243W) envisage planning for economic development and social justice by Panchayati Raj Institutions (PRIs) and Urban Local Bodies (ULBs), respectively; and, their consolidation (Article 243ZD) into District Development Plans by the District Planning Committees (DPCs), after consideration of matters of common interest.

11th Plan and Decentralized Planning

The Eleventh Plan further envisages participatory district planning process as an integral part of the preparation of State Five Year Plans and Annual Plans. Such holistic planning will result in convergence of schemes, synergistic implementation and better outcomes.

***Second administrative reform commission*:** Emphasized the importance of decentralized and participative district planning recommended;

i. Development authorities to become the technical/planning arms of the DPCs,
ii. Strict compliance of the guidelines dated 25.8.2006 issued by the Planning Commission in preparation of the district plan,
iii. Developing methodology of participatory local level planning,
iv. Integration of district plans with the state plans,
v. Clear demarcation of planning functions among the local governments and planning committees.

Manual for Integrated District Planning

The first volume of the Manual contains an exposition of the essential principles of participative district planning and sets out the steps to be taken at the state and national levels. The second volume is a Handbook for District Planning that lays down the modalities and sequence of processes for preparation of a participative district plan. It includes the formats and checklists by which the processes can be documented and data provided for different planning units.

Participative Integrated District Planning

Participative integrated planning is multi-dimensional, includes: (i) Three levels of panchayats and municipalities, (ii) Multiple sectors (*viz* health, education, nutrition, sanitation and livelihoods), (iii) A variety of funding sources (*viz* State/Centrally Sponsored Schemes, Finance Commission and own resources), (iv) Integration of departmental and programmatic machinery, and (v) A broad spectrum of stakeholders; each seeking fulfilment of its own from a plan. With increased specialisation and sectoral thrusts in development, there has been a tendency for more and more sectoral plans prepared in relative isolation, for example, District Health Plan, District Watershed Plan, District Education Plan and so on. It is important that this vertical planning process is transformed into a horizontal planning process, where local governments and other planning entities work together to develop a holistic plan, out of which sectoral plans emerge. Achieving this coordination in the face of an increasing number of schemes and fund-flows into the districts will necessitate a quantum improvement in the existing planning and implementation mechanism through local governments and DPCs.

Role of BRGF / MGNREGA in Catalyzing Decentralized Planning

In spite of various initiatives on decentralized, participative and integrated planning, the MGNREGS and BRGF remain the two main schemes for planning from below. BRGF attempts to bridge critical gaps in the infrastructure by empowering the local bodies and through appropriate capacity building to facilitate participatory planning and decision making. Under Section 16 and 17 of the MGNREGA, 2005 the Gram Panchayat and the Gram Sabha have been given key roles in planning, implementation and monitoring of the programme. Those two schemes provide good source of funds to the Gram Panchayats.

Decentralisation–Chronology of Attempts and Committee Reports

Year	*Item*	*Ideas and concepts*
First Plan, 51–56	Community Development Blocks	To break up planning exercise into national, state, district and local community levels
Second Plan, 56–61	District Development Councils	Drawing up of village plans and popular participation in planning through the process of democratic decentralization
1957	Balwant Rai Mehta Committee	Village, block, district panchayat institutions established
1967	Administrative Reforms Commission	Resources to be given/local variations accommodated, purposeful plan for Area.
1969	Planning Commission	Formulated guidelines; detailed the concept of the district plan and methodology of drawing up such a plan in the framework of annual plans, medium term plans and perspective plans
1978	Prof. M.L. Dantwala	Block level planning to form a link between village and district level planning
1983–84	Centrally Sponsored Scheme/Reseerve Bank of India	Strengthen district plan/district credit plan
1984	Hanumantha Rao Committee	Decentralisation of function, powers and finances; setting up of district planning bodies and district planning cells
1985	G V K Rao Committee	Administrative arrangements for rural development; district panchayat to manage all development programmes

Table ***Contd...***

Table ***Contd...***

Year	***Item***	***Ideas and concepts***
1993	73rd Constitutional Amendment	243G W
	74th Constitutional Amendment	243Z D district planning
1994–96	Conformity acts by state	Constitution of district planning committee in all the states
2006	Second Administrative Reform Commission	Emphasized participatory district plan
2008	MoPR and Planning Commission	Manual on integrated district plan
2009	Backward Region Grant Fund	Preparation of district plan

Methods for preparation of draft district plan

Decentralized planning is, a plan to be prepared by the rural and urban local bodies accordance with their own resources for the activities assigned to them and the national/state schemes implemented by them and, Physical integration of the plans of rural and urban local bodies with the elements of the state plan that are physically implemented within the geographic confines of that unit.

Objectives of decentralized plan

The objective of decentralized planning is to arrive at an integrated, participatory coordinated idea of development of a local area. An essential step in this direction is to ensure that each panchayat at any level or municipality is treated as a planning unit and the 'district plan' is built up through consolidation and integration of these plans as well as by considering the development of the district as a whole. It is a two-way interactive exercise, the district being viewed as a convenient local area.

Building a vision

The vision would be primarily articulated in terms of goals and outcomes and would address basically, three aspects of development, namely, human development indicators, infrastructure development and development in the productive sector. The articulation of a vision is best done in each planning unit, right down to the Gram Panchayat level, stating with respect to each area what the needs and potential are, what the attainable levels are and what the goals to be reached could be. A basic requirement is that the preparation of the vision is not conditioned by schemes and programmes. Visioning exercise is an collective dream about a region being participative nature, it would build a spirit of teamwork.

Building vision for basic human development indicators would essentially cover all the aspects of human life like health, education, women and child welfare, social justice and availability of basic minimum services. Each panchayat could propose in its envisioning exercise, that they will achieve the levels specified for each such aspect within a particular period of time. For instance, in regions which are below the national average in literacy, the first step would be to reach the average level and the next would be to attain the desirable level. Similar envisioning could be undertaken in respect of attainments regarding health, water supply and sanitation etc. Attention has to be given in gender integration and down trodden in the participatory process in order enable them to share their views and opportunities to fulfill their needs through integrated plan. The process of visioning process starts with constituting planning committees in each gram panchayat, block and district level. The secretary of the GP, all sectoral heads of the GP, NGOs, CBOs, SHG representatives, retired resource persons and other interested persons have to be called for the planning related meetings. The planning committee would be chaired by the elected head of the respective unit of GP, IP and ZP. At each level visioning exercise to be carried for developing vision, identifying problems and needs. The ward and gram sabhas will have to be involved fully in the preparation of the district vision. Undertaking participative citizen survey is itself a good way of starting the process, through giving every citizen surveyed an opportunity to voice his or her needs and vision. The district vision document should be given wide publicity. Copies and brief abstract of the same should also be made available to the people.

Data Requirement for Decentralized Planning

While doing envisioning process, a stock-taking exercise has to be conducted for assessing the human condition in the district, and to know the availability of natural, social, financial resources and infrastructure in that region. The data base prepared would be a valuable resource for the stocktaking exercise. Planning at district level require a careful study of human and natural resources along with field realities for optimum utilization and responsive planning. Varieties of data on physical resources, human and economic aspects are the pre-requisites for preparing an integrated plan for the district. The data required to prepare profile of the GP are discussed below.

Topography: It is much essential to understand the nature of topography, major physical divisions, drainage system, soil type and texture in order to quantify the resource base of a region.

Technology adoption: Level of technology adopted in agriculture and allied sectors are also to be ascertained. Technology status on infrastructure such as road network, communication facilities, power supply, financial institutions are to be identified.

Agriculture: In order to understand the agriculture status in the region, the data relating to area under cultivation, land use pattern, cropping pattern, crop cycle, nature and quality of soil, sources and adequacy of irrigation, types of farming, ownership of land, size of land holdings and the system of tenure, production and productivity are to be collected at village level.

Resource inventory: Identification of various resources available in the region like physical and natural resources are to be carried out in a proper way. Data on quantum and quality availability of local resources, their utilization and possibility of usage for various purposes have to be collected and verification to be done through from different sources.

The data required for decentralized planning can be broadly grouped into the following categories:

Natural Resources Database

i. ***Water resources***: Type of sources, quantity and quality, water availability and scarcity period etc.,

ii. ***Soil***: Type, quality, soil problems and causes,

iii. ***Flora and fauna***: Species availability and uses,

iv. ***Land use pattern***: Different uses of land in the planning region,

v. ***Livestock***: Nature, quantity, production and productivity,

vi. Cropping pattern (season-wise),

vii. ***Climate***: Variation subject to season and suitability for various options,

viii. ***Rainfall***: Rainfall rate over a period of time, temperature variations and weather conditions are to be properly assessed.

Participative Citizen Surveys and Manpower Planning

Data regarding demography of the region like male-female ratio, child population, education, employment status, caste system, land holdings, land-man ratio, wage rate, size of agricultural laborers and their migration, etc., to be collected to understand the sociological aspects while formulating a plan. Human resources are as important as physical resources. One of the reasons for the failure is under-utilization of the human resources. Therefore, the plan should clearly state the details of human resources that are available in their region. The planning team has to collect the demographical data like total population, sex, age, educational status, occupational status and skill availability. If the region has inadequate skilled laborers, then, the plan should suggest the ways to train the people to equip them with some suitable skills. If the local region has surplus labour, the plan should find ways to utilize the surplus laborers by providing suitable employment. Information is a basic tool for planning, but information relevant to each area and its population is rarely available. A citizen survey leading to a database for each gram panchayat to know more about them, developed in a participative manner, is a desirable pre-requisite for participatory planning. The process of data collection on citizens could be so dealt with that Gram Panchayats see in it, their own empowerment. This also builds a climate of participation even before the actual planning process starts. Data to be collected on the following heads.

Availability of Infrastructure Facilities

In India, still some of the remote areas and villages are not provided with adequate infrastructural facilities, to enable faster development and growth infrastructures are inevitable. Facilities like roads, communication, power supply, marketing channels, etc., are inadequate or low standard in the rural areas. Growth and development of a region or sector directly related with its quantum and quality availability of resources and infrastructure. Hence, the planning team has to collect information about the availability and requirement of infrastructural facilities. It will help the planner to prepare a suitable plan to fill up the gap before initiating implementation of any programme.

Data Required on Infrastructure - Economic and Social

Economic infrastructure

i. ***Markets*:** Types, availability, needed and location appropriateness,

ii. ***Banks/Financial Institutions*:** Numbers, area of operation, performance, etc.,

iii. ***Roads/Transport/Communication/Electricity*:** Available, working, not working,

iv. ***Agri input centers, Agri. Extn. Officers*:** Seeds, fertilizers, pesticides, Govt./Private, and
v. ***Veterinary centers*:** Numbers and services.

Social Infrastructure availability and their Utility

i. Schools/Colleges/Educational Institutions,
ii. Hospitals/Health Institutions,
iii. Community Centre/Libraries/etc,
iv. Placement of Entertainment Centers, and
v. Drinking water/Sanitation.

Trade and Industry

i. Mining and quarrying,
ii. Small scale industries,
iii. Household/Cottage industries,
iv. Handicrafts,
v. Forest, agro based industries,
vi. Wholesale/Retail trade

Availability of Financial Resources and Flow

Finance is the first and foremost criteria for putting any plan into action. Success of a plan depends on the financial provisions and its timely flow, whether a short term or long term plan; it is shaped by the fund availability. The decision regarding, when plan is to be started and to be completed, the type of machineries to be used, personnel to be employed and other related matters can be finalized only on the basis of the financial availability.

The details on various sources to be ascertained, like

i. Grants received from the State/Central Govt.,
ii. Credit from the banking at financial institutions,
iii. Local bodies general fund,
iv. Peoples contribution,
v. Loan from the financial institutions.

Identification of Problems and Needs of the People

The next important step in planning process is identification of problems and needs of the local people. For this purpose, the planning region has to be surveyed and the data must be collected from all households and discussion to be carried with resource persons and general public. Planning team has to understand the nature and acuteness of various problems through observation in that particular region. Particulars on educational status, income and expenditure, level of poverty, consumption pattern of people, living standard and life styles have to be collected. The proposed plan should be given focus on solving the identified problems through satisfying the needs of people.

Prioritization of problems

In rural areas, problems are multidimensional nature and prevail at various levels. These problems cannot be solved at one go. Certain problems may take a few years to solve and some other within a few days or months. Some problems like epidemics and other health related problems are very serious which would need the urgent attention. Whereas some others like provision of transport and communication facilities can be given next priority. Plan should prioritize and develop programmes depending upon the urgency of problems.

Identification of skills, opportunities and technological options

Development opportunities in the planning area have to be identified. If an area is facing acute unemployment problem, it has to be tackled by generating adequate employment opportunities in that area. But, where employment can be created? Whether in agriculture and allied sector? or in industrial sector? or in services sector? Answers to these questions will help to prepare a suitable plan. Then, it is essential to find out the availability of skilled persons in that particular region. Technology is another important factor in planning. Technologies adopted in agriculture and allied sector and also in industrial sector have to be identified in order to avoid overlapping of technologies. Therefore, better understanding of available opportunities, skills and technological gap is essential and linking them in a systematic way to utilize these three factors at an optimum level for better development.

Review of earlier and current programmes and projects

Another important task of planning is, before starting into the planning process, it is necessary to the review the earlier and current programmes and projects implemented by the governmental and non-governmental organizations in the region. Information regarding what kind of programmes were implemented, targets, achievements and causes of failures, level of people's participation, suitability, feasibility, type of organization, staffing pattern and source of finance have to be analyzed. Further, this information will help the planner to avoid repetition of programmes and get away from the failures. Study of ongoing programmes and strategies will help to set the targets of the proposed plan in achievable manner.

Concern on environmental sustainability

Planning at the grass root or state or at the national level should aim at sustainability in development. Instead of planning for adhoc solutions, striving towards arriving permanent solutions create much impact on the development scenario in the region. For example, if a region is having problems of unemployment and poverty, the plan should pave the ways and means to provide permanent employment opportunities, either farm or off-farm, in government or non-government organizations or by self-employment. The programmes like providing wage employment through various government schemes may satisfy the immediate requirement but will not solve the problems permanently. Therefore, planners have to do maximum efforts to solve the problems through sustainable way by alternate mechanisms with suitable strategies. At the same time, the proposed industrial or business activities should not degrade the environment.

Formulation of objectives

Formulation of objectives is one of the major tasks of planning. The important points to be considered during formulation are: it should be formulated towards solving the problems of the local people and regional prosperity. The planner should concentrate on the peculiar problems for immediate solution. The objectives should be achievable focusing on optimum utilization of locally available resources.

Designing of strategies, programmes and targets

After identification of the problems and finalizing the objectives and priorities, the team has to concentrate on preparation of proper strategies depending upon the problems encountered and objectives enunciated by involving people and acknowledging the people concerns. The strategies have to be prepared in order to deliver benefits to the local people within the stipulated time. Setting of targets is an important function in development planning. To fulfill the objectives, the targets are to be fixed in specific terms with a time frame and should be based on the availability of resources, ability of services, and capacity of the implementing mechanism and state policies.

Resource Allocation and Project Implementation

It is another important stage in the planning exercise. Resources in the form of men, material, money and energy, their proper distribution, timely delivery and steady flow of resources and finances are the vital factors contributing to the success of any plan. If any one of these resources is not available or scarcely available that will lead to delay in achieving the fixed targets. Therefore, the resources are to be properly distributed among various activities spelt out in the plan in such a way that their optimum utilization must pave the way for achieving the specified objectives. The local government component of the plan would emerge out of the resource envelope containing the following sources of funds:- (i) Own resources available for development, (ii) Transfers by State Finance Commission for development purposes, (iii) Twelfth Finance Commission grants passed on by the State Government, (iv) Untied grants for local planning, (v) Grants in respect of Centrally Sponsored, (vi) Schemes that have been assigned to the local bodies for the purposes of implementation, (vii) Grants for State Plan schemes assigned for implementation through Local Governments, (viii) Grants for externally supported schemes assigned for implementation through Local Governments, and (ix) Estimated contribution by the communities themselves.

Matching of Resources to the Plan

Ideally speaking, each Gram Panchayat should be free to allocate resources in accordance with the assessed needs. However, at this stage of our development, the local planning exercise has to take into account the diversity of sources of funds. The attempts should be to put them to best possible use. Therefore, once the order of resources for the plan are known, it is best to place them into a matrix that is divided into three categories, namely, purely untied funds, partly untied funds and tied funds. Such a matrix would give each Panchayat an idea of how it can slot its priorities into the conditionality's associated with funding. This would ensure that funds, which are inescapably tied, should be first used and then untied funds are applied.

Once needs are assessed at the panchayat level, a process of linking each need to the source of funding can be adopted, through the steps detailed below:

Step 1: Classifying each need into a matrix: Discussions with people would throw up several needs, such as housing, sending children to schools, nutrition, roads, health care etc. Each of these will need to be classified under broad headings irrespective of the source of funds.

Step 2: Assigning specific purpose grants: Having classified the needs, the next step would be to identify the specific purpose grants that address such needs and match these resources to each need.

Step 3: Assigning part-untied funds: Part-untied funds are available for certain purposes and allow for a certain measure of convergence with other schemes. Examples are funds from award of Central and State Finance Commission. These funds can be used for gap filling within limits.

Step 4: Assigning fully untied funds: The final step is the placement of fully untied funds. These are typically own sources of revenue, general or untied State Plan Grants, SFC grants.

In this connection, it would also be very useful to consider the assignment of non-monetary contributions, such as voluntary labour, as fully or partly untied resources.

Sequencing of Planning

The planning exercise ought to lead to a five-year plan for the period corresponding with the national plan period, and annual plans that define and prioritize areas and schemes from such a plan. The longer term plans would capture the overall picture of the Panchayat and allow people to understand what planning and governmental funding could hold out for them. Once a five year plan is prepared, the annual plan can be drawn out from it. Considering the size and availability of personnel of Gram Panchayats, it is obvious that they would need assistance and help in the preparation of projects and schemes, but the decision should be that of the gram sabha. Development Meets/Workshops at gram sabha level would be necessary leading to the emergence of a draft plan, with schemes and projects listed in priority.

Planning at Different Levels

Gram panchayat plan: A basic point to be stressed is that everybody should be able to understand the plan, more so the people of the village and the Gram Panchayat members. The Gram Panchayat level plan could follow a broad and simple pattern Drawn from best practices, given below is a possible framework: (i) The vision, (ii) Citizens' Profile, (iii) Natural Resources and Infrastructure Profile, (iv) The Financial Resources Profile, (v) The Anti Poverty Programme, (vi) The Gender Justice Programme, (vii) The Special Component and Tribal Programmes, (viii) Programmes for Social Security, (ix) Implementation, and (x) Monitoring and Evaluation

The planning process at the intermediate panchayat

The process and format of the Intermediate Panchayat plan will be largely the same as that suggested for the Gram Panchayats. However, the actual components would be dependent on the Activity Mapping for the Block Panchayat and the vision envisaged by the Intermediate panchayat. An important role of this level of panchayat is to act as a facilitator in the various steps of planning at the gram panchayat level. The tasks of the Intermediate Panchayat as regards planning would be: (i) Prepare five year and annual plans in accordance with activity mapping and covering inter village-panchayat issues, through a participatory process following the steps listed in the case of gram panchayats (as appropriate), (ii) Maintain multidisciplinary technical teams (which could include NGOs) for assisting gram panchayats in planning and implementation. This would especially synergize inter-tier coordination for watershed development and Rural Business Hub initiatives. There is urgent need to equip each Intermediate Panchayat with a planning support unit, (iii) Maintain and manage multi-panchayat cadres, such as teachers, engineers, watershed managers, social forestry supervisors, anganwadi supervisors, and intermediate level health supervisory workers, and (iv) Feedback from Gram Panchayats regarding works outside their purview, such as inter-village road formation and multi panchayat irrigation structures could be included in Intermediate Panchayat Plans.

The planning process at the district level

As regards district Panchayats, the role would be one of preparing plans in accordance with activity mapping and overall coordination in planning, providing capacity building and technical support, to lower levels of panchayats. The formulation of district development plan involves integration of area plans prepared by the rural and urban local bodies with development plans of the sectoral departments in the districts and credit plans prepared by the Lead Bank of the district.

Issues to be noted while preparing perspective plan

Reinforcing Administration and Planning through delegation of powers, setting up an effective grievance redressal system, and creation of necessary infrastructure, service conditions, and facilities for all personnel working in these areas would also need to be specifically addressed in the District Plan. There is need to ensure close collaboration between levels of Panchayats, without converting the relationship into either a hierarchical or an effort-duplicating one. The principle of financial subsidiarity will need to be followed, by which even if a higher level of Panchayat, such as a District or Intermediate Panchayat sanctions a work of a value less than a prescribed floor limit, it transfers the money allocated for that work to the Gram Panchayat concerned for implementation. This will lead to a clear understanding and separation of who implements what, regardless of who sanctions it. In addition, just as district and intermediate levels of panchayats would be mandated to delegate implementation of schemes below a certain outlay ceiling to the level below, it ought also be open to lower levels of panchayats to recommend to the immediate higher level such schemes that ought to be undertaken at the higher level. In addition, there is a need to enable clustering of Gram Panchayats for the purpose of building a sufficient scale for efficient planning. Some of the ground rules for planning at the intermediate level would include mandating prior consultation with Gram Panchayats. It is suggested that Intermediate and District Panchayats ought to hold meetings of all elected local government members of the levels of panchayat within its jurisdiction and carry out a detailed consultation exercise. In the case of District Panchayats a meeting of all Village Panchayat Presidents along with all elected members of the District and Block Panchayats may be held, in order to ensure a structured consultation.

FURTHER READINGS/REFERENCES

Books

Das Purnandur Sekher (2005). *Decentralized Planning and Participatory Development*, Concept Publishing Company, New Delhi.

Prasad Kamta (1988). *Planning at the Grassroots*, Sterling Publishers, New Delhi.

Articles

Rao V.M. (1989). "*Decentralised Planning Priority Economic Issues*". *Economic and Political Weekly*, 24: 1399–1405.

Sanganal Ashok, S. (2009). "District Planning Committees: An Analysis of the Roles, Responsibilities, Performance and Strengthening Measures – A Study of Mandya and Mysore District Planning Committees" Administrative Training Institute, Mysore.

Singh Rama Shankar (1990). "Decentralization of Planning: Need of the hour". *Southern Economist*, pp. 7–9.

Surendran, P. (1997). "People's Plan of Kerala". *Yojana*, 41: 34.

Reports

Institute of Social Sciences, New Delhi (1994). Decentralised Planning and Panchayati Raj.

Kerala Development Plan January Vol. 24, 2004.

Government of India (2008). Manual for Integrated District Planning, Planning Commission, Government of India, New Delhi.

Participatory Research in Asia (PRIA) 2009. Status and Functioning of District Planning Committees in India.

Government of India (2009). State and District Administration, Second Administrative Reforms Commission, Fifteenth Report, New Delhi.

5

Background of Panchayati Raj Institutions, Decentralisation and Development in Rural India

R. CHINNADURAI[1*] AND C. AJAY SHARMA[2]

ABSTRACT

In macro view or analysis development is primarily increasing national income through massive production and improving productivity concentrating in the industrial and service sector. But, micro regions may get in to imbalanced growth will be resulted in acute poverty, inequality and vulnerability. The gap between poor and rich will widen further which will seriously affect the social fabric of democracy and people governance. But the initiatives under the new Panchayati Raj Act created immense opportunities to even to the poor to raise their voice against injustice and pressure to claim their rights through Gram Sabha. In India, the process of decentralization resulted in creation of people's institutions, local self-governments known as Panchayat. Local governing institutions are granted constitutional legality as Local Government bodies responsible for socio-economic development in the rural areas. There are 29 subjects for which the panchayat is responsible with the help of Standing Committees to cover all subjects. The idea of GPDP emanated in February 2015 from Fourteenth Finance

[1] National Institute of Rural Development and Panchayati Raj, Hyderabad.
**Corresponding author:* E-mail: chinnadurai.nird@gov.in

Commission's recommendation to give Rs. 2 lakh crore to gram panchayats between 2015 and 2020. The idea was to give the panchayats the money through state governments and allow them to spend it. The Ministry of Panchayati Raj came up with the idea of Gram Panchayat Development Plan (GPDP) — an annual plan of each panchayat where the villagers would decide where the money should be spent. State government communicates the "resource envelope" to all local bodies. At the end, every panchayat knows how much money it has under different schemes and how it should plan. Once a plan is formulated, the Gram Sabha passes it. In this context, this chapter made an attempt to present the origin of decentralised planning, government of India's initiatives on vitalising the concept of Gram Panchayat Development plan and elements to be incorporated in the plan and process of development to be followed have been discussed in-depth for the benefit of wider reach.

***Key words*:** Gram panchayat development plan, Political decentralisation, People participation, Decentralised governance, Constitutional amendment, Sabki yojana and Sabka vikas.

---

1. INTRODUCTION

A number of scholars and researches have given different definition depend upon their areas of work and domain of the subjects. But, the essence of the all the definitions mean to attain a common goal and objectives focusing on bringing a positive change in various dimensions human life. It mainly aims in improving socio-economic conditions of people or a region. Improvement of human life is interlinked with various factors, therefore, the initiatives aiming towards development should focus on addressing poverty, hunger, housing, safe drinking water and sanitation. Development relies also on efforts on ensuring better health, quality education, employment, increased income, balanced ecology, appropriate use of natural resources and creating better access to various services supporting livelihood of the people in a region. The development can be resulted in creating better capabilities of the people to engage in productive functions to support their family and to contribute towards nation building.

In the era of 1990s much focus was given to the human development and it called people centric development. During this period, more concentration was given to the capacity development of the human beings. It was linked to a healthy life, education and decent standards of living. It was resulted in understanding the importance of human development, shifting the thought of development mean to only increasing national income. Regional development has got attention by fulfilment of people choices through creating better service infrastructures and involving people in the local development and decision-making. In the year 1990, the United Nations Development Programme (UNDP) has published the first global Human Development Report (HDR) and introduced the Human Development Index (HDI) as an important yardstick for measuring a country's development in addition to the existing economic and social indicators. Our country also became partner to it and made strategies to provide better education and health focus in the eighth five year plan of the nation and proclaimed to achieve Human development through incorporating in all levels of planning ranging from local development plan to national development plan.

In macro view or analysis development is primarily increasing national income through massive production and improving productivity concentrating in the industrial and service sector. But, micro regions may get in to imbalanced growth will be resulted in acute poverty, inequality and vulnerability. The gap between poor and rich will widen further which will seriously affect the social fabric of democracy and people governance. Development at a regional or village level can be attributed for easy and equal access of basic services to people including dis-advantaged, poor, vulnerable, women and religious minorities. It is to be ensured that, provision of adequate services like drinking water, sanitation, housing, energy, health, sustainable environment, education and employment.

2. THE CONCEPT OF DECENTRALISATION

Under the radical populist approach, decentralisation becomes a goal in itself for empowering the poor and the marginalised through participatory and democratic process and institutions. Under this approach, the larger aims is to bring about a structural transformation in the centralised and hierarchical systems that tend to exclude the poor and marginalised from the political and development process in a society. Democratic decentralisation for ensuring social justice for and empowerment of the poor and the marginalised is one such radical populist approach. Decentralisation will help directing the states resources towards the poor. Because the participatory approach can possibly result in increased accountability. Decentralised systems enhance accountability in many ways, *i.e.,* involvement of local people in better management of resources on which the poor are dependant. Moreover in the process of decentralisation, there is a scope for collaborative efforts among public agencies and local users resulted in synergistic outcomes. Further the decentralisation will enable the local people to participate in local decision-making process which will lead to empowerment including their skills for development roles. Ultimately, broader participation by various sections, competitive politics, and deeper economic and social transformation will make local governments more responsive to the needs of the poor and the marginalised.

Although there is greater diversity in empirical decentralisation, the basic theoretical definitions are carrying similar meaning. In general, the concept of decentralisation can be understood in three ways.

i. ***Deconcentration:*** It refers to that, the central government distribute some owned responsibilities to different its regional centres or branches without giving centralised powers to those offices. It may not be true decentralisation, but it will benefit to easy the works or responsibilities and also to extend the services to the users of beneficiaries.

ii. ***Delegation:*** It refers to that, the central government transfers certain powers and functions to its lower institutions or local bodies to make decisions and implement the strategies beneficial to its citizens. This scenario of transfer of functions, the local government institutions are having functional autonomy to implement the schemes but accountable the higher institutions.

iii. ***Devolution:*** The devolution means, the central government transfers power to decision-making, receive and mobilise resources, finance and administrative management to quasi autonomous units of local government.

The decentralisation is classified in to three categories, namely *Political decentralisation*, which means that, the political institutions collects the demands and wishes of the people and try to make the suitable polices aiming towards the welfare of the people. The *administrative decentralisation* will make ways and means to convert the policy initiatives of political institutions in to fiscal allocations and implementable regulations. *Fiscal decentralisation*, refers to powers to the local governments to levy, collect taxes, fees and spend the money for the welfare of the local communities.

3. PEOPLE PARTICIPATION (IN DECENTRALISED GOVERNANCE)

In the developing countries marginal and small farmers and the people living in slum areas are non-participants in the process of development decision-making. Their resources are very minimal and productivity is limited. Majority are poverty ridden and suppressed by the rich, the educated, and the politically well dominant. They are powerless even to claim their rightful share of society. These are the basic problems of development before introduction democratic decentralisation in India. But the initiatives under the new Panchayati Raj Act created immense opportunities to even to the poor to raise their voice against injustice and pressure to claim their rights through Gram Sabha.

In India, the process of decentralization resulted in creation of people's institutions, local self-governments known as *Panchayat*. Local governing institutions are granted constitutional legality as Local Government bodies responsible for socio-economic development in the rural areas. There are 29 subjects for which the *panchayat* is responsible with the help of Standing Committees to cover all subjects. Each standing committee has the responsibility for the financial and executive administration of the schemes and programmes within the budgetary provisions of the *panchayat*. The Gram Sabha acts as a community level accountability mechanism to ensure the functions of the PRI respond to people's needs. While fiscal devolution is a significant issue, lack of institutional modalities and clear guidelines on PRI participation and variable capacity among PRI are key lacunae.

Even though participatory planning implementation and monitoring of rural development projects is mandatory for all PRI institutions, majority of the institutions have not put full-fledged effort for mobilizing people for participation and involve them in the development process. But, a good number of Gram Panchayats in the country have been making good attempts and also attain success in implementation of development programmes and achieved expected results in the field of provision of basic needs, health and sanitation, strengthening of livelihoods, natural resource management and village self sufficiency through people participation. Available literatures show participatory planning and implementation yields good results in terms of material benefits to the stakeholders and evolve better transparency and accountability. Study of such good practices, strategies, approaches and factors of people participation in the process of planning will be very important in order to analyze for replication in other places.

4. PANCHAYATI RAJ SYSTEM IN INDIA - A BRIEF

Literatures related to Panchayati Raj System and decentralisation are available plenty all over the world and surplus materials, books, empirical and theoretical reports, articles also available on the origin and development of panchayats in India. But for the brief understanding of the readers and to give continuity of development in the field of PRIs, this chapter presents very briefly about the timelines of development in shaping the Panchayati Raj System in India and the process of decentralisation there in people participation in planning.

4.1. Statutory Provision

> *'The state shall take steps to organise village Panchayats and endow them with such powers and authority as may be necessary to enable them to function as units of self-governance'.*
>
> *(Article 40, Constitution of India)*

Historically, the institution of *Panchayat* has been an integral part of rural Indian polity and society. The idea of *Panchayats* in modern India was first evoked in the colonial period. However, during that period, *Panchayats* were primarily perceived as means of achieving village solidarity and unity, rather than as instruments of governance or development.

4.2. Balwant Rai Mehta Committee (1957)

The real impetus in the evolution of Panchayati Raj came in 1957 through the recommendations of the committee headed by Balwant Rai Mehta, former Chief Minister of Gujarat. The committee was appointed to examine the best possible way to enable people to participate in community development programs and to integrate these with PRIs. The committee observed that it was almost impossible to expect popular participation merely through extension programs. It strongly advocated the need of a "*statutory and elective body, comprehensive in its duties and functions, equipped with the necessary executive machinery and in possession of adequate resources"* in this regard.

4.3. Inauguration of "Panchayati Raj"

Following the Balwant Rai Mehta Committee recommendation, the three-tier Panchayati Raj structure first came into existence in Rajasthan on 2nd Oct. 1959. During the inauguration ceremony, it was Nehru who coined the term Panchayati Raj.

4.4. Ashoka Mehta Committee (1977)

Consequently, another committee was appointed under the chairmanship of Ashok Mehta to suggest measures for revitalising the Panchayati Raj institutions. The committee recommended that development schemes should be implemented through PRIs. Surprisingly, the committee suggested a two-tier model at district and *mandal* (cluster of villages) level covering a population of 15,000 to 20,000.

4.5. C.H. Hanumantha Rao Committee

The Planning Commission appointed a Working Group on District Planning in 1982 under the Chairmanship of C.H. Hanumantha Rao and the recommendation of this Group formed the basis for evolving the district planning and the approach was outlined in the Seventh Plan. The Seventh Plan incorporated the main ideas outlined in the recommendations of the Working Group and stated to pursue 'the decentralization of the planning process' for development. It was also realised that planning activities at the district level would vest in a single district planning body which would determine the strategies and priorities and allocate funds for various departments taking into account the planning and other capabilities available at the grassroots-level.

4.6. G.V.K. Rao Committee (1985)

The G.V.K. Rao Committee was constituted in 1985 for reviewing the administrative mechanisms for implementation of developmental programs. The committee recommended making districts the basic unit of policy planning and programming implementation. Importantly, it emphasized the necessity of holding regular elections to the Panchayats. The G.V.K. Rao Committee (CAARD) while dealing with the issue of decentralized planning endorsed the major recommendations of the Working Group on District Planning in respect of setting-up of district planning bodies and the decentralization and devolution of administrative and financial powers.

Report of the Commission on Centre-State Relations, 1988, Government of India, New Delhi, part-I, pp. 382-84. 66. Report of the CAARD, 1985, p. 30, par.4.21.

4.7. L.M. Singhvi Committee (1986)

A committee for a Concept Paper on Panchayati Raj Institutions (CCPPRI) also known as the L.M. Singhvi Committee was formed in 1987 for reviewing the functioning of Panchayati Raj institutions. It recommended the reorganization of villages for creating viable Gram Panchayats. The committee strongly recommended that greater financial resources be made available to these institutions. It opined that the Gram Sabha should be considered as the base of a decentralized democracy.

4.8. Constitution 73rd Amendment Act (1993)

The 73rd Constitutional Amendment providing constitutional status to the Panchayati Raj institutions was the fruition of the efforts and process for institutionalising the Panchayati Raj system. A vastly debated and delayed Panchayati Raj Bill was reintroduced in the parliament as the Constitution 73rd Amendment Bill. The 73rd Amendment Bill was passed by the Lok

Sabha and the Rajya Sabha with near unanimity on the 22nd and 23rd December, 1992 respectively. This Bill was ratified by 17 State Assemblies in 1993 and came into force as 'Constitution 73rd Amendment Act' from 24th April, 1993. The Act provides constitutional status to the Panchayats and gives it uniformity by making the three-tier system a permanent feature. Panchayati Raj was included in Article 243 of the Indian Constitution after the 73rd Amendment.

4.8.1. *Salient features of constitutional amendment*

- Every State has to establish panchayats in rural and municipalities in urban areas.
- The states which have population of more than two million can have three-tier system and others can have two tier systems of local governance.
- There is reservation of seats – not less than one-third seats for women.
- Reservations for SCs and STs Proportionate to their population in the region.
- The term of office for the elected body is five years.
- The local governments are entrusted the responsibility of preparation of local development plans.
- The states shall empower the panchayats and municipalities to create, collect and spend the resources through own sources like taxes, tolls, fees, rent, user charges and duties.
- The taxes collected by the state may share with the local bodies.
- The state and Central governments shall provide specific purpose grants, untied grants. Further the state can allow borrowing, accepting donations based on the suggestions of the SFC.
- The state shall establish District Planning Committee (DPC) in each district and entrust the work of preparation of district development plan by consolidating lower tier plans.

- Village assemblies' alias Gram Sabhas to be formed with the all citizens of above 18 years of age as members. The state may devolve powers of political, administrative, financial and developmental nature where in the panchayats will act proactively.
- 29 subjects are transferred to the local governments; the details of which have to be defined by the state governments. following subjects fall within the responsibilities of local governments.

5. CREATION OF THE MINISTRY OF PANCHAYATI RAJ, GOVERNMENT OF INDIA

The Ministry of Panchayati Raj was created as a separate Ministry on 27th May 2004. It has the primary objective of overseeing the implementation of Part IX of the Constitution, implementation of the provisions of the Panchayats (Extension to the Scheduled Areas) Act, 1996 (PESA) in the Fifth Schedule areas. Since under the provision in the Constitution, most of the actions including framing of laws rests with the State Governments, the Ministry strives to reach its goals with regard to improvements in the functioning of Panchayats primarily through policy interventions, advocacy, capacity building, persuasion and also through financial support.

6. V. RAMACHANDRAN COMMITTEE REPORT ON PANCHAYATS (2006)

The Report of the Working Group on Democratic Decentralisation & PRIs under the chairmanship of V. Ramachandran, former Deputy Chairman, State Planning Board, Kerala has given recommendations on different areas, mainly reviewing the panchayat legislations for appropriate size of panchayats, periodical elections to the panchayats, no need of encouraging consensus on electing the panchayat body, legalisation of DPCs election by state election commission. Activity mapping separately for each tier of panchayat. Reformation of fiscal revolution for strengthening the own source revenues for gram panchayats also vitalised. The committee specifically stressed the government of India to put forth strategies for build the capacity of the elected representatives, functionaries and members of the standing committees for full-fledged performance.

Two recommendations are more relevant to this present study, one is capacity building and other is people participation. Under capacity it suggested that, it is essential to follow as envisaged in the National Capacity Building Framework (NCBF) streamlining the NIRD as apex institution of training and capacity building. Finally, the committee has issued guidelines for preparation of local plans by the panchayats.

Deepening People's Participation

(a) In order to deepen the opportunity for more participation, States may consider establishing Ward Sabhas at the level of each ward, through appropriate legislative changes.

(b) The date, time and location for Gram Sabha meetings should be convenient for all to participate. There should be enough publicity for Gram Sabha meetings through local media and local communication methods. People attending Gram Sabha meetings should be encouraged to express their opinion freely, so that no single group dominates the proceedings. NGOs may be encouraged to promote awareness and peoples' participation.

(c) To sustain interest in Gram Sabha meetings, agendas must be circulated in advance. The Gram Sabha can be preceded with meetings of common interest groups, such as SHGs etc. Full disclosures of budgets and resources available for planning and implementation must be made.

(d) The GP Chairperson should be responsible for convening Gram Sabhas, with punitive measures of being disqualified in case of non-compliance. Relevant officers must be directed to attend Gram Sabha meetings without fail through administrative instructions.

7. CENTRAL FINANCE COMMISSION

Under Fourteenth Finance Commission (FFC) for the award period 2015– 20, grants to the tune of Rs. 2,00,292.20 crore are being devolved to Gram Panchayats constituted under Part IX of the Constitution, amounting to an assistance of Rs. 488 per capita per annum at an aggregate level for 26 States for delivering basic services, creation of reliable data base of local bodies' receipts and expenditure through audited accounts and for improvement of own source revenue. For the first time, Finance Commission grants have been decided to be given directly to Gram Panchayats and the grant is more than three times the 13th Finance Commission grant (2010-15)". The Grants provided are intended to be used to support and strengthen the delivery of basic civic services, as mentioned above, including water supply, sanitation, seepage management, sewerage and solid waste management, storm water drainage, maintenance of community assets, maintenance of roads, footpaths and street-lighting, burial, cremation grounds and any other basic service within the functions assigned to them under relevant legislations.

8. FOURTEENTH FINANCE COMMISSION (Table 1)

Table 1: Status of allocation/release under fourteenth finance commission to rural local bodies as on 31.12.2017: (Rs. in crore).

Grants	*2015–16*		*2016–17*		*2017–18*	
	Allocation	*Release*	*Allocation*	*Release*	*Allocation*	*Release*
Basic grants	21624.46	21510.46	29942.87	28529.37	34596.26	23830.20
Performance grant	—	—	3927.65	3499.45	4444.71	—
Total	21624.46	21510.46 (99.47%)	33870.52	32028.82 (94.56%)	39040.97	23830.20 (61.04%)

Fiftieth report standing committee on rural development (2017-2018) for improvement in the functioning of panchayats.

9. GRAM PANCHAYAT DEVELOPMENT PLAN (2015)

The idea of GPDP emanated in February 2015 from Fourteenth Finance Commission's recommendation to give Rs. 2 lakh crore to gram panchayats between 2015 and 2020. The idea was to give the panchayats the money through state governments and allow them to spend it. The Ministry of Panchayati Raj came up with the idea of Gram Panchayat Development Plan (GPDP) — an annual plan of each panchayat where the villagers would decide where the money should be spent. State government communicates the "resource envelope" to all local bodies. At the end, every panchayat knows how much money it has under different schemes and how it should plan. Once a plan is formulated, the gram sabha passes it. Joint Secretary Sarada G Muraleedharan, spearheading the project at the ministry, explains: "Planning is generally a very technical exercise. But here we were ready to take a leap of faith and take planning all the way to the people.

10. INTERVENTION OF THE MINISTRY OF FINANCE, GOVT. OF INDIA ON GPDP

The guidelines issued by the Ministry of Finance for the release and utilisation of funds stipulate that prior to incurring any expenditure under the FFC award, proper plans are to be prepared by the Gram Panchayats for delivery of the basic services within the functions devolved to them as per the State laws called the Gram Panchayat Development Plan (GPDP). Hence, with FFC emphasising on providing financial stability and ensuring effective planning at the grassroots level GPDP gains highest significance.

11. SUMIT BOSE COMMITTEE

The Expert Committee (Chair: Mr. Sumit Bose) submitted its report on 'Performance Based Payments for Better Outcomes in Rural Development Programmes' in January 2017. The Committee was constituted in December 2016 to look into human resources available with panchayats and suggest means by which these resources could be augmented and organised for better delivery of programmes. The Committee recommended that every panchayat should have a full time secretary, who will perform both general administration and development functions. It should also have a technical assistant, who will carry out engineering functions. To increase the social accountability of Gram Panchayats, the Committee suggested holding regular Gram Sabha meetings. Insisted to practice (i) participatory planning and budgeting; (ii) preparation of status studies for effective utilisation of earmarked budget; (iii) participatory expenditure tracking; (iv) social audit of panchayats. A system of quality monitoring should be put in place for all programmes being monitored by panchayats.

12. ORDERS ISSUED BY THE CENTRAL MINISTRIES AND FORMATION OF COORDINATION COMMITTEE

i. March 22 and May 3rd order issued by the Secretary RD for preparation of GPDP in using the Modified Plan Plus (version – 2).
ii. May 17th 2016, D/O letter issued by the Additional Secretary MoPR, on insisting the state government to appoint the CEO/ District Collector to monitor the process of preparation of GPDP for utilisation of the FFC grant.
iii. Formation of Coordination Committee at the centre level with the Secretary MoPR as chairman to supervise the progress of the utilisation of FFC grants as directed by the Ministry of Finance Govt. of India.

13. INITIATIVES OF "PEOPLE'S CAMPAIGN FOR GPDP

Sabki Yojana, Sabka Vikas People's Plan Campaign (2nd October 2018 -31st December 2018). The campaign is being undertaken on a large scale, given the number of Gram Panchayats in the country.

Special efforts have been made to ensure maximum participation of vulnerable sections of society like SC/ST/Women etc. The Gram Panchayat Development Plan aims to strengthen the role of 31 lakh elected Panchayat leaders and 2.5 crore SHG Women under DAY-NRLM in effective Gram Sabha. There will be a Public Information Campaign of all programmes in Gram Panchayat office and on Gram Samvad App. The structured Gram Sabha meetings will be spread over 2nd October - 31st December, with physical presence and presentation by frontline workers/supervisors on 29 sectors – Panchayats have a significant role to play in effective and efficient implementation of flagship schemes for transformation of rural India. The GPDP will be an intensive and structured exercise for planning at Gram Sabha level through convergence between Panchayati Raj institutions and concerned departments of the State.

14. MGNREGS CONVERGENCE WITH GPDP

The principal Secretary, Ministry of Rural Development MGNREGA Division wrote to the states insisting the MGNREGS labour budget has to be integrated with the GPDP for synergy in planning and action aiming for holistic approach within the guidelines issued by the respective states. The plan group under MGNREGS and resource groups under GPDP have to come together as one group for making integrated development plan (April, 2016).

15. REVISED GUIDELINES FOR GPDP

For the purpose of understanding and clarity the revised guidelines issued by the ministry of panchayati raj uploaded in the public website of the MoPR has been reproduced in the following sections with the minor rewriting. The stages to be followed in the process of preparation of Gram Panchayat development plan also presented with the aim of wider dissemination users and readers. Moreover, the main purpose of this study is to verify the problems and issues pertaining to GPDP as mentioned in the guidelines of developed by the MoPR. Govt. of India

15.1. Elements to be Incorporated in the GPDP

Focus on integrated gram panchayat development plan with convergence

The state may immediately take the policy decision, at the appropriate level, to operationalise GP level planning as proposed in revised guidelines issued by the MoPR. It is learned that, presently, in most states plans are prepared separately at the GP level for MGNREGS, SBM and for other schemes assigned by the States. Further, GPs are the primary agencies for identification of beneficiaries for different schemes, through Gram Sabhas. They are also given the responsibility of monitoring the projects and schemes funded by the central and state governments and also implementing purpose specific grant related activities. The panchayat representatives are represented in different committees formed by a number of parallel institutions and line departments for making decisions to implement the development and welfare projects. The panchayat also act as nodal agency activities implemented within their jurisdiction especially those related to health, sanitation, water supply, watershed management, education, nutrition, social forestry, bio-diversity and public distribution.

After commencement of FFC award, it was insisted to shift from compartmentalised planning to unified GPDP, converging all the resources over which GP has command and integrating these different functions. The important motto of this initiative is to ensure efficiency in budgeting, increased accountability in performance and better delivery of development. In addition to the FFC grant, which can be used only for basic services like sanitation, water supply, roads, street lights, play grounds, parks, burial grounds/crematoria, and other services devolved by law to the GPs.

15.2. Elements to be Considered in Preparation of Integrated GPDP

- ***Poverty reduction*:** Development efforts mainly to be focused on addressing the poverty. The poverty level is very high and vulnerability related consequences also very high in the rural areas. Therefore any development initiative has to concentrate on the reducing the poverty. The GPDP being aiming to achieve regional development must focus to incorporating poverty reduction strategies. Serious analysis on identification of patterns of poverty, identification of underlying causes and consequences of poverty will help to frame suitable strategies for improving the livelihood of the poor people. Priority has to be accorded on the basic services which support the good health and creating basic infrastructures which support the livelihood of the poorest of the poor in the panchayat region. Coordinated and concrete action on converging all the sectors, projects of central and state governments have to be harmonised in the form of realistic GPDP.
- ***Human development*:** Capacity building is a conceptual approach to development that focuses on understanding the obstacles that inhibit the people, governments, local institutions and non-governmental organisations from realising their developmental goals while enhancing the abilities that will allow them to achieve measurable and sustainable results. It is a promotion of attitudes, behaviour and competencies in individuals and partnering organisations that encourages, enable and sustains autonomy and life. Therefore, capacity building supports individuals, groups, organisations and systems to develop themselves and their social, methodological competencies and capacities to enable them to identify and prioritize their needs in order to master more effectively life and development task. Further, capacity building creates an enabling environment by providing information and opportunities about alternative ways of doing things and by assisting people to

build a different but home grown social system that reflects their desires and fulfil their needs. Therefore, before getting in to the planning process, assessment of capacity existing and capacity gap and capacity needs to be assessed to chalk out capacity building strategies. The GPDP has to build the capacity of the people, elected representatives, different committee members and SHGs for better planning for the development through GPDP.

- ***Social development*:** GPDP should be aimed at improving the wellbeing of vulnerable and marginalised groups like SCs, STs, including particularly vulnerable tribal groups and minorities, persons with disabilities, elderly people, women and children, vulnerable groups like bonded labourers, child labourers, de-notified tribes and nomads, distress-migrants, manual scavengers, transgender, victims of trafficking etc. In addition to poverty reduction and human development and economic development interventions for these categories, the GPDP should attempt to address the social determinants affecting the status of these groups.
- ***Economic development*:** In rural India, agriculture and allied sectors are the primary sector creating employment to its majority of the land holding and also landless people. The diversified activities related to forward and backward linkages of agriculture and agro based industries absorbs enormous people by providing employment including skilled and unskilled in the rural areas. Therefore strengthening agriculture and allied sectors by introducing improved technologies, innovative methods for increasing production and improving skills for better productivity will fetch more employment and income to the rural poor as well as to the farmers and also for the people engaged in supporting activities.
- ***Ecological development*:** It should include the ways of maintenance and upgradation of various eco-systems like water bodies, pastures, grass lands, catchments and local forests and conservation of biological resources and their

sustainable use like minor forest produce, fire wood, fodder, medicinal plants etc. Integrated watershed management would be the basic approach for this. All the activities taken up under GP DP should be environment friendly and bio-diversity enhancing.

- ***Public service delivery*:** The Gram Panchayat Development Plan has to develop strategies, methods and technologies to improve the service delivery to create mass access of the required services. The plan should focus on providing more services to the citizens at the same time creating own sources of income to the panchayat. The services like issuance of certificates, licenses/permits, registration of birth and death, and mediating social security pensions should be given special priority with emphasis on electronic delivery of services. No cost and low cost activities have to be listed and priority must be given to implementation at the initial stage even before receiving any activity specific funds from the external sources.
- ***Good governance*:** It refers to transparency, accountability and people participation. A necessary condition to keep the authorities accountable is to require sufficient transparency. People must be enable to have access to information, it makes actions and decisions of authorities and institutions visible and allows citizens to assess those actions and decisions. The proactive disclosure of information and free access of records and documents will ensure transparency which leads to good governance. People participation is also an important element of good governance. The GPDP should pave ways and means to create conducive environment and a platform for people to participate in decision-making and involve in development activities. Close partnership with institutions of the poor, particularly SHGs and women is also necessary. This calls for a 'Good Governance' plan for each GP including a Citizens' charter.

16. SUGGESTED STEPS FOR PREPARATION OF GPDP

Following steps should be followed for preparation of participatory GPDP:

16.1. Step 1: Panchayat Committee to Understand and Initiate the GPDP

Before beginning the process of planning it is essential to explain in detail the concept of GPDP, importance in the context of good governance and development. The processes are to be followed in GPDP also to be clearly presented before the GP Committee. The elected members of GP, members of various committees within the Gram Panchayat have to understand the process and steps in preparation of GPDP. Understanding role clarity of different committees and other stakeholders in participatory planning process need to be decided. Understanding the resource potential of the panchayat and ways and means to harness them for appropriate use for development of the panchayats has to be ascertained. Followed by, the committees have to sit and discuss letters, Government orders and circulars related to GPDP, finalisation of local publicity campaigns and deciding on formation of working groups as per the provisions of state GPDP guidelines. Listing of various activities to be carried during the process of preparation of GPDP, whom is responsible for what, timeline of the activity have to be finalised in the panchayat meeting.

Step 2: Discuss the Development Experience

Discuss the Development Experience of last five years in the GP and the current development status of the GP with focus on: Poverty, Education, Sanitation and Water supply, Public health, Local economic development, Natural Resource Management, Issues of special groups/ Persons with disabilities/Issues of SCs and STs/ Aged persons/ Children etc., Gender issues, Migration.

Step 3: Understanding the Resource Envelope of the Panchayat

GP Committee should know the resources on the basis of which it is going to prepare the GPDP. It needs to consider the financial and human resources already available/expected to be available along with the resources that can be potentially generated. At least 10 to 20% of the resources should be sought to be locally mobilised. The planned activities need to be matched with the resources.

16.2. Resource Envelope

The resource envelope of the GP, thus calculated, will contain the following sources of fund: ***Tied resources***: Swachh Bharat Mission (SBM), National Rural Health Mission (NRHM) Other centrally/ State sponsored scheme fund in which GP has command.

Untied resources: XIV Finance Commission grant, State Finance Commission grant, *Own Source of Revenue* (OSR) - taxes, non-tax, rents, fees for markets and ponds, user charges etc. MGNREGS funds, Community contribution (Cash/Kind labour), Corporate social responsibility funds, any other sources.

Human resources: The panchayat should also identify people who are willing to work for the development of the GP and make a list of them. Through this process, the GP should be able to find the human resource needed to carry out activities related to preparation of GPDP and later implementation of planned activities.

Fix the date for Gram Sabha and strategy for environment creation to mobilise maximum participation in Gram Sabha. Proper environment generation is extremely important for instilling enthusiasm among local people and ensure their participation in the GPDP process.

16.3. Step 2: Initial Gram Sabha

This Gram Sabha will be the first one in the entire process of GPDP preparation. People should be informed beforehand about the Gram Sabha to ensure maximum participation. All SHGs and functional committee members should be mobilised. Line department officials should also be invited. The objectives are: To introduce GPDP and to make local people aware about GPDP. To get approval of constitution of GPDP Committee/Working Groups. To discuss development issues separate thematic groups can be formed to discuss development issues in the Gram Sabha if attendance is sufficient. Issues to be addressed immediately along with larger issues to be addressed over time should be discussed in this Gram Sabha.

16.4. Step 3: Situation Analysis

The major objectives of situation analysis are to collect details of the existing scenario of the GP on various development issues and to assess the quality of basic civic services, infrastructure and amenities available in the GP.

Following details have to be collected during the situation analysis:

- Existing conditions and development status of the GP related to key areas like health, education, poverty, situation of vulnerable groups, etc.
- Information about the status of existing services and quality of life.

Critical information on deficiencies and gaps in basic services, infrastructure and amenities that exist in the GP are need to be identified. For conducting situational analysis, primary and secondary data need to be collected, analysed and documented. The analysis should be based on data, validated by people's knowledge.

a. In case of infrastructure, some of the gaps that could be identified with respect to roads: List of habitations without roads, length of the extension road required etc. Specify whether repair, restoration, upgrade or new construction is required.

b. In case of social development, main issues based on people's perception and expert opinion could be listed down. The issues faced by the tribal community like alienation from land, land degradation, lack of skills, lack of employment opportunities, and lack of access to public services and amenities can be listed and discussed.

c. In case of economic development, the focus should be on the potential that can be reasonably and sustainably achieved. The constraint on increasing agriculture production and productivity, linking to the markets which could add values, etc. are needed.

d. In case of the human development, deficiencies need to be assessed and addressed. Reasons for not achieving the minimum levels of learning, causes for dropout, reasons for malnutrition are also to be collected.

e. In case of civic amenities, effort should be to answer why the preferred standard of service provision and deliveries are not achieved. In case of sanitation, need for solid and liquid waste management, overall cleanliness etc.

16.5. Participatory Rural Appraisal (PRA)

Participatory Rural Appraisal or PRA is a set of techniques to assess the existing situation of the village / community. This is done by interacting with local community to understand their needs and to find out ways to cater to those needs with the help of the community itself. The purpose of PRA is to be able to learn first-hand about the status of assets, human development and services through various forms of direct consultation with people of the locality. It is a process which enables the local community to participate in their own development planning process. PRA tools may be used with the help of trained persons/organization.

***Preparation of the draft development status report of the gram panchayat*:** The collected and analysed data must be compiled and put in a report as the Draft development status report in concerned chapters.

16.6. Step 4: Gram Panchayat Meeting

After completion of the draft development status report of the Gram Panchayat development plan, the draft report has to be presented in the Gram Panchayat meeting as soon as possible. The Panchayat will get a basic idea about the community's needs and the gaps. The draft development status report should be approved by the GP committee before it is placed in the Gram Sabha. Necessary modifications can be made and the modified documents should be internalised before it is presented in the Gram Sabha.

Presentation of draft status report (DSR)

Each chapter of the DSR has to be presented and discussed separately after getting feedback from the Gram Panchayat members and line departments. In the discussion, the members should ensure that the issues and solutions drawn from the situation analysis are holistic and people centric. Subsequently, the committees and representatives of the line departments should check the feasibility and viability of the project ideas. Followed by, discussion on resource envelope and tentative resource allocation and discuss about the presentation of development report to the Gram Sabha are need to be finalised.

Discuss who would be the facilitators for presentation of each chapter to the Gram Sabha *i.e.,* Presentation of panchayat status report, Presentation on the resource envelope, Discussion on sectors/themes, Facilitation of prioritisation, Documentation of various discussion in the Gram Sabha and Discussion on plan for mobilization of people for Gram Sabha.

16.7. Step 5: Visioning and Prioritisation by the Gram Sabha

The Objectives of the Visioning and Prioritisation are to get approval for Draft Development Status Report (DSR) by the Gram Sabha, to prioritize issues based on the Draft development status report and opinion of the Gram Sabha, to identify development issues to be addressed in the annual plan, to identify development issues which needs to be addressed over five years and to identify issues that are to be addressed by other authorities/institutions. During the process the following activities to be carried.

1. ***Activity:*** Presentation, discussion and approval of DSR in Gram Sabha One of the GP Committee members/resource persons/Working Group members can read out the Development status report of the GPDP where challenges and recommendations will also be presented to make people aware about exact situations of the community. The core issues like water, sanitation, connectivity, public health etc. are to be given importance.
2. ***Visioning:*** Gram Sabha needs to discuss and develop a broad vision for improvement in identified key areas. In other words, what the local people want their GP to become in the next 5–10 years. Special focus may be given to poverty reduction, Water and Sanitation, Natural Resource Management etc. Identification of most crucial issues which need to be addressed on priority

16.8. Step 6: Draft Plan Preparation

A draft plan should be prepared based on the final DSR that was approved by the Visioning and Prioritisation Gram Sabha. This plan will contain the details about resources allocated to various sectors and projects and mode of implementation.

16.9. Step 7: Project Preparation

After the preparation of the plan and allocation of fund from respective source, detailed projects along with budget estimates need to be prepared. This should be jointly prepared by the working groups/task force, respective line department officials and GP committee.

Step 8: GP Committee Meeting

GP committee meeting is needed for validating the final plan prepared based on technically sanctioned projects and resource allocation. Panchayat committee should ensure that the plan is prepared as per the decisions of Gram Sabha and place it to Gram Sabha for final approval.

16.10. Step 9: Approval of GPDP by Gram Sabha

The GP Development Plan prepared shall be placed before the Gram Sabha either for approval or information as per state guidelines.

REFERENCES

Dashpande and Desousa Marcella (2009). Watershed Organization Trust (WOTR).

How Gram Panchayat Development Plan is Changing the Villages of India, Nidhi Sharma, ET Bureau, The Economic Times, 2016.

MoPR Report Count of GPDP, National Government Portal, Govt. of India MoPR, Govt. of India.

Panchayati Raj on the Ground – Issues in Village Level Panchayati Raj Operation Ravi.

Sumit Bose Committee on Performance Based Payments for Better Outcomes in Rural Development Programmes, PRS Legislative Research n Institute for Policy Research Studies, New Delhi.

The Working Group on Democratic Decentralisation and Panchayati Raj Institutions (2006). Planning Commission and MoPR.

Vikaspedia

6

Sustainable Housing and Urban Development

PAPPAL SUNEJA[1]*

ABSTRACT

The concept of sustainable housing is used to describe a process that applies to the housing industry. It refers to houses that are designed to reduce the overall environmental impacts, besides leaving lesser waste, more of reusing and recycling together with fewer maintenance costs and greater user satisfaction. Sustainability involves aligning economy and equity with the environment while meeting both the present and the future needs through a balance of the three components. This paper shall focus on the objectives, goals, sustainability aspects of urban housing and shall showcase a descriptive study of neighborhood unit, Clarence Perry's conception, Radburn layout, theory of new urbanism.

Key words: Housing, Reusing, User satisfaction, Sustainability.

The modern concept of sustainable development was derived from the 1987 Brundtland Report at the United Nations, which stated: *"Sustainable development is a development that meets the need of present generation without compromising the ability of future*

[1] Vishwaniketan College of Architecture, Arts & Design, Kumbhivali, Maharashtra.
**Corresponding author:* E-mail: architect.pappalsuneja@gmail.com

generation to meet their own needs". Another way of defining sustainable development is: ensuring a better quality of life for everyone now as well as for the generations to come.

The main objective of sustainable housing is:

- To produce quality homes and neighbourhood.
- To create places where people actually want to live, work and raise their families.

Also, the main goal of sustainable housing is to create high-quality places which:

- Prioritize walking, cycling, and public transport.
- Deliver a quality life, which residents and visitors are entitled to expect in terms of amenities, safety, and convenience.
- Provide a good range of community and support facilities where and when they are needed and those that are easily accessible.
- Present an attractive, well-maintained appearance with a distinct sense of place that is easily maintained.
- Promote the efficient use of land and energy and to minimize green gas emission.
- Provide an amalgamation of land uses so as to minimize transportation demands.
- Promote social integration and accommodation for a diverse range of household types and age groups.
- Enhance and protect green infrastructure and biodiversity.
- Enhance and protect the built and natural heritage.

Sustainable housing or neighbourhood should be guided by the principle of universal design *i.e.,* the design of an environment should be in such a manner that it can be accessed, understood and used to the greatest possible extent, regardless of the inhabitants' age, gender, ability or disability.

Sustainability is not confined to the physical environment only; in addition, it also includes the concept of stable integrated communities. The planning objective for this includes following main aspects:

1. The provision of communal facilities.
2. An efficient use of resources with a sustainable travel pattern, natural resources and use of land and energy.
3. The basic amenities and issues of quality of life.
4. The conservation of built and natural historical buildings and the environment.

The other concerns that need to be addressed include traffic safety, provision of public spaces and personal safety. Sustainable houses are those that are designed, built and managed as healthy, durable, safe and secure. They should be affordable for the complete spectrum of income groups. This can be attained by using low ecological energy and affordable building materials and technology. Using energy and water in an efficient way while being equipped with on-site water recycling capabilities would serve the purpose well. Also, care should be taken to protect the environment, instead of polluting it.

Furthermore, the structure should be connected to decent, safe and affordable energy, water and sanitation, and recycling facilities. It must be looked after and maintained with timely renovation and retrofitting. A good connection to jobs, healthcare facilities, shops, education and other services of a city would serve as a plus to the residents.

All in all, we can say that this is a multi-faceted concept, which is characterized by a low-density residential housing, single-use zoning and increased dependence on private automobile for transportation. It is correlated with increased energy use, pollution and traffic congestion and a decline in community concept.

The factors leading to an urban sprawl are as follows:

- The need to accommodate rising urban population.

- The economic growth and globalization.
- A desire for enlarged living space and other residential amenities.
- Attractive land and housing practices.
- Weak planning laws and single-use zoning.

Neighbourhood Unit

A neighbourhood is a geographically localised community within a larger city, town suburb or some rural area. It can be defined as a self-sustained community, which provides for maximum social interaction among the inhabitants. They are typically created by social interactions among people or the members living near one another. They are a kind of local social units, particularly larger than usual households. They are often referred to as social communities with considerably more face-to-face interaction among its members.

The fundamental components of a neighbourhood include:

- Dwelling units
- Circulation network
- Amenities
- Recreational areas/open spaces.

The term 'neighbourhood' is often used to describe the subdivision of an urban or rural settlement or the kinds of vicinity that people live in. Arnold Whittick described a neighbourhood unit as an integrated and planned urban area, related to the larger community of which it is a part and consisting of residential distinct. The neighbourhood unit is a holistic planning and design strategy that addresses the configuration of some major physical components of a community.

The four basic characteristics that define a neighbourhood unit are:

1. A mix of land uses and building types.

2. A range of mobility choices.
3. A dynamic relationship between the elements of the public and private realm.
4. A clear organizational hierarchy.

These have been described as follows:

1. A mix of uses in a neighbourhood provides the residents with opportunities to live mark and find their daily services and needs within their own community.
2. A range of mobility choices mixed land use has an important effect on the function of transportation network on a neighbour mixed land use allowing non-vehicular transportation, *i.e.,* walking and cycling, to become more viable options for residents. Complete streets facilitate the mobility choice in a neighbourhood unit.
3. The physical design of a relationship between the private and the public realm is exempted if the positive benefits of mixed uses and mobile choices are to be realised in a community. Mixed land uses can stimulate pedestrian activity, while an activated pedestrian-friendly public realm can make a mix of uses more viable.
4. The neighbourhood unit is not composed of homogeneous uses; rather, it is a configuration with a clear organizational hierarchy. Central to neighbourhood unit are public spaces or mixed-use activity centres. The basic elements that define these public spaces are streets. Further, these are connected to a larger green- or open spaces network. And further away from them, are the quiet residences within walking distance.

Talking about certain neighbourhood unit theories, we find that the neighbourhood unit, as a planning concept, evolved in response to degenerated environmental and social conditions, which fostered as a consequence of the Industrial Revolution in the early 1900s. One of the earliest authors to attempt a definition of neighbourhood unit was Clarence Perry, who was a New York planner. The concept of neighbourhood unit came up due to the advent of industrial revolution. With the latter, degradation of the city environment was witnessed, carried due to high congestion and heavy traffic movement from the city, with increasing locations of shopping and recreational activities, which further caused insecurity to school-going children. Considering all the above factors, the neighbourhood unit was evolved.

Clarence Perry's conception of a neighbourhood unit

He described neighbourhood unit as that populated area which would require and support an elementary school with a population of around 1000–1200 students; this would denote a population of 5000–6000 people. A neighbourhood is bounded by arterial roads or other boundaries with open spaces, schools community centres and local shops. He wrote that these principles if compiled well, would result in a neighbourhood community wherein the fundamental needs of family life would be met wholly. About 10% of the area would be allocated for recreational purposes and thorough traffic arteries would be confined to the surrounding streets and the internal streets, being limited to service access for the residents. In addition, a neighbourhood would be served by shopping facilities, religious areas, a library and a community centre.

Clarence Perry outlines 6 basic principles of a good neighbourhood design:

1. Major arterials and thorough traffic routes should not pass through the residential neighbourhood; rather they should provide boundaries to the neighbourhood.
2. Internal street patterns should be designed and constructed through the use of cul-de-sacs to encourage a quiet, safe and low-volume traffic movement and for the preservation of the residential atmosphere.
3. The population of the neighbourhood should be such that is sufficient to support an elementary or a primary school.

4. The focal point of a neighbourhood should be the school, which should necessarily be centrally located, along with institutions or basic facilities.
5. The maximum radius of the neighbourhood should be about one quarter of a mile *i.e.,* 400–450 m.
6. Shopping districts should be sited at the edge of the neighbourhood, preferably at the intersections of the major streets.

Street pattern, urban planning, basic facilities, walkways, sector concept

Following are the principles of neighbourhood theories:

1. ***Unit of urban planning:*** It is imperative to consider the population as a criterion for deciding the size of a neighbourhood unit, which should be in relation to the convenient walking distance to essential social services/ needs.
2. Street systems
3. ***Basic facilities:*** The neighbourhood should consist of an orderly arrangement of communal facilities.
4. ***The concept of the sector:*** A sector is a combination of two or more neighbourhoods units. In the beginning, this concept was conceived because the facilities that were not covered in a neighbourhood were to be provided in a sector. The facilities include secondary schools, major shopping units and a population of 12,000 to 18,000.
5. Neighbourhood walkways are stressed to have an independent system of pedestrian walkway complimenting the vehicular system.
6. ***Protective strips:*** These consist of the provision of green buffer areas to protect the neighbourhood unit from traffic. This also includes providing suitable facilities for developing parks, playgrounds and future expansion/widening of roads et cetera.

Radburn Layout

Radburn was founded in 1929 as a town for the major aged ones. It was planned by Ar. Clarence Stein and Henry Wright. The population shift that led to the severe housing shortage, the automobile which was becoming a mainstay in American life, added a new problem to urban living.

Radburn is America's first garden community setting a worldwide example of a harmonious blend of private and open spaces. This community was intended to be a self-sufficient unit with residential, commercial and industrial areas, each supplementing the needs of the others. The residential area included an inbuilt housing with a wide range of cost. The basic layout of the Radburn community into garden community includes the following:

- Superblock
- Cul-de-sac or cluster grouping
- Interior parklands
- Separation of pedestrian and vehicular traffic to promote safety.

The factors that influenced the planning of Radburn city were:

- Rapid industrialization after World War 1.
- The dramatic growth of various cities.
- Migration of rural population to the urban areas.
- Housing shortage.
- The need to provide housing and protection from motorized vehicle.

Radburn was initially planned for 25,000 people with an area of 149 acres, including around 400–450 single/detached houses, 90-row houses, about 100 apartment units and around 50–60 semi-detached houses.

The Architect Henry Wright enlisted the following 6 major points concerning a housing platform:

1. To plan simply, yet comprehensively. Further, the immediate area should be included. Do not stop at the property line. Adjust the sidewalks, paving to particular needs of the property. Also, arrange the buildings in such a way so as to guide light and ventilation.
2. To provide ample sites in the right places for communal use *i.e.,* social infrastructure.
3. To put factories and other industrial buildings where they can be used without wasteful transportation of goods or people.
4. The vehicular movement should be planned in such a manner so that it can be used and accessed with a minimum of danger, noise, and confusion.
5. Relationships between buildings/built-up areas should be such as to bring private and public land in relation, and the buildings in relation to each other.
6. To arrange for the occupancy of houses on a fair basis of cost and service, including the cost of what needs to be done in organising a building and maintaining the community.

The Theory of New Urbanism

New urbanism is an urban design movement which provides walkable neighbourhoods, with a range of housing and job types. This movement promotes the creation and restoration of diverse, compact, walkable and mixed-use communities; these are the components that composed conventional development too. However, these should be assembled in somewhat more integrated manner: in the form of complete communities. New urbanism promotes an increased use of public transportation systems such as trains and other Para-transit public transport. Thus, costs can be cut down. In addition, the main objective theory is about raising and creating a better place to live in.

The principles of new urbanism are given below:

- ***Walkability*:** Shady streets areas; it lays stress on providing the daily-used areas within a 10-minute walk from home or work. This goes with promoting pedestrian-friendly streets (shady, sitting areas and street lights).
- ***Connectivity*:** Inter-connected street networks; hierarchy of streets and connectivity of major land uses.
- ***Mixed uses and diversity*:** Providing mixed land-use areas at a walking distance from home. A mix of shops, offices, departments etc. On-site planning for a set of diverse people, regardless of age, income level and other conflicts et cetera.
- ***Mixed housing*:** Must suit all kinds of people. A range of type, size, and price in closer proximity.
- ***Quality architecture and urban design*:** Natural and beautiful landscapes; emphasis on the basic objectives of design such as beauty, aesthetics, human comfort. Creating a sense of place, special placement of civic uses and sites within the community.
- ***Traditional neighbourhood structure:*** Connecting interaction spaces includes public spaces; it must contain the range of uses and densities within a walking distance. It also includes distribution of areas, the high density at the centre and low density toward the end.
- ***Increased density*:** More number of buildings, residences, and shops closer to one another, for providing ease to the people.
- ***Smart transportation*:** A network of high-quality trains connecting city, towns or neighbourhood together, providing separate lanes for different modes of transportation including 4-wheeler, cycling, walking and the rest.
- ***Sustainability*:** Minimum environment impact of neighbourhood, use of energy-efficient techniques, eco-friendly technologies and cutting down on the increased pollution.

- ***The quality of life***: Emphasis on an overall raise of the quality of life by fulfilling all the basic needs such as food, shelter, employment and recreational areas.

Defining Elements of a Neighbourhood Unit

Following are the elements of a neighbourhood unit:

1. A neighbourhood unit has a central green or interaction area, or a square. A transit sector can also be located in the centre.
2. Most of the dwellings areas are within a 5-minute walk from the centre.
3. The provision of a variety of building types suit different kinds of people.
4. At the edge of the neighbourhood, there are shops, offices or any other work areas.
5. An elementary school is provided close enough so that children can walk from their homes.
6. The provision of a number of green areas/playgrounds accessible to every abode; also providing every kind of green area is a must.
7. A small ancillary building or a garage is permitted within the backyard of each house. It can be used as a rental or workplace.
8. The streets within the neighbourhood form a connected network.
9. The streets are relatively narrow and shaded by rows of trees; this can help in keeping the traffic slow and thorough.

REFERENCES

[1] Book: "*Cities in Evolution*" by Patrick Geddes.
[2] The Writings of Clarence S. Stein.
[3] New Urbanism, Available Online: *http://www.newurbanism.org/*
[4] Liveable Neighborhoods Street Layout, Design and Traffic Management Guidelines, Available Online: *https://www.planning.wa.gov.au/dop_pub_pdf/lntmg.pdf*

[5] Sustainable Housing and the Urban Poor, Available Online: *https://www.planning.wa.gov.au/dop_pub_pdf/lntmg.pdf*
[6] Book: "*Exploration of Architectural Journalism in India*" by Architect Pappal Suneja.

7

Socio-Economic Status of Slum Dwellers: An Empirical Study on the Capital City of Bangladesh

MD. KAMRUZZAMAN[1*] AND M.A. HAKIM[2]

ABSTRACT

People living in slum areas are very poor. Their socio-economic condition does not allow them to live a healthy life. They do not have access to sanitation and they cannot get safe water of water supply. They have to live in adverse conditions so why these areas had to face many health issues. The main purpose of this study was to find out socio-economic condition of slum dwellers of Dhaka city the capital of Bangladesh. Data were collected from 315 respondents by survey research method where respondents were selected by simple random sampling. A well-structured questionnaire was used to collect information. Data were analyzed through SPSS 16. Research found that people living in urban slums had bad living conditions. Owing to bad hygienic condition, health status of households was also not satisfactory. Morbidity rate was very high among studied population. It was concluded that people

[1] School of Victimology and Restorative Justice, Institute of Social Welfare and Research, University of Dhaka, Dhaka, Bangladesh.

[2] School of Food Technology and Nutritional Science, Mawlana Bhashani Science and Technology University, Tangail, Bangladesh.

**Corresponding author:* E-mail: shohag.mbstu.cps@gmail.com; info.hakim.bd @gmail.com *lived with low socio-economic conditions due to which they had to face health issues.*

Key words: Socio-economic status, Slum dwellers, Bangladesh.

1. INTRODUCTION

Slum means a heavily populated area in city[1]. Slum is that parts of the cities which are most inhabitants are in or near poverty[2]. In the early age of industrial revaluation first slums is created in the cities not so far of the center of the cities, close of factories gate[3]. In the early stage of industrialization usually lowest paid worker of industrial cities of England and the United States live in slum[4]. The latter are impoverished shanty settlements created and inhabited by squatters, many of whom are relatively recent migrants[5]. Slum areas illustrate high rates of poverty, illiteracy and bad health status. Slum dwellers have low earning. Urban areas do not provide them proper job. They do not have any formal education facilities. Dwellers of slums engaged in informal labor through which they cannot earn much. They work in environment which is harmful to them. This fact forces them to work in informal sector[6].

Lower socio-economic conditions lead them to ailing life. Living conditions of dwellers of slums are not good. Even though the living condition of slum dwellers are worse than of rural dwellers. They are more vulnerable to communicable diseases and malnutrition and at the same time exposed to greater risk of accidents at work[7,8]. Most of the slum dwellers in developing countries are living below poverty line. They do not have good source of income. An adequate supply of drinking water is basic human need[9]. Unfortunately, most of the households in slums do not have access to safe water. In some areas public water supply is available but quality of water is not so good. Sanitation system is very poor in slums[10].

The streets are narrow and unpaved; slum dwellers have to face water stagnation in rainy season. This makes the environment of that area very unhygienic. Such environment causes a number of diseases in slums[11]. One of the most important characteristics of slums is lack of ownership of land where they are living. Usually they make their houses on vacant government or public land, or marginal land parcels like railway setbacks or undesirable marshy land. When the land is not in productive use they get it as an opportunity and settle there. They are vulnerable to landslide, flood prone areas and unsafe environment[12,13].

Dhaka, the capital of Bangladesh is an over-populated city, covering near about 350 square kilometres. Dhaka is a home of over 15 million peoples[14]. Population boom couples with unplanned industrialization and urbanization spoiled the vegetation of Dhaka, triggering urban problems such as pollution, congestion and inadequate public services[15,16]. Slum is a word, a name that reflects the miseries of deprived people who have to struggle with poverty to survive[17]. Slum is a densely populated temporary residential house build lawfully and unlawfully having no water supply, sanitation facilities or electricity supply[18,19]. Most of these are one-roomed dwelling and extremely over-crowded[20]. There are approximately more than 5000 slum in Dhaka city. Most of the people who live in a slum are of Dhaka city is leads a miserable life[21,22]. The sufferings of female are more than man in that area. Another inhuman thing is female who lives in slum area of Dhaka city are considered as a lower class people and they haven't any social esteem in society[23-26].

In general, slums are the products of failed policies, bad governance, corruption, inappropriate regulation; dysfunctional land markets, unresponsive financial systems and a fundamental lack of political will[27]. States parties shall recognize for every citizen the right to benefit from social security, including social insurance and shall take the necessary measures to achieve the full realization of this right in accordance with their national law[28]. All human beings are born free and equal in dignity and rights. In

1948, the UN General Assembly passed the Universal Declaration of Human Rights, which referred to ensure a secured life for all[8,29–31]. Therefore, the current study was conducted to assess the socio-economic status of the slum dwellers in Dhaka city of Bangladesh.

2. FRAMEWORK

2.1. Study Type

The study was a pilot study.

2.2. Population Selection

There were taken a total 315 slum dwellers from different slums (Mohakhali, Komlapur, Mirpur, Tejgaon and Karwan Bazar) at Dhaka city in Bangladesh.

2.3. Study Duration

The study was conducted from July 2013 to June 2014

2.4. Sampling Method

The simple random sampling method was used to frame the slum dwellers from the study places.

2.5. Data Collecting Techniques

A planned questionnaire was developed containing both the closed and open ended query to collect data through face-to-face interview with the respondents. The questionnaire was pretested in areas far away from the sample areas and revised according to the feedback gained in the field level. The questionnaire was formed to obtain the relevant information considering personal, household, social and economic details.

2.6. Data Verification

The questionnaire was checked per day taking the interview and gain these were carefully rechecked after collecting all the data and coded prior the entrancing into computer technology. The data were edited in case of sighting discrepancy (doubt entry and wrong entry etc.)

2.7. Statistical Analysis

The data were processed to undergo statistical analysis using SPSS 16 windows program. Microsoft Word, Microsoft Excel were used to represent the tabular and chart icon.

3. RESULTS

The study presented that, most of the slum dwellers (35.50%) were between 20–24 years of age while 52.38% are female and 68.25% married. Among them 56.50% illiterate while most of them were Muslim (74.60%) and 31.11% earned livelihood as rickshaw pullers, 23.80% as beggars (Table 1).

Among the respondents 45.39% came to city for the sake of poverty and 17.46% settled in slums as inheritance while 61.90% for low income. 56.19% from village and most of them (52.38%) earned 5000 to 10000 BDT per month. 53.33% family had 6 to 8 members while 35.48% had savings below 3000 BDT (Table 2).

Most of the respondents (36.50%) lived in thatched hut while 12.69% had no electricity facility. 85.07% get water from public tap and 66.66% had sanitary latrine while 33.33% used open place of the non-sanitary latrine users. 74.36% dwellers did not take bath daily while 77.77% suffered from any disease within last two months (Table 3).

Table 1: Socio-demographic characteristics respondents (N=315).

Parameters	*Frequency*	*Percentage*
	Age (years)	
<20	35	11.11
20–24	112	35.50
25–29	55	17.46
30–34	38	12.06
35–39	32	10.15
40–44	20	6.34
45–49	14	4.44
50<	9	2.85
	Sex	
Female	165	52.38
Male	150	47.61
	Religion	
Muslim	235	74.60
Hindu	59	18.73
Christian	13	4.12
Others	8	2.53
	Marital status	
Married	215	68.25
Unmarried	79	25.07
Divorced	16	5.07
Widow	5	1.58
	Educational standard	
Illiterate	178	56.50
Primary	75	23.80
Secondary	57	18.09
Graduate	5	1.58
Postgraduate	0	0
Doctoral degree	0	0
	Occupation	
Rickshaw pullers	98	31.11
Day labors	63	20.00
Beggars	75	23.80
Small traders	38	12.06
Garments worker	32	10.05
Others	9	2.85

Table 2: Socio-economic characteristics of the respondents.

Parameters	*Frequency*	*Percentage*
Causes of coming to city		
Poverty	143	45.39
To search work	89	28.25
Natural calamities	66	20.95
Others	17	5.39
Reasons for settling in slums		
Inheritance	55	17.46
Near to work place	28	8.88
High rent in non-slum areas	37	11.74
Low income	195	61.90
Comes from		
Villages	177	56.19
Towns	138	43.80
Monthly income (BDT)		
<5000	35	11.11
5000–10000	165	52.38
10001–15000	98	31.11
>15000	17	5.39
Family members		
<3	27	8.57
3–5	108	34.28
6–8	168	53.33
>8	12	3.80
Possession of mobile phone		
Yes	282	89.52
No	33	10.47
Possession of TV		
Yes	270	85.71
No	45	14.28
Amount of savings (BDT)		
<3000	55	35.48
3000–5000	38	24.51
5001–8000	21	13.54
80001–10000	18	11.61
10000–12000	14	9.03
>12000	9	5.80

Table 3: Housing, drinking water and sanitary conditions.

Parameters	***Frequency***	***Percentage***
Housing		
Pakka	20	6.34
Semi-pucca	85	26.98
Kacha	95	30.15
Thatched hut	115	36.50
Availability of electricity		
Yes	275	87.30
No	40	12.69
Source of drinking water		
Public tap	268	85.07
Own tap	47	14.92
Sanitary latrine		
Yes	210	66.66
No	105	33.33
Type of latrine using by non-sanitary users		
Public latrine	48	45.71
Pit latrine	22	20.95
Open place	35	33.33
Daily bathing		
Yes	80	25.39
No	235	74.36
Suffered from diseases within last two months		
Yes	245	77.77
No	70	22.22

4. DISCUSSION

Slum areas are the common phenomenon in Bangladesh as well as all over the world[16,32]. These are the product of socio-economic and cultural conditions of a particular social system inhibiting the physical, mental, moral and social development of the individuals[33]. Recent years have seen a dramatic growth in the number of slums as urban populations have increased in the third world. According to a 2006 UN-HABITAT report, 327 million people live in slums in commonwealth countries, almost one in six commonwealth citizens. In a quarter of commonwealth countries (11 African, 2 Asian and 1 Pacific), more than two out of three urban dwellers live in slums and many of these countries are urbanizing rapidly. Bangladesh has the highest number of slum dwellers – 60% of the urban population – in the South Asia[34–39]. The present study found that, most of the slum dwellers (35.50%) were between 20–24 years of age while 52.38% are female and 68.25% married. Among them 56.50% illiterate while most of them were Muslim (74.60%) and 31.11% earned livelihood as rickshaw pullers, 23.80% as beggars which is supported by another study[40]. Poverty is the main companion of the slum dwellers and to earn livelihood the children also have to engage with various works[41,42]. The study also showed that, among the respondents 45.39% came to city for the sake of poverty and 17.46% settled in slums as inheritance while 61.90% for low income. 56.19% from village and most of them (52.38%) earned 5000 to 10000 BDT per month. 53.33% family had 6 to 8 members while 35.48% had savings below 3000 BDT which are similar to another study results[43–47]. According to present study, most of the respondents (36.50%) lived in thatched hut while 12.69% had no electricity facility. 85.07% get water from public tap and 66.66% had sanitary latrine while 33.33% used open place of the non-sanitary latrine users. 74.36% dwellers did not take bath daily while 77.77% suffered from any disease within last two months. While another study found that, the housing conditions in the slum present a grim scenario. About 25 percent of houses are pucca and 68.2 percent were semi-pucca in notified area and non-notified area, it is 6.4 and 79 percent respectively[48,49]. Dwellers of slums do not have adequate system of latrine cleanliness and sanitation is very poor in slum areas[50]. This clarifies that these people have unhygienic latrines[51]. They also found, more than 75% respondents replied that any of their household members had to face any illness in two months prior to study. This is a quite high ratio of illness in any area. This shows that this response degrades overall health status of this area. Most frequent illness that they faced was diarrhea and at second was the fever. It depicts that diarrhea is a problem that relates to water born ailments[52].

Considering the overall study, it felt that the life of every citizen should be safe and to improve the physical environment of the dwelling places like basic amenities of toilets, proper drainage, sewerage system and adequate water supply must be ensured for healthy life.

5. CONCLUSIONS

The rapid growth of population in urban centers since independence has led to the emergence and growth of urban slums in the country. The developmental activities in urban centers provide employment to the rural migrants as well as the local urban population. These low income groups, in the absence of proper shelter were settled in pockets of the slum areas characterized by overcrowding, dilapidated dwellings, lack of sanitation and civic amenities. Realizing the gravity of the situation governments have implemented a number of schemes and programmes to improve the living conditions of people living in slums. In a nut shell multi prolonged strategy required not only to address the needs of slum dwellers for shelter but also the problems of urban poverty, unemployment, low incomes and lack of access to basic urban services.

Conflict of Interests

The authors declare that there is no conflict of interests regarding the publication of this paper.

REFERENCES

[1] Hossain Shahadat (2013). *"Migration, Urbanization and Poverty in Dhaka"*. *Journal of Asiatic Society of Bangladesh*, 58(2): 369–382.

[2] Charles J. Stokes (1962). A *Theory of Slum, Land Economics*, 38(3): 187–197.

[3] Kumar, P. (2001). *Declining Number of Slums: Nature of Urban Growth. Economic and Political Weekly,* XlV(41): 75–77.

[4] Joshi Seema (2005). Marriage, migration and Labor market in slum areas. *Nagarlok*, 37(3): 34–49.

[5] Nautiyal (1993). Basic education in slums of Delhi: The growing menace of urban neglect. *Journal of Educational Planning and Administration,* 7(3): 453–473.
[6] Alamgir *et al.* (2009). "Assessing the livelihood of slum dwellers in Dhaka city". *J. Bangladesh Agril. Univ.,* 7(2): 373–380.
[7] Ameratunga *et al.* (2006). "Road-traffic injuries: Confronting disparities to address a global-health problem". *The Lancet,* 367(9521): 1533–1540.
[8] Kamruzzaman, M. and Hakim, M.A. (2015). Socio-economic status of child beggars in Dhaka City. *Journal of Social Sciences and Humanities,* 1(5): 516–520.
[9] Ompad *et al.* (2007). "Social determinants of the health of urban populations: Methodological considerations". *Journal of Urban Health,* 84(1): 43–52.
[10] Panda *et al.* (1993). "Health status of under-fives in a Ludhiana slum". *Health and Population - Perspectives and Issues,* 16(3&4): 133–141.
[11] Dziuban *et al.* (2010). "Surveillance for Waterborne Disease and Outbreaks Associated with Recreational Water - United States, 2003–2004". *MMWR Surveill. Summ.,* 55(12): 1–30.
[12] Siegel *et al.* (1997). "Geographic analysis of pertussis infection in an urban area: A tool for health services planning". *Amercian Journal of Public Health,* 87(12): 2022–2026.
[13] Kamruzzaman, M. (2015). Child victimization at working places in Bangladesh. *Journal of Social Sciences and Humanities,* 1(5): 516–520.
[14] Alamgir, M.S., Jaffar, N.A. and Islam, M.S. Assessing the livelihood of slum dwellers in Dhaka city.
[15] Khan, Monirul I. (2013). *Social Changes in Contemporary Bangladesh. Journal of Asiatic Society of Bangladesh (Hum.),* 58(2): 263–276.
[16] Kamruzzaman, M. and Hakim, M.A. (2015). Child criminalization at slum areas in Dhaka city. *American Journal of Psychology and Cognitive Science,* 1(4): 107–111.
[17] Wambui *et al.* (2007). "Quality of water the slum dwellers Use: The case of a Kenyan slum". *J. Urban Health,* 84(6): 829–838.
[18] Kumar Naveen and Agarwal, S.C. (2003). Patterns of consumption and poverty in Delhi slums. *Economic and Political Weekly,* 31: 5294–5300.
[19] Hakim, M.A. and Kamruzzaman, M. (2015). Nutritional status of Central Bangladesh street children. *American Journal of Food Science and Nutrition Research,* 2(5): 133–137.
[20] Hatekar Neeraj and Rode Sanjay (2003). *Truth about Hunger and Disease in Mumbai, Malnourishment among Slum Children. Economic and Political Weekly*, 38(43): 4604–4610.
[21] World Bank, "Dhaka: Improving living conditions for the urban poor". Report no. 35824-BD. Urban Development Unit South Asia Region. World Bank, Washington, DC 2006.
[22] Afsar, R. (1998). Rural-urban dichotomy and convergence: Emerging realities in Bangladesh. Institute of Development Studies, Dhaka.

[23] Sharmin Shadia and Luna Farhanaz (2015). *The Socio-Economic Condition of Female Slum Dwellers: A Study on Slums in Dhaka. IOSR Journal of Humanities and Social Science*, 20(3): 26–32.
[24] Kamruzzaman, M. and Hakim, M.A. (2015). Family planning practice among married women attending primary health care centers in Bangladesh. *International Journal of Bioinformatics and Biomedical Engineering,* 1(3): 251–255.
[25] Shirin Subarna (2012). Feminist movement and women empowerment: Bangladesh perspective. *The Journal of Social Development*, 24(1): 183–312.
[26] Alan Nankervis, Compton Robert and Baird Marian (2002). Human Resources Management (Nelson Australia Pty Limited), Second Edition.
[27] Das, B. (1997). *Slum Dwellers in Surat City: A Socio Demographic Profile. Indian Journal of Social Work*, New Delhi, Sage Publications.
[28] Convention on the Rights of the Child (1989). *http://www.ohchr.org/en/professional interest/pages/crc.aspx.*
[29] Rai Rahul (2000). Human Rights: U N Initiatives, Delhi: Authors Press, Delhi.
[30] Kolosov (2002). 'The Rights of the Child', *In:* Janusz Symonides (*ed.*), Human Rights: Concepts and Standards, Rawat, Jaipur.
[31] Tripathi, S.C. and Arora Vibha (2010). *Law Relating to Women and Children,* Allahabad: Central Law Publications.
[32] Eckstein Susan (1990). Urbanization revisited: Inner-city slum of hope and squatter settlement of despair. *World Development*, 18: 165–181.
[33] Karn, S.K., Shigeo Shikura and Hideki Harada (2003). *Living Environment and Health of Urban poor: A study in Mumbai. Economic and Political Weekly*, 38(34): 3575+3579–3586.
[34] *www.dhakatribune.com/bangladesh/2014/nov/18/study-half-u rban-population-bangladesh-slum-dwellers#sthash.rAh75COc.dpuf.*
[35] Hakim, M.A. and Kamruzzaman, M. (2015). *Nutritional Status of Central Bangladesh Street Children. American Journal of Food Science and Nutrition Research,* 2(5): 133–137.
[36] Rout, N.R. (2008). "Slum growth in Bhubaneswar: A problem or solution?" *TPI Journal,* 5(4): 59–64.
[37] Shabnam, N., Faruk, M.O. and Kamruzzaman, M. (2016). *Underlying Causes of Cyber-Criminality and Victimization: An Empirical Study on Students. Social Sciences,* 5(1): 1–6.
[38] Osephine Slater (2009). *Naked Cities - Struggle in the Global Slums, Mute*, 2(3). ISBN 0-9550664-3-3.
[39] Mony, P.K., Varghese, L. and George, A. (2006). Demography, environmental status and maternal health care in slums of Vellore town, South India. *Indian Journal of Community Medicine*, 31(4): 230–4233.

[40] Omole, K.F. (2010). "An assessment of housing condition and socio-economic life styles of slum dwellers in Akure, Nigeria". *Contemporary Management Research,* 6(4): 273–290.
[41] Brueckner, Jan K. and Selod Harris (2009). "A theory of urban squatting and land-tenure formalization in developing countries". *American Economic Journal: Economic Policy*, pp. 28–51.
[42] Mihir, G. and Geeta, K. (2000). "Socio-demographic and morbidity profile of slum area in Ahmedabad, India". *National Journal of Community Medicine,* 1(2): 106–110.
[43] Socio-demographic determinants and prevalence of tuberculosis knowledge in three slum populations of Uganda, Ekwaro Obuku *et al.* (2012). *BMC Public Health*, 12: 536.
[44] Thaker, R.N. and Dhadave, M.S. (1986). A Critique of Theories on Slums in the light of studies on Indian slums, India. *Nagarlok,* 18(3): 44–52.
[45] D'Souza, V.S. (1979). *Socio-Cultural Marginality: A Theory of Urban Slums and Poverty in India. Sociological Bulletin*, 28(1–2): 9–24.
[46] Islam, K.J. and Kumar, R. (2008). Causes and consequences of seasonal migration of rickshaw pullers. *The Human Resources Development Studies*, 1(1).
[47] D'Souza, V.S. (1979). *Socio-Cultural Marginality: A Theory of Urban Slums and Poverty in India. Sociological Bulletin,* 28(1–2): 9–24.
[48] Awadall, H.I. (2013). "*Health Effect of Slums: A Consequence of Urbanization*". *Scholarly Journal of Medicine,* 3(1): 7–14.
[49] Wambui *et al.* (2007). "*Quality of Water the Slum Dwellers Use: The Case of a Kenyan Slum*". *J. Urban Health,* 84(6): 829–838.
[50] Unger, A. and Riley, L.W. (2007). "*Slum Health: From Understanding to Action.*" *PLoS Med.,* 4(10): 1561–1566.
[51] Marengoni *et al.* (2008). "Prevalence of chronic diseases and multimorbidity among the elderly population in Sweden". *Am. J. Public Health,* 98(7): 1198–1200.
[52] Gulis *et al.* (2004). "Health status of people of slums in Nairobi, Kenya". *Environmental Research*, 96: 219–227.

8

Basic Rights on the Wane, Human Rights on Brown Study: A Case Study on Thrown Away Children in Bangladesh

M. KAMRUZZAMAN[1,2,4*] AND M.A. HAKIM[3]

ABSTRACT

The aim of this study was to shed light on the predicaments of the thrown away children in their street life and also the situational analysis of basic and human rights of those children in Bangladesh. The primary objective of this paper is highlighting the response of community, UNICEF and ILO about homeless children in Bangladesh. The secondary objective of this paper is drawing successful strategies to make exploitation free life on the basis of the existing laws to eradicate the child abuse arranging safe childhood.

Key words: Thrown away children, Basic Rights, Human Rights, UNICEF, Case study, Bangladesh.

[1] School of Victimology and Restorative Justice, Institute of Social Welfare and Research, University of Dhaka, Dhaka, Bangladesh.

[2] School of Criminology and Police Science, Mawlana Bhashani Science and Technology University, Tangail, Bangladesh.

[3] School of Food Technology and Nutritional Science, Mawlana Bhashani Science and Technology University, Tangail, Bangladesh.

[4] School of Law, National University, Gazipur, Bangladesh.

[*] *Corresponding author:* E-mail: shohag.mbstu.cps@gmail.com

1. INTRODUCTION

The greatest English Poet William Butler Yeats, a Nobel in Literature once says,

> "Come away, O human child!
> To the waters and the wild
> With a fairy, hand in hand,
> For the world's more full of weeping
> Than you can understand"[1].

Children 'lost, stolen and disappearing' and 'robbed' of their childhood below 18 years old living, working, playing and sleeping on the street who are deprived of basic rights are the thrown away children[2–4]. Like all other children although they have the basic rights to develop, survive and thrive, they encounter innumerable problems and their predicaments are shocking and surprisingly most of the people in Bangladesh even do not "bat an eye at street children sleeping in the mid-afternoon sun"[5]. So now it is time: let their plight be known to all- let the conscience of humanity revolt[6,7]. According to Bangladesh Bureau of Statistics among a total child population (5–17 years old) of 42.39 million the total number of working children in urban areas of Bangladesh is estimated 1.5 million. Many of these children living, working, playing and sleeping on the streets and are deprived of their human rights[8]. There are numerous children live as street children in the big cities and towns particularly in Dhaka city. They live an inhuman life and a significant portion of them are involved in begging[9,10]. These homeless children who lack the proper requirements of life and they are tagged as 'severely deprived' children. These severe deprivations can be found with their not having the adequate services in the provision of shelter, food, sanitation, water, information, nutrition, education, and health etc. Despite constitutional recognition of the right to shelter for all citizens, 41% of all children are deprived of adequate shelter[11,12]. The street children are in vogue as a part of thrown away (forced to leave home) children in more developed nations more likely to come from single-parent homes[13] or due to the consequence of polygamy in different societies across the world. These fellow children are often subject to abuse, neglect, exploitation, or extreme cases, murder by clean-up squad hired by businessmen, criminal gang and very often the police to retain great business benefit[14,15].

Bangladesh has a high incidence of throw way children because half of its population living below poverty line. For this reason children have to work for their families survive. Poverty and child labor are associated with each other and these have significant impacts on childhood malnutrition and incompetent labor force of a nation[16–18].

Besides, there are many conspicuous causes behind the harsh curtain of their life, such as overpopulation, family disintegration, unemployment, illiteracy, unplanned urbanization, landlessness, natural disasters, oppression of step father or mother[19–21] etc., which are indeed quite pathetic and matters of investigation. Those problems are to be tackled in the best possible ways for the overall betterment of these ill-fated children[22].

In 2015 it is found that 42.6% thrown away children worked in hotel, 22% in garage, 12% in workshop 7% in factories and 6% in vehicles. Kamruzzaman and Hakim (2015) summarizes that among the homeless children 32.9% work in restaurant, 18.8% in industry, Transport 11.8% and Industries 18.8% in Dhaka city[15]. Summon (2007) summarizes that there are five factors that can lead to child labor in Bangladesh. The author said that poverty is the major cause of child labor. He also said that illiterate and poor are interring related[23]. The thrown away children are poor because they are illiterate and illiterate because they are poor. Social factor that can be include dynamics of parents and children as a family unit and socio-economic inequality that can be lead to child labor in Bangladesh[24–27]. International Labor Organization (ILO) also estimated that there are 30% of children's in Bangladesh are economically active[28].

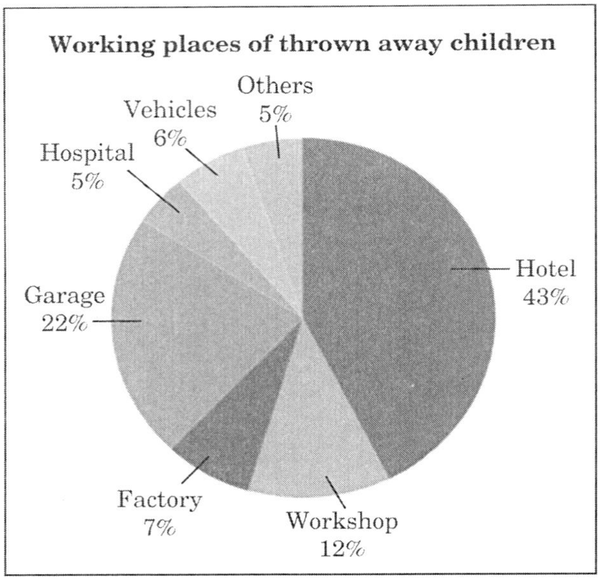

Fig. 1: Working places of thrown away children in Bangladesh[15].

2. SITUATIONAL ANALYSIS OF THROWN AWAY CHILDREN IN BANGLADESH

Bangladesh is an agriculture based country. In this most of the people are poor and the average family size is six persons. Most of the families' father works as a rickshaw puller or day laborer and the mother as a domestic help. Poverty leads to quarrels, tension and can ultimately result in cruel treatment of children[29] which result in thrown away. The huge percentage of homeless children is found to be the malnutrition gainers by dint of lacked access to safe drinking water, inadequate nutritious foods, lack of hygiene practices and shelter[30–32]. These thrown away children are the different diseases sufferers on the basis of seasonal variation and some are chronic health disorders sufferers according to their dwelling topographic variation. About 73% of street children in Dhaka city suffer from chronic malnutrition while mortality and morbidity status among street dwellers has reached an alarming level for lack of basic health and nutritional care services[33]. In line with this, the homeless population in Dhaka, of which a significant number is the child beggars; is known to face extortion, erratic unemployment, exposure to violence, sexual harassment, and to engage in high-risk behaviors[9,34]. Sometimes they are engaged in various kinds of criminal activities by touch of criminal gang and peers[15]. These thrown away children are in deprivation to their rights to rights to survival, education and safe childhood[35].

3. PERSPECTIVE OF UNICEF

UNICEF already started works with the Government of Bangladesh to reduce child labor and establish learning in urban area because in urban area a lot of thrown away children working in garments industry and textile mills. They through a project called Basic Education for Hard to Reach Urban Working Children (BEHTRUWC). Their learning centers provide basic education in Bangle, English, Social Science and Mathematics. They also learn life-skills education, interpersonal relationships, critical thinking and decision making that can be help to children future life. The basic education course duration is 40 months and there are five learning cycles of eight months. Students work and study in small groups. These groups are making according their skill level and sometimes random selection to encourage peer to peer learning[36]. This program contributes to national efforts to eliminate the worst forms of child labor in Bangladesh. In 2010 UNICEF also developed National Children Policy and its specific objective is to protect children from child labor. UNICEF has been advocating for the creation of a children code in order to harmonize domestic legislation with the convention on the right of the child including Article 32 on child labor[37]. They also work with Ministry of Social Welfare and other Ministry and NGOs to undertake mapping and assessment of Bangladesh child protection system.

4. PERSPECTIVE OF ILO

In 1999 Bangladesh has ratified the ILO Worst Forms of Child

Labor Convention (No. 182) but in 1973 has not ratified the Minimum Age Convention (No. 138). They say that corruption and weak institutional capacity is the main problem in the monitoring process of the government in Bangladesh. The monitoring system addresses only the formal sectors, where as child labor is in the informal economy. Bangladesh government has not taken action to reduce commercial sex with children. ILO Convention No. 182 requires the government to take effective and time bound measures to:

- Prevent the engagement of children in the worst forms of child labor
- Provide the necessary and appropriate direct assistance for the removal of children from the worst forms of child labor and for their rehabilitation and social integration
- Ensure access to free basic education and, wherever possible and appropriate, vocational training, for all children removed from the worst forms of child labor
- Identify and reach out to children at special risk
- Take account of the special situation of girls.

In 2001 after ratifying the convention Bangladesh government takes a project to combat the worst forms of child labor in urban areas. At the same time ILO and Royal Netherlands Embassy help a pilot project to develop a Time Bounded Program (TBM) to reduce the worst forms of child labor[38].

5. PERSPECTIVE OF AIN O SALISH KENDRA (ASK)

Ain o Salish Kendra (ASK), a national legal aid and human rights organization, provides legal and social support to the disempowered, particularly women, working children and workers. Its goal is to create a society based on equality, social and gender justice and rule of law. It seeks to create an environment for accountability and transparency of governance institutions. It is working to establish human rights especially the child rights in

Bangladesh. To fulfill their objectives they arrange seminars, round-table dialogue, monthly publications of human rights report across the country to aware the general people and the policy makers.

6. PERSPECTIVE OF APORAJEO BANGLA

This non-government organization Aporajeo Bangla works mainly to protect child rights. From the very beginning they are taking various programmes for the development of street children of the capital city of Bangladesh. For better it needs collaboration of government and communities.

7. PERSPECTIVE OF BELA

Bangladesh Environmental Lawyers Association (BELA) emphasizes on the sustainable development with the protection of environment. In the very present time they raise voice to ensure eco-health for the future generation mostly the rootless children.

8. APPLICATION OF HUMAN RIGHTS FRAMEWORK TO CURB THE SORRY TALES OF THE THROWN AWAY CHILDREN IN BANGLADESH

All human beings are born free and equal in dignity and rights. In 1948, the UN General Assembly passed the Universal Declaration of Human Rights (UDHR), which referred in Article 25 to childhood as entitled to "special care and assistance"[9,39–41]. Bangladesh is obliged under both national and international law to protect and promote the rights and interests of children. According to the Articles 17 and 19 of the constitution of Bangladesh, the state should take proper measures of free and compulsory education for the children along with equal economic development throughout the country and to fulfilling this condition; the government of Bangladesh under the Ministry of Social Welfare builds up five vagrancy centers. But most of the beggars do not want to spend their time into the vagrancy centers because of various problems along with insufficient food facility, treatment opportunity, rehabilitation insecurity, recreational lacking and so on. In 1990 Bangladesh government passed the primary education Act and in 1993 it established the compulsory primary education system for children age 6 years and above. In 1991 to 1996 the government of Bangladesh adopted the National Children Policy (NCP) and formulated the national plane of action for children[42]. The constitution of Bangladesh and Children's Act 1974 guarantees basic and fundamental human rights and ensures affirmative action for children. The rights are the guiding principles for formulating policies and laws to protect restricting development and hazardous work that can help children to develop in free way. As a result Bangladesh government has taken initially a number of policies and plans to promote equitable inclusive and high quality education to reduce child labor. Bangladesh is a signatory to and has ratified most of the major international convention related to children except for the ILO (International Labor Organization) Minimum Age Convention (No. 138)[43]. Bangladesh has signed and ratified the convention of the Right of the Child (1989) which indicates to protect and promote the rights and interests of the child, such as the right to a compulsory and free education (Articles 28 and 29) the right to be protect from exploitative work or performing any work that may be considered hazardous, interferes with the child's education or is harmful to the child's development (Article 32) and right to an adequate standard of living (Article 27). Bangladesh is also the first South Asia country to ratify the Worst Forms of Child Labor Convention (No. 182) in March 2001 which imposes an obligation upon to "take immediate and effective measures to secure the prohibition and elimination of the worst forms of child labor as a matter of urgency" (Article 1). Such as all forms of slavery or practices similar to slavery child prostitution, child pornography, using children for illicit activities and work which would harm the physical, social and moral development of children (Article 3)[44]. The Government of Bangladesh also ratified the UN Convention on the Rights of Persons with Disabilities (CRPD) and its Optional Protocol as well. Article 7 of UN CRPD ensures the rights of Children with disabilities[45].

9. DISCUSSION

There are many causes like poverty, culture and tradition, barriers to education, market demand, the effect of income shocks on householder and lack of legislation or poor enforcement of existing legislation that can led unsafe childhood in developing country like Bangladesh. Thrown away children has no minimum standard of living so they are forced to go earn livelihood through child labor, that can destroys children creativity and innocence because at that time they need to learn something. It can also damaged children physical and mental health and involves children bad activities like drugs, robbery etc. Child labor can also reduce to get good job opportunity because in this life time they need to have a good education. It can also decrease the efficiency of the work force because more uneducated workforce[46]. In developing countries like Bangladesh most of the people are poor and uneducated they are live from hand to mouth. So child labor is a solution to poverty. A survey states that there are 70% of child labor in Bangladesh is members of landless and floating families to reduce poverty. It is seemed that child labor is very harmful of children in Bangladesh that can lead no right way to grow and develop in free way. It can also damage children physical and mental health[47]. We know that children of today become the adults of the future and need invest to protect them. It is also believed that poverty is a great problem in our country that can lead increase child labor but I don't support this responses that if father is a farmer then his children do work in the field to help them we can change this tradition. Bangladesh is a small country but population size increases day by day so population is the main problem in Bangladesh for this reason most of the people are poor and they cannot proper take care for their children's[48]. So at first we have to control our population size and ensuring education for all children. Family planning can reduce our population size. We have to building awareness of the parents who are sending their children factory and textile mills for money. I also think that some time they are victim by natural disaster and send their children different kinds of works[49–51]. In rural areas so many child labor here so they have to take another project for rural children to reduce rural child labor and give same opportunity like urban children. They have also taken another project like National Children Policy it can obviously reduce child labor I support this project. UNICEF also helps to improved birth registration and at last they are able to give birth certificates everyone in Bangladesh I believe that this will also reduce child labor[52,53]. ILO and Netherlands Embassy also help Time-Bounded Program (TBM) it can reduce the worst forms of child labor because it is includes awareness-raising and advocacy, policy and legal reform, urban informal economy, rural informal economy, basic education, technical education, poverty reduction and unconditional worst forms of homeless children. We know that child labor is a great problem in Bangladesh[53–57].

At first Bangladesh government immediately take action on corruption because if government has corruption then any one cannot apply their policy. UNICEF, ILO can also communicate with local NGOs to apply their policy. They also can take another project food for education. For example if the parents send their children for education then they will get food. So most of the parents who are poor they will send their children for education. In this way we can reduce child labor in Bangladesh.

10. CONCLUSIONS

Bangladesh is one of the poor countries in South Asia. Most of the families are poor who don't get basic rights. The situation of thrown away children is in beggar description. So, to make a safe childhood basic and human rights must be ensured for them. We can make employers and families aware and sensitize regarding child rights. We can also make partnership, collaboration and co-operation among stakeholders and their commitment also we can knowledge sharing, mobilizing technical and financial support and strengthening capacity to reduce violence against children and exploitation. We have to increase public spending on safe shelter, food, education, expand access and quality of technical and vocational education. At last everyone should love and care for children not to ignore.

REFERENCES

[1] Good reads: Quotes about Children. Retrieved from: http://www.goodreads.com/ quotes/tag/children? p. 2.

[2] Stephens, S. (1995). *Children and the Politics of Culture in Late Capitalism*, *In:* Stephens, S. (*eds.*) Princeton University Press, pp. 8–9.

[3] Hecht, T. (1998). *At Home in the Street: Street Children of Northeast Brazil*. New York: Cambridge University Press, pp. 8–9.

[4] ARISE, Baseline Survey of Street Children in Six Divisional Cities of Bangladesh, Edited by A. R. f. I. S. C. Environment. Dhaka: Department of Social Services, Ministry of Social Welfare, Government of Bangladesh (2001).

[5] Timmerman, K. (2012). *Where am I Wearing? A Global Tour to the Countries, Factories, and People that Make Our Clothes*. Hoboken, N.J.: Willey, p. 26.

[6] Aderinto, A.A. (2000). Social correlates and coping measures of street children: A comparative study of street and non-street children in South-Western Nigeria. *Child Abuse and Neglect,* 43(4): 1199–1213.

[7] Agneli, S. (1986). Street Children: A Growing Urban Tragedy: A Report for the Independent Commission on International Humanitarian Issues. London: Weidenfeld and Nicolson, Prologue.

[8] Black, M. (1996). *Children First: The Story of UNICEF, Past and Present*. USA: Oxford University Press, pp. 119–147.

[9] Kamruzzaman, M. and Hakim, M.A. (2015). Socio-economic status of child beggars in Dhaka city. *Journal of Social Sciences and Humanities,* 1(5): 516–520.

[10] Conticini and Hulme (2005). As cited by Nawaz, 2011.

[11] National Report of Bangladesh on 'Global Study on Child Poverty and Disparities'; UNICEF (2009).

[12] Hakim, M.A. and Kamruzzaman, M. (2015). Nutritional status of Central Bangladesh street children. *American Journal of Food Science and Nutrition Research,* 2(5): 133–137.

[13] Flowers (2010). pp. 20–21.

[14] Evgenia Berezina (1997). Victimization and Abuse of Street Children Worldwide. Youth Advocate Program International Resource Paper, Yapi. Retrieved November 30, 2012.

[15] Kamruzzaman, M. and Hakim, M.A. (2015). Child criminalization at slum areas in Dhaka city. *American Journal of Psychology and Cognitive Science*, 1(4): 107–111.

[16] Rahman, A. and Chowdhury, S. (2007). Determinants of chronic malnutrition among preschool children in Bangladesh. *Journal of Biosocial Science,* 39(2): 161–173.
[17] Rahman, A. and Biswas, S.C. (2009). Nutritional status of under-5 children in Bangladesh. *South Asian Journal of Population and Health,* 2(1): 1–11.
[18] Hakim, M.A. and Kamruzzaman, M. (2015). Nutritional status of preschoolers in four selected fisher communities. *American Journal of Life Sciences,* 3(4): 332–336.
[19] Islam, T., Haque, M.M. and Tarik, S.R. (2001). Developing Skill and Improving Environment of the Street Children at Aricha and Daulatdia Ferry Ghats. Mohammadpur: ACLAB, pp. 10–11.
[20] Kamruzzaman, M. (2015). Child victimization at working places in Bangladesh. *Journal of Social Sciences and Humanities*; 1(5): 516–520.
[21] Kamruzzaman, M. (2015). Dowry related violence against rural women in Bangladesh. *American Journal of Psychology and Cognitive Science,* 1(4): 112–116.
[22] Hai, M.A. (2014). Problems faced by the street children: A study on some selected places in Dhaka City, Bangladesh. *International Journal of Scientific and Technology Research,* 3(10): 45–56.
[23] Sumon, A.I. (2007). "Informal Economy in Dhaka City: Automobile Workshop and Hazardous Child Labor". *Pakistan Journal of Social Sciences*, 4(6): 711–720.
[24] Rahman, A. and Kuddus, A. (2014). A new model to study on physical behavior among susceptible infective removal population. *Far East Journal of Theoretical Statistics*, 46(2): 115–135.
[25] Rahman, A. and Sapkota, M. (2014). Knowledge on vitamin A rich foods among mothers of preschool children in Nepal: Impacts on public health and policy concerns. *Science Journal of Public Health*, 2(4): 316–322.
[26] Megabiaw, B. and Rahman, A. (2013). Prevalence and determinants of chronic malnutrition among under-5 children in Ethiopia. *International Journal of Child Health and Nutrition*, 2(3): 230–236.
[27] Kamruzzaman, M. and Hakim, M.A. (2015). Livelihood Status of Fishing Community of Dhaleshwari River in Central Bangladesh. *International Journal of Bioinformatics and Biomedical Engineering,* 2(1): 25–29.
[28] Bangladesh Bureau Statistics (BBS) (2003). Child labor in Bangladesh.
[29] Nazrul, I. (2010). Sociological perspective of poverty. *Bangladesh e-Journal of Sociology*, 7(2): 57–60.
[30] Rahman, A. and Hakim, M.A. (2016). Malnutrition Prevalence and Health Practices of Homeless Children: A Cross-Sectional Study in Bangladesh. *Science Journal of Public Health,* 4(1–1): 10–15.
[31] Hakim, M.A. and Kamruzzaman, M. (2015). Nutritional status of preschoolers in four selected fisher communities. *American Journal of Life Sciences,* 3(4): 332–336.

[32] Hakim, M.A. and Rahman, A. (2016). Health and nutritional condition of street children of Dhaka city: An empirical study in Bangladesh. *Science Journal of Public Health,* 4(1–1): 6–9.
[33] ICDDR, B. (2010). Street dwellers performance for health care services in Dhaka, Bangladesh. Dhaka: ICDDR, B.
[34] Beggars in Dhaka city: Profession or compulsion (2014). *Asian Journal of Business and Economics,* 4(4.3) Quarter III. ISSN: 2231–3699.
[35] Mamun Rashid (2005). "Banking for beggars", The Daily Star (*www.thedailystar.net*).
[36] UNICEF, ILO, World Bank Group (2009). Understanding Children's Work in Bangladesh.
[37] UNICEF (2008). Opinions of Children of Bangladesh on Corporal Punishment.
[38] Karen, D. and Abdul, H.M. (2010). The decent work country program Bangladesh 2006–2009. ILO Regional Office for Asia and Pacific.
[39] Rai Rahul (2000). Human Rights: UN Initiatives, Delhi: Authors Press, Delhi.
[40] Kolosov (2002). 'The Rights of the Child', *In:* Janusz Symonides (*ed.*), *Human Rights: Concepts and Standards*, Rawat, Jaipur.
[41] Tripathi, S.C. and Arora Vibha (2010). *Law Relating to Women and Children*, Allahabad: Central Law Publications.
[42] Rabiul, H. (2009). "A baseline study on situation of child labor and potential to be child labour among children with disabilities". Centre for Services and Information on Disability (CSID).
[43] Nazrul, I. (2010). Sociological perspective of poverty. *Bangladesh e-Journal of sociology*, 7(2): 57–60.
[44] Bangladesh Population Census and Labor Force Survey (1974). *Child Labor in Bangladesh: Trends, Patterns and Policy*.
[45] ILO (2013) *Working Out of Poverty*. International Labor office, Geneva, Switzerland.
[46] ILO (2013) Working out of poverty. International Labor office, Geneva, Switzerland.
[47] United Nation (2012). How would empowering people help achieve poverty eradication? United Nations Department of Economic and Social Affairs. Islam, J., Quazi, A. and Rahman, A. (2011). Nexus between cultural dissonance, management accounting systems and managerial effectiveness: Evidence from an Asian developing country. *Journal of Asia Pacific Business,* 12(3): 280–303.
[48] Hakim, M.A. and Talukder, M.J. (2016). An assessment of health status of street children in Tangail, Bangladesh. *Science Journal of Public Health,* 4(1–1): 1–5.
[49] Kamruzzaman, M. and Hakim, M.A. (2015). Family planning practices among married women attending primary health care centers in Bangladesh. *International Journal of Bioinformatics and Biomedical Engineering,* 1(3): 251–255.

[50] Aptekar, L. (1994). *Street Children in the Developing World: A Review of Their Conditions. Cross-Cultural Research*, 28(3): 195–224.
[51] Kellett, P. and Moore, J. (2003). Routes to home: Homelessness and home-making in contrasting societies. *Habitat International*, 27: 123–141.
[52] Hasan, R. (2009). A baseline study on situation of child labour and potential to be child labour among children with disabilities. Centre for Services and Information on Disability CSID), Dhaka.
[53] Rahman, A. and Kuddus, A. (2014). A new model to study on physical behaviour among susceptible infective removal population. *Far East Journal of Theoretical Statistics,* 46(2): 115–135.
[54] Rahman, A. and Chowdhury, S. (2007). Determinants of chronic malnutrition among preschool children in Bangladesh. *Journal of Biosocial Science,* 39(2): 161–173.
[55] Plan Bangladesh, Child Protection Policy – Say No to Child Abuse: Plan‘s Policy to Child Protection, 1 January 2005. Dhaka: Plan Bangladesh, 2005.
[56] White, B. (1996). Globalization and the child labour problem. *Journal of International Development*, 8(6): 829–839.
[57] Rahman, A., Harding, A., Tanton, R. and Liu, S. (2013). Simulating the characteristics of populations at the small area level: New validation techniques for a spatial micro simulation model in Australia. *Computational Statistics and Data Analysis,* 57(1): 149–165.

9

The Plight of Acid Crime and Victimization: A Case Study in South Asia

MD. KAMRUZZAMAN[1,3,4*] AND MD. ABDUL HAKIM[2]

ABSTRACT

The study was conducted to shed light on the acid crime and victims in South Asian developing countries (i.e., demographic subdivision Bangladesh). The objective of this paper is drawing successful strategies to make exploitation free life on the basis of the existing laws to eradicate the peril. The data were collected mainly from secondary sources. The perceived causes of acid violence included dowry, family dispute, property dispute, marital dispute, refusal of love etc. After victimization, the survivors were deprived from basic social services and human rights. Subsequently, the consequences incorporated death, disfigurement, disability, chronic poverty, isolation from job, family and community, lack of security and so on. As a result, the prevention, reintegration and the legal rights of the survivors were not ensured at all stages of their life. The study was recommended to take a collaborative action to all

[1] School of Victimology and Restorative Justice, Institute of Social Welfare and Research, University of Dhaka, Dhaka, Bangladesh.
[2] School of Igloo Dairy Limited, Abdul Monem Limited, Dhaka, Bangladesh.
[3] School of Criminology and Police Science, Mawlana Bhashani Science and Technology University, Tangail, Bangladesh.
[4] School of Law, National University, Gazipur, Bangladesh.
**Corresponding author:* E-mail: shohag.mbstu.cps@gmail.com

the stakeholders to create awareness to the family and society enforcing laws by government to eclipse these sorry tales.

Key words: Acid crime, Violence against women, Victimization, Case study, South Asian countries.

1. INTRODUCTION

Acid attacks occur throughout the world. Bangladesh has some of the highest recorded incidence of acid violence. According to Acid Survivors Foundation (ASF) Bangladesh, there have been 3,662 reported acid attack victims in the country during 1999 to 2015[1]. Acid violence involves intentional acts of violence in which perpetrators throw, spray, or pour acid on to victims' faces and bodies[2]. It also describes an attack against an individual in which sulfuric, hydrochloric, or nitric acid is employed as a weapon to cause severe burns. The results are permanent disfigurement, often blindness and sometimes hearing loss, depending on where the acid falls. Overall, the findings revealed that the incidence of acid attacks is escalating as reported more frequently in the press. Yet, in the country, arrest and conviction of perpetrators are low and the police require persuasion to pursue a case. Most survivors, predominantly women, being from poor families with little access to education, are ignorant of their legal rights and the judicial system and so rely on legal aid organizations to assist them. It is also found that acid is readily available to perpetrators, mostly men who are aggrieved because they have experienced rejection of their advances[3–6].

When acid is thrown on a person, the results can be horrifying. Nitric, hydrochloric, or sulfuric acids all have a catastrophic effect on human flesh. It causes the skin tissue to melt, often exposing the bones below the flesh, sometimes even dissolving the bone. When acid attacks the eyes, it damages these vital organs permanently. Many acid attack survivors have lost the use of one or both eyes. The victim in traumatized physically, psychologically and socially[7,8].

An acid attack on your body would dramatically change your life. Most survivors of an acid attack are forced to give up their education, their occupation and other important activities in their lives. This is because recovering from the trauma takes up most of their time and because the disfigurement they have to bear debilitates and handicaps them in every conceivable way. Bangladesh enacted two laws in 2002—one that heightens criminal penalties and improves criminal procedures and another that attempts to decrease the availability of acid. Acid attacks have decreased by 15% to 20% in Bangladesh each year after the country adopted specific laws to address acid violence[9–11]. With the aim of contributing to efforts to design effective laws and policies to combat acid violence, the study analysis of acid attack perpetrators, motives, victims, and the impact of attacks on victims in Bangladesh[12–14].

2. CAUSES OF ACID ATTACK

Similar to other form of gender based violence, the acid violence have several causes, which was interlinked with the various social problems of Bangladesh. The root causes, were patriarchal society which developed based on power. The ostensible causes were dowry, family dispute, property dispute, marital dispute, refusal of love etc. The causes of acid attack varies case to case basis and more than one person could be attacked by a single incident. As such, more people's life and livelihood could be spoiled due to a single incident of acid violence[15,16].

3. CONSEQUENCES OF ACID VIOLENCE

The victim of acid attack suffered physically, psychologically, socially and economically. Also, they had to struggle at every stages of life after being a survivor. From home to outside, they had been ignored and neglected by some portion of the people. Thus rights were not ensured proportionately for the acid survivors. The survivors could not return fully to the previous life where they lived with all supports from the family and community. The acid attack not only disfigured the faces, but also spoiled the full and secure life over a multitude of dimensions. The consequences of acid violence were numerous, some major consequences had been revealed by the study. The consequences include disfigurement, negligence from family and society, separation from job and education, marital barrier, disability, poverty etc.

3.1. Biological Consequences

Acid causes skin tissues and soft bones to melt. Acid injures were usually much deeper and acid effects the skin tissues faster than flames. Furthermore flame burns were affecting the tissues and soft bones not the hard bones, while acid is aggressive enough to cause permanent damage even to hard bones. Any parts of the body could be injured through acid throwing. The face, however, was the most targeted area of the miscreants. In many cases, some parts of the body were being disabled by acid throwing. The eyes, ears, nose, face were mostly injured in and around the cases of acid violence. Those sensitive areas were also vulnerable to be disfigured quickly. As the faces are always open in nature, the organs of this area have greater possibility to be disabled.

3.2. Security Issues

In the community, the perpetrators were threatening the survivors for withdrawing the cases against them. Sometimes, it was found that the survivor and their family had been attacked more than one time because of continuing acid case. Moreover, due to lower social status and economic power of the survivors, they faced trouble to survive at their locality by ignoring the threat of the perpetrator. Sometimes due to the threat from the perpetrators the victims might also lose their homes and shelter[11]. According to the follow-up report of ASF, 2009, it was found that around 40% survivors were threatened by the perpetrators[1].

3.3. Sociological Consequences

Due to disfigurement, sometimes the family and society could not treat an acid victim as earlier. Besides, social stigma was another cause of negligence from family and community, which results separation from family or divorce etc. The victims became anxious, uncertain or even depressed because of their separation of the family and society. Chronic illness, social conflict, husbands' torture, family torture etc., were other forms of negligence to survivors creating separation[17–20].

3.3.1. *Separation from job and education*

After becoming an acid victim, the survivors were under-valued by their peers, colleague and friends and also from the community. Besides they had to struggle to get the earlier environment at their institutions or school/college. Even in some cases, they could not get the family and community support as they wanted. Sometimes the employer was not satisfied to survivors because of their disfigured out looking/face. Thus, the survivors were mentally depressed causing separated from their jobs and drop out from education[21–24].

3.3.2. *Marital barrier*

Due to the facial disfigurement in most cases, the youngest girls were deprived from marriage[1]. The victim's family, community and local people hand less interest to arrange marriage for an acid victim. This condition, furthermore, morally depressed the survivors to involve with their earlier community.

3.3.3. *Lack of participation at social and cultural programs*

Gender violence represents an expression of human behaviors and attitudes and is deep rooted in the society[11]. In the case of acid violence, the survivors got less importance in participating at social and cultural festival because of their physical and psychological condition. This also created a permanent problem in the survivor's mind that again falls in mental shock. Sometimes the survivors were not interested to participate in the social and cultural gathering due to their facial disfigurement and the fragmented social environment[25–27].

3.4. Economical Consequences

Acid attacks had hurtful effect-physically, psychologically and socially. This disability obstructed the survivors to work continuously and thus they cannot earn as earlier. A survivor cannot work long time under the sun as their affected areas get in infections, which reduced their working ability tremendously in home and outside, causing poor to poorest as most of the survivors living under the poverty line. It was found that 65% survivors were living under poverty line as per the calculation as per poverty definition cited at HIES, 2005. While 28 percent populations live under poverty line[7]. After becoming an acid victim, ones could not meet their family demand. Sometime the survivors had to depend on external support for their survival. Bi-variate analysis also reiterated the strong relationship between domestic violence and poverty[11]. Violence both systematic and random was part of the condition of poverty in as much as poverty is associated with relative powerlessness and the poor are least able to defend themselves or to remove themselves from threatening situations[10].

4. LEGAL REMEDIES OF ACID VICTIMIZATION

Section 4 of Acid Crime Control Act, 2002, causes the death of another person by a person acid such person shall be punishable with death or imprisonment for life and shall be liable in excess of these exceeding on lakh BDT[28].

Section 5 says that if any other person in anyway hurt by acid:

a) Wholly or partly lost sight or hearing, or face, breasts or genitalia is mutilated or destroyed such person shall be liable to imprisonment for death of imprisonment for life.

b) The body's other organs, glands or in part is deformed or damaged, or anywhere in the body, then that person was injured, but not less than seven years' rigorous imprisonment for a term which may extend to fourteen years and it shall be liable to an additional term not exceeding fifty thousand taka.

c) If any person, or to any other person sough on the acid, then do so because of the person's physical, mental or otherwise, do no harm, though, but at least three years' rigorous imprisonment for a term which may extend to seven years and shall be liable to fine of fifty thousand taka[29,30].

5. STATISTICAL FINDINGS

Fig. 1 shows that, in 2015 total number of acid attack were 59 and the 74 persons were victimized. In October, the number of acid victimization was highest in this year and lowest were in December while most of them were women.

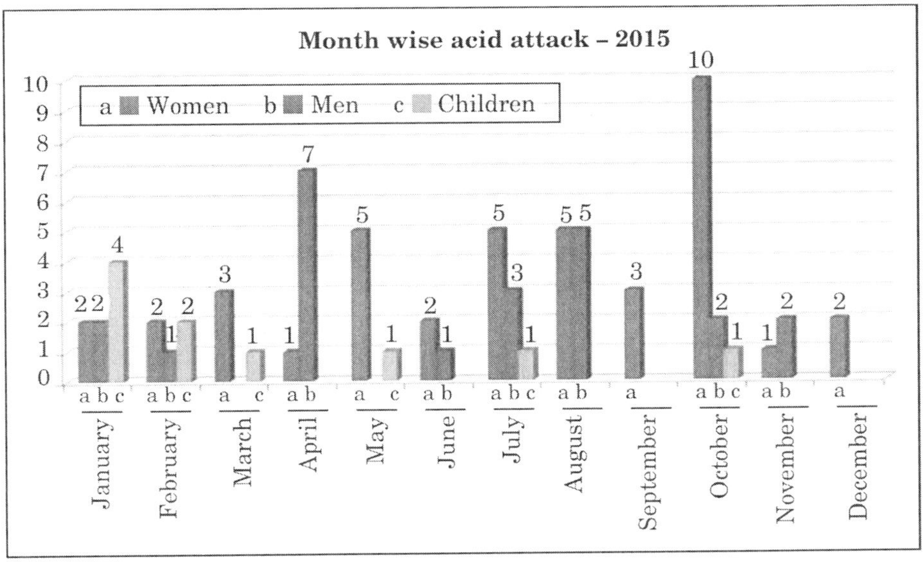

Fig. 1: Acid attack statistics-2015[1].

Fig. 2 display year basis number of acid attack from 1999 to 2015. There were reported 3303 incidents and total 3662 victims during that period. According to this statistics the number of acid attack were gradually increased in 1999 to 2002. However, after 2002 the number of acid attack is decreasing respectively by the year.

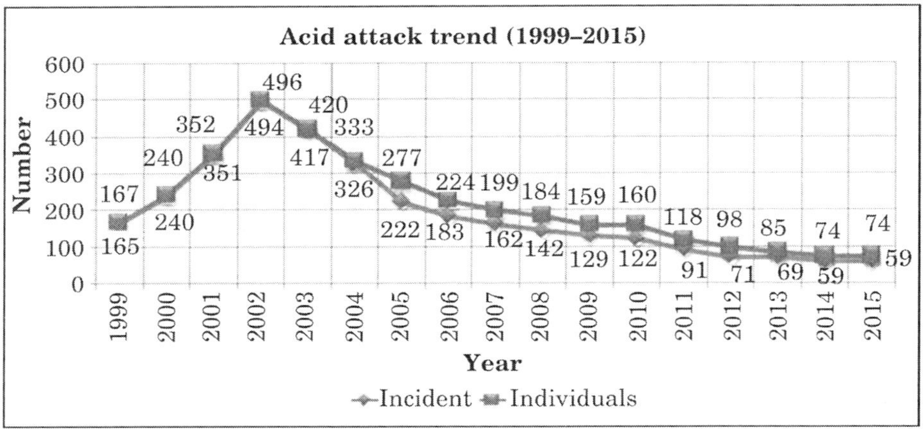

Fig. 2: Acid attack statistics (1999–2015)[1].

In 2015 total number of acid victim was 74 including 24 males and others 50 females. Maximum women victim were between 26 to 35 years of age (Table 1).

Table 1: Age group of acid victims 2015[1].

Age group of acid survivors – 2015		
Age group	***Male***	***Female***
Under 18	1	9
19–25	5	10
26–35	9	17
36–45	3	6
46–55	2	8
Over 55	4	–
Total:	24	50
Grand Total:	74	

Table 2 presented that, dowry, family related dispute and property dispute works mostly as motivational factor for acid attacks.

Table 2: Motivation of acid attack 2015[1].

Motivation of acid attack – 2015			
Reasons	***Man***	***Woman***	***Children***
Dowry	–	5	–
Family related dispute	3	6	–
Land/property/money dispute	8	8	–
Marital dispute	1	8	–
Refusal/rejection of love	–	2	3
Refusal/rejection of marriage	1	1	5
Refusal/rejection of sex	–	2	–
Not know	8	6	–
Others	2	3	2
Total:	23	41	10

It is found that, total 2019 cases were filed to law enforcing agency and court from 2002 to October 2015. Including those only 325 perpetrators had convicted of 185 cases. Among them 14 perpetrator convicted to death sentence and 117 perpetrators had convicted to life time imprisonment (Fig. 3).

6. DISCUSSION

There were reported 3,303 incidents during 1999 to 2015 in Bangladesh. More than 3,662 people had been attacked due to acid violence in that period. Around 90%survivors were victimized before 40 years of age. Of the total, 68% victim of acid attack was women and children and 32% victim was men and boys (ASF, 2015)[1]. Besides, 65% had been living under poverty line and half of them did not study at any level of education. In 2000, the number of acid victim were 234 and the acid attack increased rapidly in the next year and in 2002, it reached at apex where 490 people were attacked by acid throwing. After 2002, the acid attack reduced

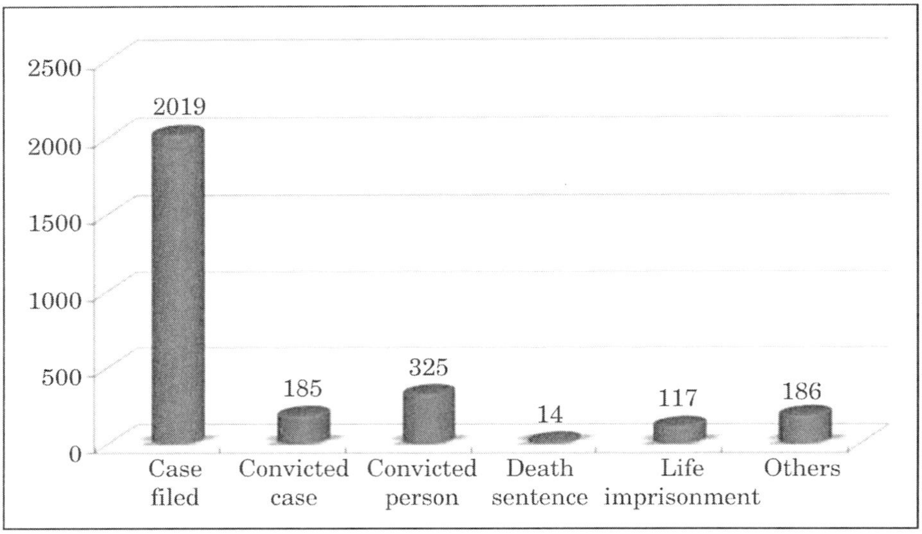

Fig. 3: Conviction Status (2002 to October 2015)[1]

dramatically and in 2003, it was 411 people and this trend continued up to 2015. In 2015 the number of acid attack was 74 people.

7. RECOMMENDATIONS

To eradicate acid violence, governments must address its root causes: gender inequality and discrimination, the availability of acid, and the impunity of perpetrators. Below we provide concrete recommendations that government and corporations can immediately undertake in an effort to combat acid violence.

Government: In furtherance of their duty to exercise due diligence to prevent acid violence, governments should:

- Enact criminal laws that specifically address acid violence and effectively regulate the production, distribution, use, sale, and handling of acid;
- Effectively enforce and implement laws designed to deter acid violence; and

- Provide victim redress, including compensation for healthcare costs.

Non-Government Organizations: In furtherance of their emerging duty to exercise due diligence to minimize the negative human rights impacts of their activities, companies that produce, distribute, use, or otherwise handle acid should:

- Assess the ways in which they can reduce the negative human rights impacts of their activities; and
- Support industry and government efforts to regulate the safe-handling, storage, labeling, transfer and disposal of acid by manufacturers, distributors, and other business and individual users of acid in order to deter the unauthorized use of acid.

8. CONCLUSIONS

Acid violence is a prohibited form of gender-based violence under national and international law that both reflects discrimination against women and perpetuates it. Even if acid violence increased at an alarming rate in Bangladesh, by the passage of time this rate decreased significantly after the initiative of the government of Bangladesh, donors and NGO's. The education and awareness levels of the victims were not reached up to the mark for claiming the rights. Due to un-empowered socially and commercially, they had been deprived even from the basic civic amenities and human rights while most of them were lived under the poverty level. So, a collaborative action is badly needed by all the stakeholders to create awareness and enforcing laws to curb the global peril arranging a safe life.

REFERENCES

[1] Acid Survivors Foundation Publications (2002 – 2015). *www. Acidsurvirors.org*.

[2] AGCW (The Avon Global Center for Women) (2011). Combating Acid Violence in Bangladesh, India and Cambodia- A report by the Avon Global Center for Women, UK.

[3] Abedin, J. (2008). Women Empowerment in Bangladesh. Dhaka, Bangladesh.
[4] Kamruzzaman, M. (2015). Dowry related violence against rural women in Bangladesh. *American Journal of Psychology and Cognitive Science*, 1(4): 112–116.
[5] BBS (Bangladesh Bureau of Statistics) (2001). Population and Housing Census, Government of Bangladesh.
[6] Begum, H.A. and Nahar, S. (2006). A study on acid violence in Mymensingh, Dhaka, Bangladesh.
[7] BBS (Bangladesh Bureau of Statistics) (2011). Population and Housing Census, Government of Bangladesh.
[8] Hossain, K.T. and Sumon, S.R. (2013). *Violence against Women: Nature, Causes and Dimensions in Contemporary Bangladesh. Bangladesh e-Journal of Sociology*, 10(1).
[9] Hossain, K.T., Imam, M.H. and Khair, S. (2001). Males' Perception on Violence against Women in Bangladesh (mimeo). Dhaka: British Council.
[10] Kabeer, N. (1989). Monitoring poverty as if gender mattered a methodology for rural Bangladesh. Institute of Development Studies in Brighton, England.
[11] Nariphokko and Bangaladesh Mahila Parishad (1995). Baseline report on violence against women in Bangladesh.
[12] Save the Children (2003). Gender-based violence. Care and protection of children in emergencies, Afield guide.
[13] Kamruzzaman, M. (2015). Child victimization at working places in Bangladesh. *American Journal of Applied Psychology*, 4(6): 146–159.
[14] Kamruzzaman, M. (2016). A criminological study on the dark figure of crime as a socio-ecological bulk of victimization. *American Journal of Business, Economics and Management,* 4(4): 35–39.
[15] UN (United Nations) (2005). "Violence against women: A statistical overview, challenges and gaps in data appendix-interview checklist collection and methodology and approaches for overcoming them". Expert Group Meeting. Organized by: UN Division for the Advancement of Women.
[16] Kamruzzaman, M. and Hakim, M.A. (2016). Factors associated with the suicidal tsunami as a mental illness: Findings from an epidemiological study. *American Journal of Environment and Sustainable Development*, 1(1):1–5.
[17] Kamruzzaman, M. and Hakim, M.A. (2016). Prostitution going spiral: The myth of commercial child sex. *International Journal of Biomedical and Clinical Sciences*, 1(1): 1–6.
[18] Das, S.K., Khan, M.B.U. and Kamruzzaman, M. (2016). Preventive Detention and Section 54 of the Code of Criminal Procedure: The Violation of Human Rights in Bangladesh. *American Journal of Business and Society*, 1(3): 60–67.

[19] Kamruzzaman, M. and Hakim, M.A. (2015). Child criminalization at slum areas in Dhaka city. *American Journal of Psychology and Cognitive Science*, 1(4): 107–111.

[20] UN (United Nations) (2013). Special Rapporteur on violence against women, its causes and consequences finalizes country mission to Bangladesh.

[21] WHO (World Health Organization) (2011). Campaigns against acid violence spur change. Special News, WHO. Retrieved from *http://www.who.int/bulletin/volumes/89/1/11-020111.pdf.*

[22] Kamruzzaman, M. and Hakim, M.A. (2016). Socio-economic status of slum dwellers: An empirical study on the capital city of Bangladesh. *American Journal of Business and Society*, 1(2): 13–18.

[23] Kamruzzaman, M. and Hakim, M.A. (2016). Condom using prevalence and phobia on sexually transmitted diseases among sex-buyers in Bangladesh. *American Journal of Environmental and Occupational Health*, 1(1): 1–5.

[24] Kamruzzaman, M. and Hakim, M.A. (2015). Socio-economic status of child beggars in Dhaka city. *Journal of Social Sciences and Humanities*,1 (5): 516–520.

[25] Kamruzzaman, M. and Hakim, M.A. (2015). Family planning practices among married women attending primary health care centers in Bangladesh. *International Journal of Bioinformatics and Biomedical Engineering*, 1(3): 251–255.

[26] Kamruzzaman, M. and Hakim, M.A. (2015). Livelihood Status of Fishing Community of Dhaleshwari River in Central Bangladesh. *International Journal of Bioinformatics and Biomedical Engineering*, 2(1): 25–29.

[27] Md. Shahidul Bari and Md. Iqbal Mahmud Choudhury (2001). *Acid Burns in Bangladesh, Annals of Burns and Fire Disasters*, 14: 115.

[28] Bangladesh. Acid Control Act (ACA), Ch. 4, No. 1 of 2002.

[29] *www.minlaw.gov.bd.*

[30] Zafreen Farzana*et al.* (2010). Socio-demographic characteristics of acid victims in Bangladesh. *J. Armed Forces Med. College Bangladesh*, 6: 12–14.

10

Women, Conflict and Peace Building in Ethiopia: The Case Study of Traditional Gumuz Community in Metekel, North Western Ethiopia

DAGNACHEW AYENEW YESHIWAS[1]*

ABSTRACT

The Gumuz are Nilo-Saharan speaking people who live in northwestern lowlands of Ethiopia. The social fabrics of the Gumuz and their interaction with neighbors have been attracting numerous sociologists and anthropologists. However, this study is designed to investigate the role of women in conflict and peace building process among the Gumuz community omitted by the studies conducted so far. To understand the contribution of women in the process, it has employed ethnographic research design. The data which have been collected through in-depth interview, observation, and review of documents is analysed thematically. Accordingly, the study revealed that women of Gumuz play key roles in both instigating conflicts and facilitating the resolution process. Women are often behind conflicts occurring among the traditional community of Gumuz. In spite of this, women among the Gumuz are also transmitters of cultural values of peace to future

[1] Department of Peace and Development Studies, School of Governance, Wollo University, Dessie, Ethiopia.

**Corresponding author:* E-mail: dagnualem@gmail.com;

generations. They act as messengers of peace and intermediaries in settling violent conflicts, undertaking reconnaissance missions to assess possibilities of peace and facilitating communication. Furthermore, they are 'bridge building' blocks between hostile communities; through 'inter clan marriage' where a woman from a clan is given in marriage to a man of another clan as away of sealing alliance for reconciliation in post violent conflict reconstruction period. However, despite possessing these wealthy of experience, insights and key role in conflict resolution and peace building process, the Gumuz women have been marginalized from formal peace building and decision-making process. Therefore, a holistic attempt to constructively deal with conflicts in the area should always consider these time tested traditional roles of the Gumuz woman.

Key words: Gumuz, Women of Gumuz, Conflict, Conflict resolution, Reconciliation, Peace building.

---

1. INTRODUCTION

Ethiopia is a multi-ethnic state endowed with people of diversified culture, language, faith, religion and long history of state hood. Nilo-Saharan speaking people of Gumuz in northwestern lowlands of Ethiopia are one among many others. Although they scattered in various parts of northwestern Ethiopia such as Awi nationality zone and North Gondar zone, majority of Gumuz population is living in Metekel and Khamashi zones of BGRS. Roughly, Gumuz of Metekel represents 80 percent of Gumuzs' total population living in the area (Teferi, 2014). Their oral traditions indicated that they are Pre-Cushitic settlers of highland areas of Ethiopia. Similarly, Bruce opines that the people of Gumuz are aborigines' of the region; he calls them Western '*Shanqila*[1]' (cited in James, 1977:1).

---

[1] A derogatory generic name connotes black skinned people occupying West and North West of Ethiopia (Teferi, 2014).

The Gumuz people have their own traditional religion. They believe in poly spirit super natural being called *mussa* and *gaheya* / *gaffiya* believed to be the mediator (Tsega, 2006). *Musa* presents spirits which are omniscient and omnipotent considered to be benevolent, kind and redeemer. There are a number of *muss as* operating in daily acts of life prevailing over different objects, phenomena, and actions. Some of them are *mussa-aya* (river spirit), *mussa kuancha* (sorghum spirit), *mussa patua* (pumpkin spirit), *mussa bokola* (corn spirit), *mussa omboh* (spirit of laughing), and the like (Woldesellassie, 2004[2]). Mussa is everything for the Gumuz; there is a festival which is celebrated two times in a year called *keya Musa* (*tella* (local beer) of God) to bless *mussa*; the first is celebrated when the rains starts and the second one comes forth when food crops get ready for consumption.

When *mussa* is disappointed, it causes sufferings and deaths among the community. In such a time, the *gaheya / gaffiya* recommends the appropriate offerings to be made for the *mussa,* and ceremonies and rituals to be performed. In every village, there are more than two prayer houses for the *mussa* where prayers and sacrifices are offered at times of disease, crop failure, natural disaster and the like. The *gaheya / gaffiya* is responsible for leading the prayer and as a mediator between man and *mussa* and he/she is often consulted and his/her words are strictly adhered to.

The Gumuz are egalitarian community and their nucleus of social organization is clan. It is their primary unit of initiating cooperation and establishing common defence against others (Desalegn, 2010). Traditionally, they are identified by different general local divisions such as the Gumuz of Mandura, the Gumuz of Metekel, the Gumuz of Kamashi and the like (Woldesellassie, 2004). These local politics are further sub-divided into other small units of sub-local clans. For example, Gumuz of Dangur is divided as Gumuz of Kitili, Gumuz of Aypapo... and each clan has it traditional elders called *ganza* (elders). Among the Gumuz, no one is adjudged as an isolated entity; every one is the protector of his

[2] and Informants, Ato Anteneh and Ato Gesese

brother. If someone did wrong, say if he kills a person from another clan, the whole members of the clan are responsible and – they cover all the compensations for the victim's family.

The prevailing system in marriage arrangement is sister exchange marriage (always exogamous and polygamy); if a man wants to get married he has to give a female relative or his sister for the family where he brought his wife. A man can also inherit wives from his died brother. Predominant sources of livelihood among the Gumuz are shifting cultivation usually supplemented by fishing, hunting and gathering. They use slash and burn farming; they cultivate crops at a certain size in some year and leave to another farm land until the previous recovers.

To this end, the Gumuz are amongst traditional societies of Ethiopia attracting numerous anthropologists, sociologists and historians. Listing academic literatures conducted on the Gumuz community is not an easy task. Large number of studies has been conducted regarding their history, social and political structures (*e.g.*, James, 1977; Abdussamad, 1995; Berihun, 2004; Desalegn, 2010 and others). Other studies give emphasis for historical and existing interaction of the Gumuz with their neighbours (Alemayehu, 2015; Teferi, 2014; Tsega, 2006; Woldesellassie, 2004 and others). Still others focus on issues behind conflicts prevailed in the area and their remedies (*e.g.*, Dagnachew, 2018). Almost all of the studies indicated that Metekel zone where majority of the Gumuz population resides is one among conflict prone areas of Ethiopia. Hence, any study attempted to investigate gender dimension of those conflicts and their remedies founds to be imperative.

2. STATEMENT OF THE PROBLEM

Inconventional wisdom of conflict studies, the role of women to conflict and peace building process is undermined by many researchers (Lihamba, 2003). It is perceived that since it is men who fight wars, it is men who (should) sit together and make peace.

But, in fact while men make up majority of combatants, they could hardly do without their women supporting them. Besides, many women have been active in the front lines of wars in Africa as well as in other parts of the world[3].

Moreover, peace cannot also be maintained only because men have stopped fighting each other (Lihamba, 2003). But, condition for peace come from systems of societal equilibrium which is maintained by norms and values acquired by individuals beginning from their early childhood experiences. Women are thus with opportunities to mould those norms and values on children because children spent most of their formative age with their mothers than fathers (Ntahobari and Ndayiziga, 2003). Violence will also overburden and causes more suffering for female than male. Women will look after their family, supply labour, administer their home and in times of crisis they may also be victims of gender based violence which targets women such as rape, kidnapping, forced pregnancy, sexual slavery and others (Bayrne, 1996; Naraghi-Anderlini, 2006). As such, women have more appetite to peace than men and in many societies they have significant contributions on its prevalence (Conaway and Sen, 2005).

However, while women have actively engaged in conflict and peace process, their role has largely been neglected. Similarly, despite possessing wealthy of experiences, insights and playing key roles in conflict and peace building process, the Gumuz women have got no attention from the studies conducted so far. Hence, this study concerns involvement of women in the course of conflicts and their key roles played to maintain peace and stability among the Gumuz community. Accordingly, this study has the following objectives;

- To investigate how Gumuz women appear as causes and instigators of conflict.

[3] In this regard, mentioning Empress Taytu Betul during the war of Adwa is note worthy.

- To assess indigenous institutions and systems of conflict resolution and peace building among traditional Gumuz community.
- To identify key roles played by Gumuz woman in the conflict resolution and peace building process

3. SETTING OF THE STUDY AREA

The name 'Metekel' is derived from one of the seven Agew clans, *awi lagneta*[4]. It represents a vast territory in northwest Ethiopia from the border of Sudan to the north of Abbay River (Blue Nile). It is bordered on the North by North Gonder Zone and in the East by Awi Nationality Zone. To the South and South West, it is bordered with Khamashi Zone, while to the West it adjoins with the Sudan.

In the pre-1991 state structure, Metekel region, known as Metekel *Awraja*, was part of Gojjam province. At present, however, although it kept its former district with some rearrangements, it has become a zone under BGRS. Some parts of the former district of Guangua with the capital, Chagni, and a portion of Debate districts are included to Awi Nationality Zone of Amhara National Regional State. Since the end of 2000, Gilgel beles town, which is 546 Kilometres away from Addis Ababa, is the capital of the zone. The name Metekel, therefore, is used in the study to refer districts included after the area was designed as administrative zone in 1991. These are Bullen, Dangur, Dibate, Guba, Mandura, Wembera and Pawi.

The major ethnic groups that inhabited the area are Gumuz (36.78%), Shinasha (21.6%), Agew (11.65%), Amhara (17.39%) and Oromo (11.09) (CSA, 2007). There are also other folk ethnic

[4] Studies and oral tradition of the people indicates that seven fathers of Agew arrived to Gojjam originally from Waghimira, Wollo, namely Ankasha, Banja, Zigem, Kuakura, Metekel, Azena and Chara (Tsega, 2006; Taddesse, 1988).

divisions which are relevant for the study such as *qey* and *tikur*[5], *nebar* (early inhabitant) and *mete* (recent migrant), highlanders and lowlanders, *yekilil balebet* (indigenous) and *leloch hizboch* (non-indigenous). Above all, Metekel is one among conflict prone areas of Ethiopia where both inter and intra ethnic conflicts are frequently reported (Dagnachew, 2018).

4. METHODOLOGY OF THE STUDY

This study has employed ethnographic research design. The rational to the selection of ethnographic research design was due to the fact that issues described in the research require field work techniques in which the topic can be understood in the holistic description of cultural traits related to the objectives of the study. Ethnographic research methods are ideally suited to describe or analyze cultural practices, human beliefs and behaviours, and socio-cultural changes over time. This study was also designed to describe and analyse the traditional role of Gumuz woman in conflict and peace building activities. Accordingly, the data that have been collected through the following techniques is analyzed thematically.

- ***In Depth-Interview:*** The researcher undertakes a series of extensive interview which is unstructured type and open ended questions with key informants. The selection of key informants was through purposive sampling that targeted individuals well embraced with culture, socio-cultural practices and history of the people such as elders, members of elder's council (*mangama*), local leaders and religious leaders.
- ***Observation:*** The researcher has also spent his time to observe daily activities of the people. Activities which take

[5] 'qey' and 'Tikur' are colour dichotomies of people in the area. 'qey', in Amharic, refers to people of the area with comparatively brighter colour while 'Tikur', also in Amharic, represents 'black'. Accordingly, Gumuz in the area are identified as 'Tikur.'

place in villages, market areas, tea rooms, religious/ cultural ceremonies, *tela* houses, *bourde* houses and so forth were major targets.

- ***Document Review:*** Available documents (statistical data, letters, minutes, archives, proclamations and policies...) and prior works which are relevant to this study were also consulted and cross checked against the data obtained from primary sources.

5. RESULTS AND DISCUSSION

5.1. Women and Major Causes of Conflict among the Gumuz

Conflicts and warfare exist among human beings since time of antiquity. Conflict is an inevitable human phenomenon as far as interaction exists. Tsega (2006) stated that inter-clan relations among the Gumuz are manifested in conflicts than peaceful coexistence. Among the Gumuz community, as discussed later, it can be argued that women are major issues and sources of conflict. Conflict may appear for various reasons, but the most common causes of conflict in the Gumuz include, traditional marriage arrangement, abducting girls, adultery, deliberate killing for fame, insult and resource use[6].

A. Marriage arrangement

Exchanging of sisters for wife is the common system of marriage among the Gumuz (Woldesellassie, 2004). It means if a man wants to get married he has to give a female relative or his sister for the family where he brought his wife. Therefore, Gumuz women are married off unwillingly without having much option, which sometimes forced them to run away from their husbands and return to their family (Tsega, 2006). They are to live with the husbands they have never seen, and there are many cases of repeatedly returning women.

[6] Informants; Aba Polis, Ato Bekele and Ato Cheru.

Moreover, exchanged wives are expected to be active, hardworking, virgin and fertile. If a girl is not a virgin at a time of marriage and fertile after marriage, members of the husband's family will refuse her[7]. She will be given very low social status; she will be maltreated by her husband and despised by the society. Thus, she will be forced to return to her parents and her husband in his turn will request for replacement or to return his sister. If members' of wife's family refused the claim of husband, conflict will erupt soon between the two clans.

Moreover, traditional marriage arrangement of the community prohibits a young man with no sisters to exchange to start a family. Therefore, to start a family, kidnapping a girl appears as the only remaining alternative of men with no sisters. When it occurs, unless the girl is freed or all the necessary negotiations are made, fighting between clan members of both sides will continue. If someone from the girl's family happens to kill one of the abductors, he will have special acceptance and reputation among community members.

In times of marriage, the girl is also expected to be virgin. If the girl is not found virgin, in addition to maltreatment and dehumanization from husband's side, she holds a duty to tell when, how and by whom she has lost her virginity to her husband. Unless all the necessary negotiations and compensations are made, conflict will appear and continue between the clans of the husband and the man who had illicit sexual relationship with the girl before her marriage. Thus, marriage arrangements and expectations of the Gumuz usually cause inter-clan tensions and conflicts.

B. Adultery

As mentioned before, among the Gumuz, the identity of a person is always marked by his/her membership to a clan. The clan is composed of various neighbourhood members claimed to have blood relations along patrilineal descent and its territory is strongly defended from outsiders. Therefore, anybody having illicit

[7] Informant; W/ro Yeshi

relationships with some one's wife is strongly hated, and if found becomes subject to serious punishments and a potential cause of conflict. For example, in 1882, among Gumuz of Guba, Italian visitor Luigi Mondo has observed the procedure of punishment for committing adultery and reported the following;

> .... Everyone was dressed in their best and looked war like with their beautiful round convex shields made of buffalo skin and their spleen did spears wound round with snake skin. What sort of festival could this be? They told me quietly that the wife of the sheikh had just been killed because on that very morning she was guilty of adultery. Her lover was sentenced to be sold as a slave but the wife's throat was cut on the spot where the mound had been built and her body was thrown in to the river... (James, 1977:7).

However, now a time, if adultery is committed among traditional community of the Gumuz, the woman will be subject to punishments passed by clan elders and her illicit lover will receive the punishment from the husband. Among the Gumuz, the husband of the woman having illicit relationship is expected to take revenge against the man who commits the adultery. If revenge is not taken, women insult the husband and he will lose his acceptance from the community particularly among the women. Therefore, he is forced to take the revenge and actions taken him may lead to inter-clan conflicts beyond personal disputes as clan members in the side of the illicit lover will also stand to provide protection to their member.

C. Deliberate killings

For the Gumuz, killers and hunters are highly respected and considered as warrior patriots. Therefore, killing for fame among the Gumuz have a special place and people are encouraged to kill. The killer is called *gunza* which means 'male'. *Gunza* is a hero; he would have special status and priority in social activities, his own separate drinking vessel and seat[8]. If he kills the killer of his brother, he would get priority to obtain his wife and property. Their wives also encourage their husbands to kill since respect and fame extends up to them, for example they will have priority in fetching water and sitting at festivals.

Abdussamad (1995) has also reported that 'when they [Gumuz] succeeded in killing a person, they cut off his right arm, dried it with smoke and beat their drums with it; this gives great honour to the killer'. Previously, one had also to kill to marry and they were traditionally required to bring men's genital organs (Tsega, 2006). However, such killings are always allowed only against non-relatives particularly highlanders and if a Gumuz suddenly kills relatives he will be isolated from the community[9].

D. Revenge

Taking revenge is also another chief cause of conflict within the Gumuz. If someone killed another, relatives of the victim are expected to take revenge. If such actions are not taken, women insult their husbands for not taking revenges and the husband will lose his acceptance from the community particularly among the women. Therefore, day and night men of the Gumuz prepare themselves to take revenges. As a result of multiple killings for kidnapping, against adultery, for fame and so on... revenge is a common cause of conflict with in the Gumuz community.

From the discussion, it can be concluded that women are behind major causes to conflicts which appear among traditional community of Gumuz. In marriage arrangements and adultery, inter-clan conflicts usually erupt following behaviours observed and actions undertaken by women. Furthermore, women of Gumuz have also instigated conflicts between their men through encouraging their husbands for deliberate killing and revenge, and insulting those men who are reluctant to do so.

---

[8] Observed in Dibati town in *Tella* (local beer) house.
[9] Informants; Ato Nega and Ato Wendu.

Furthermore, once a conflict happens between clans, women will also use various ways of instigating men to go to war. They praise men who join the war without hesitation and at the same time they also ridicule, nag and abuse those who are reluctant to join the war. They bless conflicts and prepare food before hand and welcome those who return with blessings, songs and dances. During conflicts they provide moral support to and initiate their men.

5.2. Traditional Conflict Resolution and Peace Building Institutions of the Gumuz: *Siyaha* and *Mangama*

Conflict in itself is neither good nor bad, but the way it is handled makes it either constructive or destructive. If conflicts are dealt positively, they become engines for constructive social change. If they are not properly resolved, they become sources of destruction. Accordingly, every society has developed its own traditional mechanisms and institutions for curing conflicts. Among the Gumuz, there are time tested and effective customary conflict resolution systems and institutions namely *Siyaha* and *Mangama*.

A. Siyaha

Siyaha is traditional institution of governance and conflict management among traditional community Gumuz[10]. Members of the clan elect a respected person for the overall leadership of the Gumuz in a given locality and he is called *Tissa*. The *Tissa* wears a white and red cloth sheet on his forehead which symbolizes his authority and this sheet of cloth is called *Siyaha,* from which the name of the institution is derived. The *Tissa* has his deputy called *Gantic Tissa* assigned to deal with conflicts among the community and represents *Tissa* during his absence. After *Tissa* and *Gantic Tissa* are elected, the head of the peace keeping force, *Tis muhin* and the peace keeping force known as *Lagawidan* will be assigned. *Tis muhin* and *Lagawidan* are traditionally allowed

[10] Informants; Aba Polis and W/ro Yeshi.

to be armed for keeping peace. Tsega (2006) stated that the term of office for any official member of *Siyaha* cannot be for more than 4 years.

According to informants, though the leadership role of *Siyaha* is replaced by formal institutions, its active role in handling conflicts and keeping peace is still accepted and respected among traditional community of Gumuz. Tsega (2006) has mentioned the following major roles of *Siyaha* in the traditional community of Gumuz;

- Maintaining justice and conflict resolution.
- Ensuring security of life and property.
- Safeguarding positive values of the society and educating the young.
- Providing appropriate guidance and leadership.
- Emphasizing the prevalence of respect, equality and human rights within the community.

B. Mangama

Mangama literally means assembly that is composed of elders elected by villagers. They are responsible for managing conflicts arise in villages, among clan members and within family. Higher level inter-clan conflicts will be reported to *Tissa*, which in turn will inform to selected elders. According to informants, elders are to be selected from non-feuding neutral clans who did not have earlier conflicts with either of conflicting clans. Elders among the Gumuz are considered pillars of the community who are concerned about peaceful coexistence of the community above anybody. They cure any from conflicts in the form of abducting, killing or else; embark on reconciliation efforts until the grudges are healed.

If the case is death, before bringing the primary conflicting parties together, greater effort has to be made for facilitating the process with the closest relatives. Then, a separate location outside the village of the two feuding clans will be selected for the main *mangama* council, usually around a river. A clan who committed the worst act will be required by elders to bring goat and the bull to be slaughtered and sacrificed during the process. Before, the process get started a goat will be slaughtered with blessing from elders to appease the *mussa*. The blood of the goat will be let to flow away in the river which symbolizes washing away of violence.

Guided by elders, the two conflicting individuals will come to each other at the river. They will be covered by a garment so that they cannot see each other until towards the end of the process. The two feuding individuals are expected to shave their hairs and needed to wash and clean their body during the reconciliation day. Towards the end of the process the two feuding parties will be brought to each other and unveiled by elders and finally embrace each other. They swear an oath not to break the reconciliation and a bull is slaughtered for consumption[11].

For more complete reconciliation and peaceful coexistence, the two clans will continue another feast ceremony. It will be conducted on two different occasions to allow members of the two clans to enter each other's village and house. The first clan to arrange the feast is the one that caused more causality and loses fewer members. At the feast with the appearance of peace – facilitating elders, food and drink will be served as they embrace and kiss each other. The process will be completed when the second clan arranges the same feast ceremony[12].

5.3. Basic Features and Principles of Traditional Conflict Resolution and Peace Building Practices of Gumuz

Primarily, conflict resolution among the Gumuz is not a task to be arbitrarily conducted. It is time selective without affecting home responsibilities of individuals who are involved in the process. Thus, according to informants, conflict resolution is done during those sections of time when there is mental allotment, intellectual

[11] Informants; Ato Nega, Aba Polis, W/ro Yeshi, Ato Bekele.
[12] Ibid

bliss and spiritual conveniences. River banks and shadows of big trees are usually places where the process of conflict resolution takes place.

Another important feature of conflict resolution process among the Gumuz is that the involvement of super natural beings in the process. Among the Gumuz, there is a belief for the existence of beings such as super natural beings, ancestors and deities in the process of conflict resolution. Therefore, the process begins through blessings and sacrifices made to appease them. The *gahiya/gaffiya* is also consulted regarding the appropriate time when they will intervene in the handling conflicts. This belief has also created a corresponding duty on the combatants to adhere to the decisions made by the council believed to receive advices from supernatural beings, their ancestors and deities. It is believed that breaking the reconciliation process undertaken by elders is equivalent with disrespecting their ancestors and deities. Thus, decisions made and passed by elders in the process will be final and expected to be accepted by parties to the conflict unconditionally.

Conflict resolution practices among the Gumuz are also characterized by the dramatization of the process. The stage for the scene of drama is often arranged around river banks and shadows of big tree performed and attended by adjudicators (council of elders), *siyaha* members, religious leaders *(gahiya/gaffiya),* conflicting parties and their clan members, witnesses and the larger crowd. The level of performance by the council of elders is triangular, focusing or viewing the parties to the conflict, witnesses and the audience (large crowd). The assigned individuals are obliged not to leave the scene until resolution has found. Apart from the dramatic scene, proverbs, maxims and poems of the society are also used. Hence, the performance level of conflict resolution in Gumuz enabled participants in the ensuing drama to further understand and appreciate that customs and norms bequeathed to them by their ancestors.

An interesting aspect of the scene in the drama of conflict resolution is the celebration of reconciliation by the attendants.

At the end of the process, conflicting parties as well as observant will eat, drink, dance, sing and chant all together. The ceremonial steps, swilling appearance and embracing gestures exchanged among the hitherto aggressive parties to the conflict provided fun fair with a mood of pomp and pageantry at the closing session of the stage craft. It is one way of sealing the reconciliation and bringing the healthiest relationship of conflicting parties.

Furthermore, traditional conflict resolution and peace building methods practiced in Gumuz community are governed by the following principles;

Truth: According to informants, truth is the fundamental ingredient in every affair of the community. It is associated with the positive conduct of life and it is observable in every aspect of life. The people of Gumuz indoctrinated that their ancestors loved and embraced truth as covenant ego. Hence, it has been upheld as salient principle and suitable verification to authentic verdict in traditional conflict resolution processes of the Gumuz.

Collective responsibility: As a matter of fact, in Gumuz, the identity of an individual is determined by his/her membership to a clan and no one is adjudged as an isolated entity. Every one is the protector his brother, this is why the principle of collective responsibility is in place. Thus, the conflicting parties submit themselves to the process of conflict resolution with full confidence on the assigned individuals as well as principles which would be applied to the conflict. During the process, the populace will also follow both parties with concern born out of sympathy and respect for them. Compensations expected from those parties which are guilty for more causality are also shared by the whole members of their clan.

Impartiality and transparency: A principle adopted by ancestors of Gumuz to show tensions associated with conflict resolution and peace building. Indeed, actors of the resolution process need these principles to stand the test of time towards ensuring completeness of verifying truth and asserting vibrant claims. For example, if the process is to deal with higher level inter clan conflicts then members of adjudicators are elected from neutral clans which did not have previously a record of conflict with either of the conflicting clans. It will also take place in a separate location outside the village of both feuding clans. The process goes in an open air in which attendants and conflicting parties observe and follow the whole process until reconciliation is reached. Thus, council of elders upheld these principles towards playing safe and restoring peace in the muddy atmosphere.

***Equity and fairness*:** During the resolution process, parties to the conflict are always given fair hearing and representation (through witness). No one has its case treated in absentia as during so announced to misplace of justice and assault to the enforcer of justice (*nussa*). Parties to the conflict are also always afforded reasonable time to state the issues of conflict and their claims. Failure to ever appear at the scene of conflict resolution regarded as contempt of court. The end of justice usually reconciliation, therefore, justified the principles of conflict resolution in the Gumuz. Thus, the parties to the conflict enjoined to give peace a chance by shifting the ground of conflict and limping towards peace and harmony in a principle of "give little, get little".

***Forgiveness and tolerance*:** During the process, both sides of the conflict appear at the scene being ready to tolerate their differences and to forgive all the things went wrong at the time of their hostile relationship. Their goal of appearance is not to revenge, no to make others liable or not to see when the other party is subject to punishment but to reconcile and to bring back their healthiest relationships. Hence, tolerance and forgiveness are major ingredients of traditional conflict resolution of the Gumuz to attain its goal; reconciliation and restoration of harmonious relationships.

5.4. The Role of Women in Traditional Peace Building and Conflict Resolution Practices of Gumuz

Within the Gumuz women are behind the causes to many types of conflicts appeared in the community. However, despite their role in initiating and encouraging their men to go to war, they also play key roles in ending violent conflicts and facilitating the peace process. Women of Gumuz are transmitters of cultural values of peace to future generations. They also act as intermediaries in conflict situations, undertaking reconnaissance missions to assess possibilities of peace and subsequently facilitating communication and peace negotiations. They are also 'bridge building' blocks between hostile communities; through 'inter clan marriage' where by a woman of a clan is given in marriage to a man of another clan as a way of sealing alliance for peace and reconciliation in post violent conflict reconstruction period. Accordingly, the following are major roles played by the Gumuz woman in traditional peace building and conflict resolution practices.

5.4.1. *Women and peace education*

In many traditional African societies, it is believed that peace is the result of socialization; peace is made not born. In such societies, the culture of peace will be implanted in a child through responsible upbringing and socialization undertaken and supervised by mothers (Ntahobari and Ndayiziga, 2003). Hence, in traditional African societies peace is expected to be established and strengthened little by little in young minds and mounded in the behaviour and personality of the young through the agency of the mother. Mohammed (2003) stated that mother is the first and most valuable school in life through whom our early childhood experience is shaped.

Among the Gumuz, women strive to bring their children with positive norms and ethos to lay the foundation for a healthy and stable society. At their formative age, children of Gumuz remained with their mothers and other group of women. As such, each child is exposed to a variety of songs, stories proverbs and sayings directed by mothers and conveyed at fire place or after evening meals, aimed at how to minimize conflicts and promote peace. The themes of stories and songs teach children to develop traits of responsibility through reciprocity, honesty, loyalty, faith and controlling one's own appetite for the benefit of the society.

Generally the central message is about how greed and self-interest can be sources of conflict; therefore young children are expected to behave against these voices. Regarding this, an informant from *kitili* clan said that,

> Children live within the village where they are born, observing what is done, watching their parents, clan members and elders and following their role models. This extended period of observation is always to be supervised by the mother, who has her young children constantly at her side, so that from an early age, children come to acquire an appetite for those virtues valuable to the society, that remind a good upbringing.

There are also disciplinary measures taken even for very young, to set them on the right road in the early ages. Girls grow up with practical moral trainings, their mothers are expected to be careful about it, because it is their pride if their daughters are prized for their moral excellence and a mother would be disappointed if her daughter is denigrated[13]. Mothers have a responsibility to make sure their daughters are successful in their married life. In the Gumuz traditional society, a woman is reprimanded for her bad manners and if she is not virgin at marriage. Consequently, among the Gumuz, a mother's advice to her daughter is calculated to reinforce and strengthen those values that would make her successful in her married life.

In general, women of Gumuz have always played a critical role in maintaining equilibrium in their society by bringing up their children as responsible members of the community. Women taught their daughters and sons the right behaviour and norms of society, and inculcated into them the importance of such values as honesty, uprightness, generosity, civic mindedness and the necessity to compromise. In doing so, women of Gumuz are transmitters of cultural values of peace to future generations, which can be referred to as peace education.

[13] Informant; W/ro Yeshi

5.4.2. *Women as mediators and messengers of peace*

Primarily, the role of women in mediating conflicts among the Gumuz is attributed to their role emanated from the marriage system of the society. In a polygamous marriage of Gumuz, the senior wife is key mediator to conflicts appearing at family level. She is responsible to restore peace in situations of conflict between junior wives, or between husband and one of the wives. Women of Gumuz are also able to persuade their men to stop fighting and settle their differences through negotiations.

Furthermore, giving respect to women (particularly to the elderly) is the main feature of Gumuz culture. Hence, elder women played a key role in crisis management and peace-making. In times of war, for example, they are the only ones who can move freely in conflict zones without experiencing danger. This is because, among the Gumuz, committing violence against women is shame full. An informant from *Dibati* said, 'why you dare to attack a woman? Is that, because she is giving a child for you?' This cultural norm of the Gumuz provides to women an opportunity to freely engage in settling violent conflicts between their men.

Therefore, in times of war, studying the situation, assessing opportunities of peace, and facilitating communication between the warring parties become major roles of women. For example, if either of the warring clans has an appetite to end the war, old woman will be searched and sent to the second clan with *kuancha* (sorghum), which is the most respected food crop and symbol of peace. If the invitation for peace is welcomed by the second clan then the woman will return with another *kuancha,* otherwise she will came up with *berbere* (peppercorn)[14]. When the woman returns with *berbere*, the second clan has rejected the peace plan and the war will be continued.

[14] *berbere* (peppercorn) among the Gumuz symbolizes conflict/war/violence, for example, if a clan of Gumuz has engaged in to conflict with another ethnic group then old woman will be sent to each clan of the Gumuz to be ready against their enemy. It is cited by informants as the major reason to escalation and expansion of group conflicts in the study area.

However, if the call for peace is refused by either of the warring clans, women will employ desperate measures in order to end the violent conflict. An elder woman with *kuancha* will came up and stand in the middle of warring parties and refused to leave until the two groups backed down[15]. The Gumuz men who have respect for both *kuancha* and woman will immediately stop the war. This action provides an environment that enabled the warring clans to talk over their differences and searching peaceful solution. Then the case will be transferred to and administered by procedures in *Siyaha* and *Mangama*. Thus, elder women who are respected by all among the Gumuz play a key role in crisis management and peacemaking.

5.4.3. *Women as builders of bridges*

In addition to positive upbringing of children and managing crisis and conflict, the role of a Gumuz woman goes up to building bridges between clans. A traditional Gumuz society does not allow marriage arrangements with in a clan. As a result, marriage is always arranged between people who are far to each other in terms of genealogy and territory. This type of marriage brought together and bonded two previously unrelated clans which in turn will minimize the possibility of inter-clan tensions.

Moreover, the role of women in peace building and conflict resolution extends up to post violent conflict reconstruction strategies. Among the Gumuz, during inter-clan conflict, if death happens then a marriage involving the warring clans will be arranged[16]. This kind of marriage occurs between a man who lost a brother or close relative and a girl from the opposing side. The marriage is organized to heal the wounds and cement agreement or settlement reached by the two parties, as a married woman will give a birth which can replace the life lost in the battle. This will strengthen the bond of the two groups and minimize the possibility of another conflict erupting between them.

---

[15] Informanst; Ato Bekele and Aba Polis
[16] Informants; Aba Polis and W/ro Yeshi

6. CONCLUSIONS AND IMPLICATIONS

It is indicated that inter-clan relations among the Gumuz are characterized by conflict than peace full coexistence. Women are behind many sources of conflict such as marriage arrangements, abduction, revenge, fame and others. But, despite their contribution in instigating conflict, women of the Gumuz have also key roles played during resolving conflicts and peace building process. Among others, women of Gumuz are transmitters of cultural values of peace to future generations. They also act as messengers of peace, intermediaries in settling violence, undertaking reconnaissance missions to assess possibilities of peace and subsequently facilitating communication and peace negotiations. They are also 'bridge building' blocks between hostile communities; through 'inter clan marriage' as a way of sealing alliance for peace and reconciliation in post violent conflict reconstruction period.

However, the field work revealed that despite possessing these wealthy of experience, insights and key role in conflict resolution and peace building process the Gumuz women have been marginalized from formal peace building and decision-making process. As noted before, Metekel is one among conflict prone areas of Ethiopia. Therefore, a holistic attempt to deal with conflicts in the area should consider this time tested traditional role of the Gumuz woman. This can be achieved through;

- Enabling women to take active part in formal conflict resolution and peace building process in the area.
- Introducing the values and attributes that maintained and reinforced the balance of traditional society which is possessed by women into the formal education curriculum.
- Creating awareness among the young generation of the Gumuz community regarding peace values that Gumuz women possess. This might be done through education, media, organizing seminars and workshops or other suitable communication channels.

- Although there are number of distinguished women among the Gumuz community in peace building process, their achievements are neglected. Therefore, recording their history of achievements in their sphere and introducing awards and giving recognition is another important step.
- Conducting further studies regarding the issue. Any effort which came up to manipulate these time tested experiences and attributes of women in peace process should be preceded by academic engagements. So far, this is the first study conducted on the role of Gumuz woman in traditional conflict resolution and peace building efforts in the community. Thus, further academic engagements on the issue will came up with better and comprehensive understandings that can be inputs to policy making at various levels.

REFERENCES

Abdussamed, A. (1995). The Gumuz of the lowlands of Western Gojjam: The Frontier in History: 1900-1935. *Africa*, 50(1): 53–67.

Alemayehu, E. (2015). Inter ethnic relation among Awi and Gumuz North Western Ethiopia, since 1975: A shift from hostile to peace full co existence. *African Journal of History and culture.*

Asnake, K. (2013). *Federalism and Ethnic Conflict in Ethiopia: A Comparative Regional Study*. New York: Routledge.

Berihun, M. (1996). Spontaneous Settlement and Inter-Ethnic Relations in Metekel, North West Ethiopia. MA thesis, Social Anthropology, Addis Ababa University.

Byrne, B. (1996). *Gender, Conflict and Development. Volume I Overview.* BRIDGE Report No. 34. December 1995, revised July 1996. Brighton, Institute of Development Studies, University of Sussex.

Conaway, C. and Sen, A. (2005). *Beyond Conflict Prevention: How Women Prevent Violence and Build Sustainable Peace.* New York, Global Action to Prevent War; Geneva, Women's International League for Peace and Freedom.

Dagnachew, A. (2018). Relative deprivation: An explanation to inter ethnic conflicts in Metekel Zone, North Western Ethiopia, Since 1991. *IJPDS,* 9(1–14).

Desalegn, A. (2010). *Awi-Gumuz relations: The Dynamics of Ethnicity in Ethiopia.* Saarbrucken: VDM Verlag Dr. Mueller.

Desalegn, A. (2014). *Ethiopian Ethnic Federalism: A "God-Sent" Opportunity for All Ethnic Groups? Modern Africa: Politics, History Soc.,* 2(2): 63–92.

Desalegn, R. (1988). Some Notes on Settlement and Resettlement in Metekkel Awraja (Gojam Province). *PICES*, 9(1): 116–134.

James, W. (1977). Notes on the Gumuz: Their Culture, History and Survival. *Paper to be Presented at the Conference on Ethiopian Origins to be Held at the School of Oriental and African Studies on 28th and 29th June 1977.*

Lihamba, A. (2003). Women's Peace Building and Conflict Resolution Skills, Morogoro Region, Tanzania. *In*: UNESCO, *Women and Peace in Africa*, pp. 111–131. Paris: UNSCO Workshops. Retrieved January 20, 2017 from: *http://www.afrikaworld.net/afrel/chinwenwoye.html*

Mohamed, A.M. (2003). The role of Somali Women in the search for peace. *In*: UNESCO, *War and Peace in Africa*, pp. 75–110. Paris: UNESCO Workshops. Retrieved January 20, 2017 from: *http://www.osisa.org/sites/default/files/sup_files/peace_building.pdf*

Naraghi-Anderlini, S. (2006). Mainstreaming gender in conflict analysis: Issues and recommendations. *Social Development Papers on Conflict Prevention and Reconstruction,* No. 33. New York, The World Bank.

Ntahobari, J. and Ndayiziga, B. (2003). The Role of Burundian Women in the Peaceful Settlement of Conflicts. *In*: UNESCO, *Women and Peace in Africa*, pp. 11–26. Paris: UNESCO Workshops. Retrieved January 20, 2017 from: *http://www.academia.edu/5333880*

Ruibal, A.G., Xurxo, M. and Aparicio, A.F. (2006). Deep- mapping the Gumuz house. Retrieved October 20, 2015 from: *https://moduloxurxoayan.files*

Taddesse, T. (1988a). Nilo-Saharan Interaction with Neighboring Highlanders: The Case of Gumuz of Gojjam and Wallega", Proceedings of the Workshop on Famine Experience and *Resettlement in Ethiopia, Addis Ababa, Addis Ababa University.*

Teferi, M. (2014). The Gumuz of Matakal and their Agaw Neighbours: A Historical Survey of Ethnic Interaction, 1898-1974. *Proceedings of the Second Annual Workshop of the Institute of Ethiopian Studies. Addis Ababa: Addis Ababa University Press.*

Tsega, E. (2006). Inter ethnic interaction on Frontier: Mettekel (Ethiopia) 1898-1991. Germany: Otto Harrassowitz and Co. KG. Wiesbaden.

Woldesellassie, A. (2004). Gumuz and Highland Resettlers: *Differing Strategies of Livelihood and Ethnic Relations in Metekkel*, Northwestern Ethiopia. PhD Dissertation, Gottingen, University of Gottingen.

11

Federalism and Ethnic Based Conflict; Case from The Oromo and Somali Communities in Ethiopia

TAKELE BEKELE BAYU[1*]

ABSTRACT

Since 1991 Ethiopia has made a paradigm shift favoring federalism against the centralized hierarchical power to radically respond to the problem of diversity and better recognize and accommodate the country's ethno-linguistic and cultural diversity. Consequently, the 1995 constitution has redefined the country along ethnic lines with the creation of nine ethnic-based regional states and two federally administered city-states in an effort to create a more prosperous, just and representative state for its entire people. However, the adoption of ethnic federalism, which provided a high level of autonomy to each nationality, as a diagnosis and response to the Ethiopia's century long divisions between nationalities and history of exploitation has created further challenges, particularly localized conflicts, at various levels in the country. This study has attempted to investigate conflict dynamics between Somalis and Oromo communities in the context of ethnic federalism while employing primary and secondary data collection and analysis methodology. The study found out that unintended effects of ethnic federalism,

[1] National University of Public Service, Budapest, Hungary.
**Corresponding author:* E-mail: Takeb21983@gmail.com

the restructuring of administration merely along ethnic lines goes against the realities of the region; unclear administration boundary along the shared boarders; ethnic politicization; mega ethnic syndrome within the society and the lack of integration between federalism and democracy in the process of implementation are major causes behind the recurrent conflict between the two neighboring communities.

***Key words*:** Ethnic Federation, Ethnic Politicization, Conflict, Oromo Communities, Somali Communities.

---

1. INTRODUCTION

Ethiopia is a diverse nation with more than 80 ethnic groups with their own distinct socio-cultural and linguistic elements. Paradoxically, since its modern existence, the second half of the 19th century, the political and administrational system of the country had been arranged against the existence of the country's socio- cultural and linguistic diversity. In 1991 a multi-national force led by Ethiopian People Revolutionary Front (EPRDF) has adopted ethnic federalism and institutionally accommodate and constitutionally recognize the issue of nationalities in Ethiopia[1]. This is a paradigm shift and departure from the previous centralized monarchical and military rules in the sense that in the new ethnic federalism the sovereignty of the state resides in the nations, nationalities, and peoples of Ethiopia[2]. The Oromo and the Somali regional administrations are among the nine ethnically divided regions in the country under the new federal restructuring sharing more than 1000 km long boundary, geographically from the Jigjiga highlands in the Northeast to the Ethiopian-Kenyan borderlands in the Southeast. Historically, Somalis and Oromo have a long tradition of co-existence and strong socio-cultural integrations as well as antagonistic relationships and intermittent conflicts[3,4,5,6]. However, since Early September 2017 ethnic based crisis that had never seen in the history of the country has erupted around the border areas of Oromia and Somali regions displacing nearly 857,000 people[7]. Surprisingly, the conflict has changed its shape and nature over time from local level territorial conflict to intra-federal boundary dispute from a simple confrontation by using traditional weapons to war-like scenarios with modern and more sophisticated weaponry resulting in mass death and displacement[4)] Therefore, this study has made an attempt to investigate the conflict dynamics between the two neighbors' in the context of ethnic federalism.

2. ANALYSIS AND EXPLANATION TO THE CURRENT OROMO- SOMALI CONFLICT DYNAMICS

As well known the introduction of ethnic federalism in Ethiopia has created regions along ethnic line and in effect the two ethnic groups living along the shared boarder have been separated by administrative boundaries. It is unfortunate that neither the 1992 proclamation, nor the 1995 FDRE constitution nor any other law said anything about how the administrative boundaries should be demarcated. Disagreements over exactly where the Oromia-Somali border should lie have resulted in several referenda including the 2004 in which Oromia won about 80% of the disputed areas, but implementation and full demarcation has never occurred which is fueling the ongoing conflict[4,8]. In effect, the conflict that has erupted along the shared boarder of the Oromia and Somali regional state since early September 2017, which is still ongoing, affected all districts along the regional borders causing mass devastation and displacement never seen in the history of inter-communal conflict in the country, displacing nearly 857,000 from both ethnic communities[7]. The current Somali-Oromo conflict must be seen in the context of changing political and administrative dynamics at macro and micro level including the unintended effects of ethnic federalism, the restructuring of administration merely along ethnic lines goes against the realities of the region; unclear administration boundary along the shared boarders; ethnic politicization; mega ethnic syndrome within the society, problem related to leadership and governance system are major forces behind the recurrent conflict between the two neighboring communities. Therefore, this section has identified and analyzed issues of ethnic federalism that have complicated the current conflict dynamics in the region.

I. The Unintended Effects of Ethnic Federalism

The implementation of ethnic federalism in Ethiopia is accused of centering ethnic differences than focusing on similarities and commonly shared values and identities. In effect, it has caused unintended effects leading to inter group friction by promoting differences and hardness inter-ethnic boundaries which actually yielded the construction of the self and the other.

In sharp contrast with past efforts of constructing Ethiopian identity while setting aside ethnic identity, the new political arrangement – ethnic federalism – since 1991 exclusively focused on the construction and promotion of ethnic identity at the cost of Ethiopian identity. Paradoxically, much have been done to make people feel different and unique in their lingo-cultural elements at the cost of what communities commonly share as a society living in the same state. Consequently, people started to build their identity and values in a way that threaten the existence and identity of others. In connection with this, ethnic federalism left hardness inter-ethnic boundaries in which case in the contemporary Ethiopia ethnic boundary is not just an administrative boundary rather it ideologically and practically tied and identified with identity. These circumstances have created ethnic dichotomy, ethnic 'likes' and ethnic 'others' resulting in mass death and displacement on the part of the ethnic 'others'. This is exactly what characterizes the current Ethiopian Somali and Oromo conflict. In this regard, the personal interviews conducted on both groups revealed that Oromo are displaced from the disputed districts because they are living on the Ethiopian Somali territory and *vice versa*. The system confused and blurred the difference between administration boundary and political boarder and in effect administrative boundary is viewed as a political and ethnic differentiator between two largest regions. It indeed has complicated the nature, intensity, scope and consequences of ethnic tension and conflict in the shared border areas where the two ethnic groups reside.

II. The Restructuring of Administration Merely along Ethnic Lines Goes against the Realities of the Region

As indicated on the introductory part, Oromo and Somali share a lot in common. However, state restructuring since 1991 has taken only ethnic dimension. The restructuring of administration only along an ethno national basis was disadvantageous for both the Oromo and Ethiopian Somali communities who have been living along the shared boarder since they have much in common than elements that separate them. Both groups who live along the shared boarder largely identify themselves with a joint Somali-Oromo identity. This means that the new federal arrangements went against the history, social capital, political system, religious affiliation and economic relations and contexts of the two people. Hence, Somali-Oromo brotherliness was disrupted when communities had to settle for affiliation with the Somali or the Oromia region and concomitant, a Somali or Oromo identity. Hence, the demarcation has took only ethnic dimension leaving aside other variables like close linguistic affinity and bilingualism, geographical setting, economic interdependence and business relationships, common vision and destiny, shared socio-cultural practices including intermarriage and customary institutions, they all are helpful in promoting peaceful coexistence and building sustainable society. The personal interviews from both sides indicated that in the past they all (people who live along the shared boarder) have relied on common Muslim–Cushitic identity, but this has disrupted due to the changing political and administrative structure at macro and micro level forcing people to choose either the Somali identity or the Oromo identity[9]. In effect, this has promoted ethnic differences while building ethnic antagonism within the community leading to ethnic tension and conflict in the region.

III. Unclear Administration Boundary along the Shared Borders

As well known the introduction of ethnic federalism in Ethiopia has created regions along ethnic line and in effect the two ethnic groups living along the shared boarder have been separated by administrative boundaries. It is unfortunate that neither the 1992 proclamation nor the 1995 FDRE constitution nor any other law said anything about how the administrative boundaries should be demarcated[6]. The personal interviews conducted with both groups have indicated that there is unclear administration boundary along the shared boarder which contributes to the conflict between the two ethnic communities[10]. Disagreements over exactly where the Oromia-Somali border should lie have resulted in several referenda including the 2004 in which Oromia won about 80% of the disputed areas, but implementation and full demarcation has never occurred, which fundamentally contributed to the ongoing stresses and at the end of the day eruption of violent conflict along the shared boarders of the two regions[3,6,8,9]. Hence, the administrative boundaries between the Oromo and Somali regional states should be demarcated in a way that ensures the freedom of movement of pastoral groups and does not exacerbate resource competition between them.

IV. Ethnic Politicization

The political economy which organized alone the ethnic line has paved the way for elites in the country to take the advantage of exploiting the cultures, values, and practices of ethnic groups and thereby mobilize the same to realize their private dream of controlling political power and economic resources. Ethnic elites in different parts of the country have succeeded in building their private life at the cost of the well-being of their ethnic groups while diverting public resources in favor of their gain. However, at the time when the political elites removed from power due to mismanagement and incompetence then they inform and equip them with false and wrong information as if the group ignored, mistreated and misrepresented in different areas. In this way they mobilize their particular ethnic groups and thereby incite conflict with other ethnic groups who coexisted with them for many years. In connection with this it is common to observed shift of identity among the political elites in the two regions. Political elites in the two regions are opportunist changing their identity on the basis of the opportunities provided by either the Ethiopian Somali or Oromia region. For instance, at a time the Oromia region provides them a political position then they mobilize their ethnic group/ clan to join the Oromia region and *vice versa*[11,12]. The process is not peaceful rather conducted by igniting conflict amongst the different clan in the region. In effect loss of life, human and animal and displacement is common in the region. Thus, from this perspective and what actually observed on the ground it is possible to conclude that what has been called ethnic conflict in the region is elite-driven conflict, rather than people to people confrontations. In this regard, Local political elites have the power to stimulate ethnic difference and thereby worsen ethnic tensions[13,14]. Further, though the 1995 Federal Democratic Republic of Ethiopia (FDRE) Constitution guarantees the equality and rights of'nations, nationalities, and people to self-administration[2], practically observation shows that this principle have been abused by local and regional officials across the country as they are advancing their mere interest in the name of the group whom they claim represent even if it is at the expense of the interests of other groups. This kind of behavior and action has worsened the conflict situation between ethnic groups throughout the country. Hence, it is common to see in many parts of the country that an elite-driven conflict has changing its phase from conflicts between small elites into prevalent conflict among the greater population causing mass death, displacement and looting, worth mentioning in this case is the Oromo-Somali conflict.

V. Mega Ethnic Syndrome within the Society

Ethiopia is now characterized by young generation who grew up and educated in the currently implementing ethnic based political system. In effect, there is widespread mindset problem in relation to the perception, understanding and facts about ethnic identity. Particularly, the young generation made to see the world from their ethnic identity perspectives. For instance, when someone assigned to a government position/political power it is common to hear from the public questions like from which ethnic group/local area is he/she from, instead of questioning the professional and ethical qualities, experiences that the individual has. In the same token, when someone has caught because of his/her alleged crime including corruption it is common to blame the government in that the individual held because he/she belongs to our ethnic group. Further, the system has done much effort and work to make citizen think ethnically while less effort has been exerted to promote their Ethiopian identity. This has created a favorable ground for the ethnic elites to mobilize the young generation instrumentally to use them for their power dream and capital accumulation. This is now become a normal way of doing things in Ethiopia almost in every corner of the nation. The personal interviews conducted on both groups have revealed that when one ethnic Somali gets in personal conflict due to different reason with his/her counter Oromo background then the conflict is portrayed as if it happened between the two Ethnic groups on the basis of ethnic antagonism[10]. However, the truth of the matter is that they simply appeared as ethnic conflicts just because they happened to bear the names of participant ethnic groups. In effect, the personal conflict takes ethnic form causing much devastation on both sides.

VI. Leadership Problem and Lack of Good Governance at Different Level

As a country, Ethiopia is characterized by the lack of good governance as manifested in the form of absence of rule of law, accountability and transparency in the system. Different documents including the government reports have indicated that bad governance and mass unemployment are the two main forces challenging the country's positive economic growth and accelerating poverty reduction. The situation is more complex and challenging as one move to the lower level of administration.

The federal government has failed to protect the constitutional rights of citizens; the right of people's movement across the nation. Eviction and displacement of the so called "non-indigenous citizens" by local and regional government officials and even sometimes in conspiration with top federal officials is common in Ethiopia. A case to mention is the Oromo eviction from the Ethiopian Somali regional state and *vice versa* before the eruption of the all-out conflict between the two ethnic groups. And surprisingly no one has held responsible. Particularly, the Ethiopian Somali regional government led by Abdi Mohammed Omar was reluctant to take order from the federal government and calm down the issue since he and his groups receives all rounded support from top EPRDF old guards and military generals in return for his commitment in promoting and protecting their private interest, illicit trading and contraband which is common in the region. This indeed stimulated ethnic tension and thus conflicts to be erupted between the two ethnic groups.

Unclear boundary formation is considered as the fundamental cause for the recent conflict between the two groups. To settle the disputed district along the shared boarder, in 2004 the federal government through its institution - the House of Federation - has carried out the referendum[11]. The House of the Federation, which is composed of representatives of nations, nationalities and peoples, has the powers and functions including interpreting the Constitution, striving to find solutions to disputes or misunderstandings that may arise between States and ordering federal intervention if any State, in violation of this Constitution, endangers the constitutional order among others Article 62[2]. It is consistent with this provision that the House of Federation had carried out political referendum in 463 kebele along the contested borders of the Oromia and the Somali regions[11]. However, the house has failed to enforce the result of the referendum. This failure whatever the reason behind has resulted in the eruption of violent conflict that has never been seen between the two ethnic groups. Hence, weak institutional enforcement as well as lack of political commitment at the federal government level can be mentioned worthwhile behind the recent conflict between the two groups. Further, as revealed in the personal interviews conducted with both groups there is a lack of timely intervention and resolution by the federal government[10].

On the part of the respective regional governments, officials from both regions instead of working incoordination on the ground in minimizing the hatred and mistrust between the two communities they are fueling the conflict by emotional and irrational claim and counterclaims. Indeed, the two regions have signed a peace pact in April 2017 with the view to calm down the situation and bringing peace along the shared boarder. During the agreement, the two leaders' (Lema Megersa of Oromia and Abdi Mohammed of Somali) displayed a historic gesture of unity where the two regions appeared to have resolved their issues and were said to have reached an agreement to complete the border demarcation process pursuant of the 2004/5 referendum. However, they failed to respect the terms of the pact. Instead of finding common solution to their common problem, they have traded blame about the main cause of the recent clashes. Consequently, the two regions immersed into another round of conflict and severe political confrontation unprecedented in contemporary Ethiopian history. Therefore, if there is good will, political commitment and leadership skills on both sides it could be possible to manage the conflicts before it turns out into wild violence to the end normalize relationship amongst the group.

Weak control and regulation of the federal government over region's use and mobilization of funds in the peripheral regions including the Ethiopian Somali state has created a breeding ground for corruption and misuse of fund for unintended purpose in the name of peace and security. Further, poor control of the movements of light and heavy arms and weapons along the Ethiopia's border with neighboring such as Kenya and Somalia as well as weak internal control along the shared border between the two regions has created easy access to military equipment[15]. In this regard, it is true that conflicts in the past in the areas were less devastating as they mainly involved the use of traditional weapons such as bows, arrows and spears. However, the widespread availability of small arms and light weapons has significantly increased devastations in the region. That is why the recent conflict virtually looks like warfare when we look at the number of causalities from both sides.

3. CONCLUSIONS

The Oromo and Ethiopian Somali Community, due to their century's interactions, have developed great common traditions and shared socio-cultural values. In the same token, the two ethnic groups have experienced antagonistic relationships and intermittent conflicts throughout their history of existence, though the nature, behaviors and trends of conflict varied from time to time taking a new forms and dynamics with huge repercussion. Traditionally, the main sources of conflict amongst clans in the region are identified as competition over scarce resources, territorial expansion, livestock raids and counter raids, kidnap for marriage purpose and the revenge tradition. However, after the newly introduce political and structural changes in the country (Ethnic Federalism), the existed conflicts over natural resources has been transformed into inter-regional boundary dispute and conflict involving multiple driving factors and forces. This has increased the complexity and intractability of the conflict between the Oromo and the Somali communities. Therefore, for the current Oromo-Somali Conflict in Ethiopia can be attributed to factors associated with ethnic federalism including unintended effects of ethnic federalism, the restructuring of administration merely along ethnic lines goes against the realities of the region; unclear administration boundary along the shared boarders; ethnic politicization; mega ethnic syndrome within the society and leadership problem and lack of good governance.

4. RECOMMENDATIONS

Since the conflict in the region is much more complex than the dominant narrative of resource scarcity, open democratic dialogue, genuine consultation and negotiation at different level with various interest groups, stakeholders the community representative, militant groups operating in the areas is paramount importance to ease the increasing ethnic tension and political crisis to the end building sustainable peace in the region.

The government must practically commit itself to constitutionalism and democratic federalism; implement the constitution and its federal system within the framework of reconciling national identity with ethnic identity, adjust the federal system given the socio-cultural and linguistic realities of communities, and above all hold political referendum on the constitution and its federal system so as to win national consensus.

Federalism alone cannot bring peace and stability if not implemented along with democracy and good governance. In this regard, both qualities lack in the Ethiopian federalism and in effect, government must work hard not only in ensuring democracy and good governance across the nation but also must take the lion share in democratizing society's culture. Hence, this paper urges the need to establish legitimate, capable, accountable and democratic authorities and leadership at all level so as to build social harmony and community spirit paving the way for peace and stable nation building.

5. REFERENCES

[1] Tewfik, H. (2010). "*Transition to Federalism: The Ethiopian Experience*". *In*: Forum of Federations, Ottawa, Canada. *http://www.forumfed.org/pubs/occasional*

[2] FDRE (1995). The Proclamation of FDRE Constitution. Addis Ababa: Berhanena Selam Printing Press.

[3] Mesfin Getachew (2006). 'Ethnicity and Ethnic-Conflict in Post-Federal Ethiopia: A case of Ma'eso District Conflict between Oromos and Somalis'. EPU Research Papers Issue.

[4] Mohammud Abdulahi (2005). The changing nature of pastoral conûicts in south-eastern Ethiopia: The case of the Boran and Digodi pastoralists;

Africa peace forum, Pastoralist Concern Association Ethiopia, InterAfrica Group, Saferworld, pp. 7–17.

[5] Ali, K. (2005). 'Conflict and conflict resolution in Somali regional state' Final consultancy report for GTZ, Capacity Building in Governance Conflict Prevention 1 Transformation CPT, under Ministry of Federal Affairs (MFA), Addis-Ababa, Ethiopia, p. 39.

[6] Shide, A. (2004). 'Conflicts along Oromia-Somali States Boundaries: The case study of Babile districts'. *First National Conference on Federalism, Conflict, and Peace Building, Organized by the Ethio-German Co-operation (GTZ) of The Federal Governance Development Project in collaboration with the Ministry of Federal Affairs. Addis-Ababa, Ethiopia.*

[7] OCHA and the National Disaster Risk Management Commission (NDR MC). Ethiopia: Conflict Displacement Situation Report, 23 January 2018.

[8] Faisal Roble (2017). Roots to the Somali Massacre: Challenging False Narrative; WardheerNews.

[9] Muhyadin Odowa Liban (2006). Local conflicts between Somali and Oromo people in the context of political decentralization in Ethiopia. Comparative case study on Ma'eso and Babile Districts. MA thesis unpublished. Institute of Social Studies Kortenaerkade 12 2518 AX The Hague, The Netherlands.

[10] Personal Interview: Displaced ethnic Oromo and Somali, Dire Dawa, 19 July -18 August 2018.

[11] Asnake Kefale (2013). Federalism and Ethnic Conflict in Ethiopia. Comp arative Regional Study. Routledge series in federal studies. Inter-regional conûicts: Accessed 21 September 2018 at *https: / / www.taylorfra ncis.com / books / 9781135017989 / chapters / 10.4324%2F 9780203759530–14.*

[12] Tobias Hagmann and Didier Peclard (2011). *Negotiating Statehood Dynamics of Power and Domination in Africa.* Federal restructuring in Ethiopia: Renegotiating Identity and Boards along the Oromo-Somali Ethnic Frontier. *Development and Change*, 41(4). The Institute of Social Studies. Blackwell Publishing Ltd.

[13] Salih, M. (2006). "Ethnic conflicts, the nation-state and beyond" course 4217, Handout: Lecture 5. The Hague, The Netherlands.

[14] Assefa, A. (1996). 'Ethnic conflict in the Horn of Aji-ica: Myth and reality'. *In*: Kumar Rupesinghe and Tishkov Valery, A. (*eds.*), *'Ethnicity and Power in the Contemporary World'.* United Nations University Press. Accessed at:*http: / / www.unu.edu / unupress / unupbooks / uuI2ee / uuI2e eOO.htm#Contents*

[15] Getachew, K. (2002). 'An overview of root causes of problems that currently affect Bor'ana pastoralists of southern Ethiopia'. *In:* Babiker Mustafa (*ed.*) *'Resource Alienation, Militarization and Development: Case studies from East African Drylands'. Proceedings of the Regional Workshops on East African Drylands: Khartoum and Addis-Ababa,* pp. 67–76.

12

Third Force in Malaysian Political Landscape

ZAWIYAH MOHD ZAIN[1]* AND MOHAMMAD AGUS YUSOFF[2]

ABSTRACT

This paper aims to discuss the emergence of third force in Malaysia. The analysis in this paper is qualitative and derived from primary and secondary data. The primary data is generated through in-depth interviews with individuals who are experienced and knowledgeable about the subjects under study. The secondary data is obtained from previous studies. Analysis shows that: First, third force became popular in 2008 general election. They were the parties that did not support either the Government or the opposition. Second, the role of third force in Malaysia is to highlight current political issues in order to influence the voters. Finally, even though they try to highlight the issues, their voices are not good enough. This is because the two-party system has not been established yet. However, on 14th General Election held on May 2018, for the first time the coalition of the opposition which is Pakatan Harapan won and formed a new government and ultimately open space to the two-party system in Malaysia.

[1] School of Government, College of Law, Government and International Studies, Universiti Utara Malaysia, Sintok, 06010 Kedah, Malaysia.

[2] School of History, Politics and Strategy, Faculty of Social Sciences and Humanities, Universiti Kebangsaan Malaysia, Bangi, 43600 Selangor, Malaysia.

**Corresponding author:* E-mail: zawie98@yahoo.com

Key words: Third force, Election, Two-party system, Civil disobedience, Democratization.

INTRODUCTION

Malaysia is a democratic country that has a stable political system since independence. Since the first election in 1959 until the 13th General Election in 2013, Barisan Nasional (National Front) has governed the country. Malaysian politics, despite being stable, sometimes found itself in a rather tensed situation. Political tensions allow certain parties such as opposition political parties, third force and Non-Governmental Organization (NGOs) to unite to oppose the government party which is Barisan Nasional. The first attempt in establishing formal cooperation between the opposition was in 1990, while the second was in 1999. Starting from 2008 until 2015, the opposition has cooperated under the Pakatan Rakyat (People Coalition). From September 2015 until now the opposition have a new coalition which is Pakatan Harapan (Alliance of Hope). The effort made by the parties is a method for creating a two-party system in the country to challenge the dominant coalition Barisan Nasional (BN).On 14th General Election on May 9, 2018 for the first time opposition which is Pakatan Harapan won the election and form the new government. There are several studies related to third force, however, the study of the third force in Malaysia is not so prominent.The objective of the study is first; identify the actors that form a third force. Second, analyze the role of the third force in Malaysian politics and its impact on the democratization process.

METHODOLOGY

This article used qualitative method. The primary data is generated through in-depth interviews with individuals who are experienced and knowledgeable about the subjects under study. They are representative of the government political party, the Barisan Nasional (before May 9 2018), opposition party (before May

9 2018), and NGOs. The Barisan Nasional Coalition includes United Malays National Organization (UMNO), Malaysian Chinese Association (MCA) and Malayan Indian Congress (MIC). The oppositon party includes People's Justice Party (PKR), Malaysia Islamic Party (PAS) and Democratic Action Party (DAP). NGOs that are involved in this study include PERKASA and ABIM. The secondary data is obtained from books, journals and previous studies. Data from interview was analyzed using the specific theme set by researcher.

LITERATURE REVIEW

Third Force

Third force is a grouping (as of political parties or international powers) intermediate between two opposing political forces (Merriam Webster Dictionary, 2014). Refer to the Webster's New World College Dictionary (2010), third force is a third element, group, bloc, etc., functioning as a counter-balancing, neutralizing, or moderating force or influence in a struggle between two established powers.

In developed countries like the United States (US) and United Kingdom (UK), the third force has been long established and refers to smaller parties that are formed because of the weakness of the two-party system that exists in these countries. Small parties or also referred to as third parties are also contesting elections against the power of the first and second power. Due to the weakness of the first and second powers, the smaller parties which are regarded as the third force, has attracted the support of the people. For example in the UK, during the parliamentary elections in May 2010 the first and second power which contesting was the Labour Party which is the government party and also the conservative party. While other smaller parties considered as third parties contested in the elections, such as the Liberal Democratic Party, Plaid Cymru and the United Kingdom Independent Party (Ritchie, 2010:1).

The results of the election shows that the Labour Party, the government party which previously only obtained 258 seats with only 29 percent of the popular vote and the Conservatives won 305 seats with 36.1 percent of the popular vote from the 650 seats contested. This decision requires the Conservative Party to join the third force composed of other smaller parties to form a government. As a result the Liberal Democratic Party, which won 57 seats with the support of 23 percent has emerged as the third force which joined the Conservative Party to form the government (Amory, 2010:1; Thurston, 2010:1). It shows in developed countries, third force has a big fan base so it can stand as a political party that can match the first and second powers.In this case also, the third force has managed to form a government when they joined the Conservative Party.

In Burma, the term third force appeared only in November 2010 when the government was holding general elections. These elections were the first elections in two decades since the victory of Aung San Suu Kyi in 1990. This followed the new constitution approved in a referendum in 2008 in which the people chose to hold elections to form government in Burma. In the general elections, the first power, the government party, Solidarity and Development Party and the second power, the opposition National League for Democracy were the influential parties that compete between them. While the third force refers to small newly formed parties that do not have strong support. However, they still took part in the elections, to challenge the first and second forces. The party consisted of a group of veteran politicians, former student activists and former communist who had established political party to contest in the 2010 elections. The election results show the government party, Solidarity and Development Party won more than 70 percent of the vote (BBC News February 4, 2011). This shows that the third force in Burma is not a power that can undermine the power of the first and second forces in the country's political system as in developed countries. This is because the first force, the government party, has a strong influence and support in these countries which make it difficult to be challenged.

In conclusion, the third force in a political system exist in a country where there are particular groups who oppose or disagree with the first or second force. However, the influence of the third force depends on the strength of the first force, which is the government party.

Civil Disobedience

Civil disobedience is a form of people dissent against the government or its officers, as there are certain points that they are not satisfied with. According to Rawls (1971:363), civil disobedience is a public, non-violent, conscientious yet political act contrary to law, which is usually done with the aim of bringing about a change in the law or policies of a government. In his arguments Rawls state that first, civil disobedience is a political act not only in the sense that it is addressed to the majority that hold political power, but also because it is an act guided and justified by a political principle which is principle of justice. Second, civil disobedience is a public act, not only it is addressed to principles, it is done in public and not covert or secretive. Third, civil disobedience is non-violent.

Quigley and Bahmueller (1991:629) define civil disobedience as a deliberate, public, conscientious, and non-violent act that breaks a law in which the person accepts responsibility and punishment. It is an act of non-violent protest undertaken to alleviate some injustice, usually with an appeal to some higher principle or law. Based on this definition, the act considered as civil disobedience is first that the citizen must disobey a law, most often the law that is being broken is considered unjust. Second, the citizen would have to deliberately and publicly disobey the law. The citizen must be acting to serve the common good, not the personal interest. Third, the citizen must act conscientiously, in that he or she has an honest belief that his or her actions are intended to correct a grave injustice. Finally, the act must be non-violent and the citizen must be willing to accept the consequences of his or her action. Quigley and Bahmueller also stress that there are two types of civil disobedience, which are individual or moral disobedience and organized or social civil disobedience.

Democratization

Huntington (1991:15) asserted that democratization is a group of transitions from non-democratic to democratic regimes that occur within a specified period of time. Democratization is a new phenomenon that started in the 19th century, emerging from a wave of democratization. Indeed, there were three waves of democratization in the modern world. Each of the first two waves of democratization was followed by a reserved wave. These waves of democratization and the reverse wave occurred as follows: the first wave of democratization (1828–1926), the first reverse wave (1922–1942), the second wave of democratization (1943–1962), the second reverse wave (1958–1975), and the third wave of democratization (1974–1989). Huntington states that the process of democratization is due to five major factors namely, declining autocratic government, global economic development, changes in church activities, new policy on human rights and snowballing effects.

According to Doorenspleet (2006:42), democratization is defined as a group of transition from authoritarian regimes to democracies that occur within a specified period of time and that significantly outnumber transitions in the opposite direction. Doorenspleet added that economic factors have an influence on the democratization process. His study shows that the impact of economic development on democratization was drastic, especially during the third wave of democratization (1976–1989).

In sum, the definition of democratization by scholars show that they agree that democratization is a process of transition from a non-democratic regime to a democratic regime that occurred within a specific period of time. According to them, democratization occurs due to certain factors. For example, for Huntington (1991), there are five main factors leading to democratization. These are declining autocratic government, global economic development, changes in church activities, new policy on human rights and snowballing effects. Doorenspleet (2006) however, said that the one major factor that helps accelerate the democratization process is economic development.

FINDINGS AND DISCUSSION

Background of Third Force in Malaysian Politics

In Malaysia, the third force only began to be discussed seriously at 12th General Election in 2008. In the 2008 general elections, the main opposition party contesting, PAS, PKR and DAP had collaborated in putting up a candidate against the Barisan Nasional. However, at that time there was not a formal pact between them. The success of the opposition to deny the Barisan Nasional the two-thirds majority in parliamentary led to the opposition to form a formal collaboration and declared the five states they ruled - Kelantan, Kedah, Penang, Selangor and Perak as the Pakatan Rakyat (People's Coalition) states. The formation of the Pakatan Rakyat or People's Coalition has opened up an opportunity for the existence of the two-party system in Malaysia. After that, every time during the general elections, the opposition will present themselves as the coalition which is Pakatan Rakyat against Barisan Nasional. This is because the opposition pact which eventually established Pakatan Rakyat has provided an alternative for voters to choose between Barisan Nasional and Pakatan Rakyat. Following this development, the Barisan Nasional and Pakatan Rakyat have been always competing to win the support of the people and most notably seen in By Election in the aftermath of 2008 general elections. It is in the midst of this competition between the government and the opposition parties that emerged a third force which did not agree with both the first and the second force and warms the atmosphere of politics in Malaysia.

The question is which actor formed the third force? First, those who disagree with the policies and administration of Pakatan Rakyat. For example, the elite from PKR who decided to leave

Pakatan Rakyat and declared themselves as independent members of Parliament. Among them are the members of parliament Bayan Baru, Zaharin Mohd Hashim, Nibong Tebal, Tan Tee Beng, Kulim Bandar Baharu, Zulkifli Nordin, Wangsa Maju and Wee Chee Keong. Apart from that, there were also PKR elites who have left the party because they did not agree with the struggle of PKR and in the event formed a new part led by Zaid Ibrahim. Zaid Ibrahim announced his resignation and left PKR in October 2010 and formed a new party called the Kesejahteraan Insan Tanah Air (KITA) in December 2010 (Malaysiakini, 15 Disember 2011).

In addition to that, they were also part of the activists who supported the Pakatan Rakyat during general election of 2008 including Raja Petra Kamaruddin and Haris Ibrahim who had formed the Malaysian Civil Liberties Movement (MCLM). This is also due to the fact that they were not happy with several PKR policies such as the lack of opportunity to lead the party which is controlled by Anwar's family, not happy with the election of the top leadership which is seen to involve nepotism and also the weakness of PKR in the administration of states, especially Selangor (Shaharul Shafie, 2010; Loh, 2011). MCLM did not have the intention to contest in the general elections, however, they planned to elect their own candidate who they think as having integrity to contest on People's Coalition ticket. It is when their candidate is not accepted, only then they will contest for the general elections.

Secondly, the actors who formed this third force were individuals who previously supported the Barisan National or government party, but there were several issues which they did not agree with and made them formed NGO to struggle for their cause. For instance, PERKASA, AMANAH and Majlis Perundingan Melayu (Malay Consultative Council). PERKASA was founded by Ibrahim Ali, the member of Parliament of Pasir Mas who won on PAS ticket and later declared himself as independent Parliamentarian but support BN. The Malay Consultative Council was a coalition of 72 Malay NGOs which was formed in March 2011 to defend the position and sovereignty of Malay Sultanate.

AMANAH is an NGO which was formed by Tengku Razaleigh Hamzah in July 2011 with the aim of fighting corruption, cronyism and communalism in Barisan Nasional. Apart from that, there were also others who formed political parties for struggle, such as Human Rights Party (HRP) which appeared following the dissatisfaction towards MIC which was accused of failing to represent the Indian community by defending their plight in BN.

The third is the university students. This is because they were the group which did not belong to any party and did not favour any side, but they look more on the arising issues. However, their movement and voice was limited due to Universities and University Colleges Act 1971 (UUCA). The activities of university students after the implementation of UUCA became somehow rigid until they appeared again in the political arena in 1998.Yet, the stern action by the government towards those who involve with politics, such as suspension from university and stern warning made the university students to isolate themselves from politics. However, starting from 2009, university students presented themselves with political parties because of three main reasons.

Firsly, there was announcement from government (after being desperate) to amend UUCA. Secondly, universities were becoming free from the clutches of the goverment. This is because of many new universities being established as a result of Barisan Nasional own policies. When many universities were established, there was less competition to obtain admission into the universities as it was in the era of the 1980s and 1990s and dismissing students for taking part in political activities was less, rather universities were desperate in getting students. Therefore, the university is not in a condition to suppress the students again rather they are depressed. This means that the system has indirectly liberalized the university. Third, Barisan Nasional and UMNO are tired and not able anymore to sponsor candidates as before, and this makes the students to obtain a pretty good field to compete in campus politics. As a result, during the 2011 campus election, those who have always been considered as pro-opposition obtained victory in several universities such as the University of Malaya (UM) and Universiti Putra Malaysia (UPM).

In addition, the emergence of new media has also led campus atmosphere to become so rife with freedom. Students have dared to speak as a coalition which fight for various issues relating to democracy. For example, in October 2011 when the International Islamic University Malaysia (IIUM) Professor Abdul Aziz Bari was suspended from his duties for seditious comment on the Royal Institution, students and other young people rose up and demanded justice. They held a demonstration after Friday prayers in IIUM and it also involved alumni who insist that the suspension is withdrawn. In addition, students also made various comments in the alternative media which did not agree with IIUM's action and defended Abdul Aziz Bari by opening a Facebook account, "We together support Prof Aziz Bari" which received the support of over 1000 people in about two weeks.

Referring to the above explanation, this third force is not new in Malaysia after the 2008 elections, but it has existed for long. However, before the elections in 2008 the group did not have any effect and was not considered as a third force because there was not a two-party system in Malaysia. However, every time there is an election, this group either consisting of NGOs, fragmented political parties and student groups also play a role in the election campaign either directly or indirectly. At the 13th election third force has been giving support to the opposition, namely Pakatan Rakyat. This is because when the Pakatan Rakyat denied two-thirds victory of BN in Parliament at 12th General Election it has given new hope to the third force. The hope is that Malaysians had the awareness to evaluate issues that occurred regarding the administration of the country. They should be given support and convinced that it is time to establish democratic processes and political maturity in Malaysia. One of the NGOs which are considered as the third force is the BERSIH. BERSIH held a rally to attract community support, so that they realize that there are many restrictions made by the government such as restrictions on press freedom, injustice in the election campaign and so on.The question is, to what extent did this third force affecting the general elction result as well as the democratization in Malaysia?

The Impact of Third Force Toward Malaysian General Election

12th General election

With a variety of issues that arose by third force in the administration of Abdullah Badawi in the period 2006 to 2007, it was expected that BN would face a tough general election. As a result, in 12th General Election BN failed to win two-thirds majority of parliamentary seats. BN also lost Kedah, Penang, Perak and Selangor and failed to recapture Kelantan. In the Federal Territory of Kuala Lumpur BN lost 10 of the 11 parliamentary seats. Such scenario led political analysts to say that Malaysia has been hit by a political tsunami. BN won 140 seats out of the total 222 parliamentary seats contested, while the opposition gained 82 seats which consists of the People's Justice Party (PKR) (31), DAP (28) and PAS (23) (Table 1).

Table 1: Parliamentary seats won by political party in the 2008 general election.

State	*BN*	*DAP*	*PAS*	*PKR*
Perlis	3	–	–	–
Kedah	4	–	6	5
Pulau Pinang	2	7	–	4
Perak	13	6	2	3
Kelantan	2	–	9	3
Terengganu	7	–	1	–
Pahang	12	–	–	2
Selangor	5	4	4	9
Negeri Sembilan	5	2	–	1
Melaka	5	1	–	–
Johor	25	1	–	–
Sabah	24	1	–	–

Table 1: (*Contd...*)

Table 1: (*Contd...*)

State	*BN*	*DAP*	*PAS*	*PKR*
Sarawak	30	1	–	–
Federal Territories (K.L, Labuan dan Putrajaya)	3	5	1	4
Jumlah	140	28	23	31

Source: The Election Commission (2008).

The weaknesses of the leadership of Abdullah Badawi had contributed to the failure of the BN to defend two-thirds majority seats of parliament since 1974. This is because Abdullah Badawi failed to deliver on campaign PRU 2004, failed to solve economic problems, problems of racism and the occurrence of family intervention in its administration. All the matter has raised people's discontent and lead to the occurrence of the protests. The protest is the way through demonstrations and the use of the internet. Between the protests that occurred at that time was Bersih and Hindraf rally in November 2007.

13th General election

On the other hand at 13th General Election under Najib Razak, BN results worse than 12th General Election. This is because the BN failed to get a majority of two-thirds of the parliamentary seats. BN only won 133 seats out of 222 parliamentary seats, while the people's coalition got 89 seats (38 DAP, PKR and PAS 21) (See Table 2).

Table 2: Parliamentary seats and State assembly seat won by political party in the 2008 general election.

	Parliament seat				*State assembly seat*				
Negeri	*BN*	*PAS*	*DAP*	*PKR*	*BN*	*PAS*	*DAP*	*PKR*	*BEBAS*
Perlis	3	–	–	–	13	1	–	1	
Kedah	10	1	–	4	21	9	2	4	
Pulau Pinang	3	–	7	3	10	1	19	10	

Table 2: (*Contd...*)

Table 2: (*Contd...*)

	Parliament seat				***State assembly seat***				
Negeri	***BN***	***PAS***	***DAP***	***PKR***	***BN***	***PAS***	***DAP***	***PKR***	***BEBAS***
Perak	12	2	7	3	31	5	18	5	
Selangor	5	4	4	9	12	15	15	14	
Kelantan	5	9	–		11	32	–	1	
Terengganu	4	4	–	–	17	14	–	1	
Pahang	10	1	1	2	30	3	7	2	
Negeri Sembilan	5	–	2	1	22	–	11	3	
Melaka	4	–	1	1	21	1	6	–	
Johor	21	–	4	1	38	4	13	1	
Sabah	22	–	2	1	48	–	4	–	1
Sarawak	25	–	5	1	–	–	–	–	
Wilayah Persekutuan Putrajaya	1	–	–	–	–	–	–	–	
Wilayah Persekutuan Kuala Lumpur	2	–	5	4	–	–	–	–	
Wilayah Persekutuan Labuan	1	–	–	–	–	–	–	–	
Jumlah	133	21	38	30	275	85	95	49	1

Source: The Election Commission (2013).

14th General election

Malaysian 14th General Election was held on 9 May 2018. At the election, there is intense competition between government parties which is the Barisan Nasional and also the coalition of opposition parties which is Pakatan Harapan.The coalition of Pakatan Harapan includes PKR, DAP, PAN, BERSATU and support by WARISAN political party. Baraisan Nasional who has won 13 times general election forced struggling with various issues in the year 2015. Among the issues are the abuse of power, corruption, the issue of corruption in 1Malaysian Development Berhad and the implementation of good and services tax. These issues have been raised by various parties including third party. The results of the election shows that Pakatan Harapan managed to get a simple majority of parliamentary seats, and formed the new Government (See Table 3). The success of the Pakatan Harapan in the election have brought Malaysia to the new era of giving priority to

Table 3: Parliamentary seats won by political party in the 2018 general election.

NEGIRI	*PKR*	*BN*	*PAS*	*DAP*	*Warsian*	*Bebas*	*Solidariti*	*Jumlah*
Perlis	1	2	0	0	0	0	0	3
Kedah	10	2	3	0	0	0	0	15
Kelantan	0	5	9	0	0	0	0	14
Terengganu	0	2	6	0	0	0	0	8
Pulau Pinag	11	2	0	0	0	0	0	13
Perak	13	11	0	0	0	0	0	24
Pahang	5	9	0	0	0	0	0	14
Selangor	20	2	0	0	0	0	0	22
W.P. Kuala Lumpur	10	0	0	0	0	1	0	11
W.P. Putrajaya	0	1	0	0	0	0	0	1
Negeri Sembilan	5	3	0	0	0	0	0	8
Melaka	4	2	0	0	0	0	0	6
Johor	18	8	0	0	0	0	0	26
W.P. Labuan	0	1	0	0	0	0	0	1
Sabah	3	10	0	3	8	0	1	25
Sarawak	4	19	0	6	0	2	0	31
Jumlah	104	79	18	9	8	3	1	222

Source: The Election Commission (2018).

transparency, justice, against corruption, against the abuse of power, has the freedom of the media and restructure administrative institutions.

The Role of Third Force and Its Impact to The Process of Democratization

Referring to the discussion above, third force is a form of civil disobedience that appears in Malaysia either as individual or organized civil disobedience. The third force is said to be one form of civil disobedience because these are the people who started looking for political influence in Malaysia after the 2008 general elections and were involved in efforts to engage in protest against the government. Among those who often get media attention is PERKASA which often appear to express their grievances against the government. For example, in relation to the objection of gambling license in 2010, the government's proposal to make Malaysia as a hub for nightlife and also protest against the government suspension of a school principal in Johor who was alleged to have made racist remarks in 2010. As for students, they also often come forward involving in civil disobedience during Najib Razak's era, including objections to the UCCA, Internal Security Act, Education Financing Scheme and Good and Services Tax (Malaysiakini, August 22 2012; December 22 2012).

While third force is one form of civil disobedience, but its effectiveness in bringing about the process of democratization is still at a minimum. This is because they still do not have a lot of supporters at the grassroots level, whether to mobilize civil disobedience or get the government's attention in a particular issue. In addition, they are also bound by the restrictions through a variety of acts that restrict political rights and the rights of citizens to freedom of assembly and expression, such as Internal Security Act - replaced with the Peaceful Assembly Act 2011 and the Security Offences (Special Measures) Act 2012. However, with the success of opposition parties which is Pakatan Harapan at 14th General Electionon May 2018 it has opened a new sheet to the third force to be more outspoken and contribute to democratic processes. This is because the new governmnet has promised to create a new Malaysia which is at Justice, transparency, and independent media.

CONCLUSIONS

This article discusses the new power in politics, the third force. The first and second powers refer to the political parties which has long been strong and being contesting in general elections. While the third force is smaller parties or NGOs that emerged following their dissatisfaction with the first and second powers. In Malaysia, although the third force has long existed, they only began to receive attention in 2008.This is because the general election held has produced many shocking results. In the general election, the ruling coalition failed to win two-thirds majority in the parliament. Consequently, the opposition parties united to form the Pakatan Rakyat an alternative to Barisan Nasional, and they managed to rule some states in Malaysia. At the latest election on May 2018 the opposition which is Pakatan Harapan won the election and form the new government. The third force that emerged in Malaysia is made up of; first, those who originally supported the government party, but ultimately there are things that made them formed a group, or a new party because they are not satisfied with the government. Second, those who initially supported the opposition parties, but set up a new group because they are no longer with the opposition. Third, NGOs and groups of students who have different ideas with the first and second party. Referring to the role of the third force, they consist of a mechanism to bring about the democratization process in Malaysia especially after 14th General Election.

REFERENCES

Amory, E.H. (2010). Resounding rejection of labour: Voters don't want another four years of Gordon Brown or his party. 7 Mei. *http://www.dailymail.co.uk/debate/election/article-1274259/UK-ELECTION-RESULTS-2010-Gordon-Brown-Labour-resoundingly-rejected.html [3Oktober 2011]*

BBC News Online (2011). Burma ex-Prime Minister Thein Sein named New President. BBC News 4 February. *http://www.bbc.co.uk/news/world-asia-pacific-12362745 [30Oktober 2011]*

Bedau, H.A. (1991a). Civil disobedience and personal responsibility for injustice. *In:* Bedau, H.A. (*ed.*), *Civil Disobedience in Focus,* London: Routledge, pp. 49–67.

Bedau, H.A. (1991b). Introduction. Dlm. H.A. Bedau (pnyt.). *Civil Disobedience in Focus,* London: Routledge, pp. 1–13.

Doorenspleet, R. (2006). *Democratic Transitions: Exploring the Structural Sources of the Fourth Wave.* New Delhi: Viva Books.

Huntington, S.P. (1991). Democracy's third wave. *Journal of Democracy,* 2(2): 13–34.

Loh Richard (2011). Rakyat the 'third force' or 'the main force'. *http://blog.limkitsiang.com/2011/07/29/rakyat-the-third-force-0r-the-main-force/[31 Oktober 2011]*

Malaysiakini (2011). *http://www.malaysiakini.com ,15 Disember [5 January 2012]*

Malaysiakini (2012). *http://www.malaysiakini, com22 Ogos [12 October 2013]*

Merriam-Webster Online: Dictionary and Thesaurus (2014). *www.merriam-webster.com*

Quigley, C.N. and Bahmueller, C.F. (2001). *Civitas: A Framework for Civic Education*, Center for Civic Education: Calabasas, CA.

Rawls, J. (1971). A *Theory of Justice*. Massachusetts: Belknap Press.

Ritchie, A. (2010). *New UK Government Holds First Cabinet Meeting. The Sydney Morning Herald 13 Mei.http://news.smh.com.au/breaking-news-world/new-uk-govt-holds-first-cabinet-meeting-20100513-v0k1.html [3 Oktober 2011]*

Shaharul Shafie (2010). Mampukah kuasa ketiga ubah politik negara? (Can third force change the Malaysian Political Landscape). *http://wrl.blogspot.com/2010/12/mampukah-kuasa-ketiga-ubah-politik.html [1 November 2011]*

Sheldon, G.W. (2005). *The Encyclopedia of Political Thought*. New Delhi: Viva Books.

The Election Commission Malaysia (2008). 12thGeneral Elction Report. Kuala Lumpur: Percetakan Nasional Malaysia.

The Election Commission Malaysia (2013). *https://www.spr.gov.my/[30 April 2013]*

The Election Commission Malaysia (2018).*https://www.spr.gov.my/ [1 Jun 2018]*

Thurston, M. (2010). Britain's conservatives in power pact talks after poll deadlock. *http://news.smh.com.au/breaking-news-world/britains-conservatives-in-power-pact-talksafter-poll-deadlock-20100508-ujzo.html [3 Oktober 2011]*

Webster's New World College Dictionary (2010). *websters. yourdictionary.com [17 November 2014]*

Whiteley, P., Seyd, P. and Billinghurst, A. (2005). *Third Force Politics: Liberal Democrats at the Grassroots*. New York: Oxford University Press.

13

Future Overall Social Progress: Will There Be An Era of Sustainable Transformation?

ARKADY MARTYNOV[1,2*]

ABSTRACT

The paper is devoted to fundamental issues concerning the ideology of the future sustainable development. Its implementation has available in the first place proceeding from the recognized framework concept of Sustainable Development (SD). At the same time, this concept requires serious improvement. As follows from the argumentation, a realistic design of institutional changes in connection with resource and organizational / behavioral changes needed for SD is called for to realize in the line of overall social system transformation. Its adequate understanding presupposes an exhaustive study of interconnected transformations in the main social fields as system processes taking into account the influence of relatively exogenous factors (technological, demographic and climate changes). According to the author, the transition to global sustainable social transformation is achievable. Main attention focuses on a number of possible fundamental shifts, the synergetic implementation of which will make such a transition possible. As follows from the arguments, the sustainable reproduction of the economy of a mature post-industrial type, including the green

[1] International Institute for Social Development, Moscow, Russia.
[2] Institute of Economics, Russian Academy of Sciences, Moscow, Russia.
**Corresponding author:* E-mail: socpolamv@mail.ru

sectors, implies its stable and quiet growth, although the rapid growth of individual markets, especially innovative ones, may take place. The main findings also include the substantiation in favor of the choice of the national middle way model as the most appropriate for the corresponding sustainable system transformation of society.

Key words: Social system, Sustainable development, Overall social transformation, Resilience, New Normal, Inclusive institutions, World balance of power, Adaptation to new technologies, Fair pay of labor, Favorable distribution of capital, Multi polar political order, Middle class positions, Middle way, Post-materialistic consciousness, Convergence of "capitalism and socialism".

1. INTRODUCTION

Until recently, world development in the present post crisis decade has characterized by a lack of significant technological and institutional progress. In the current period, the growth of capital in conventional markets is the most significant factor of economic development in almost all developed countries. Macro effect of growth of existing high-tech and knowledge-intensive capital and, in particular, investments in information technology of today's generation actually reached saturation for a long time ago. In general, an almost gloomy picture of the stagnation of technological and institutional progress has taken place, judging, at least, from the dynamics of indicators recognized at the international level - total level - total or multi - factor productivity. In fact, the inertial trend of economic development unambiguously prevails associating with a stagnation in the global dynamics of personal well-being.

Without exaggeration, the world community and the majority of its members - sovereign countries - face a choice of urgent and fully realistic long-term solutions that allow them to concentrate their efforts on overcoming the arisen barriers to progress. To justify these decisions, it is necessary to take into account a whole series of economic and other social changes.

It is worth noting that in recent and resonance reports of international organizations a purely pragmatic vision of the collision of modern economic and general social development prevails[1–4]. The focus is on the imperative of simultaneously achieving maximum economic productivity - efficiency and social inclusion in its broad sense (taking into account the value relations between generations) in the observed future. Based on this approach, a set of long-term solutions have proposed for traditional areas of economic and social policy with the participation of the state, business and public organizations. However, with such a selective, two-scalar approach in the spirit of the "main link" a number of critical problems appear to be in the background. Among them, it is enough to name at least the problems of adaptation of different categories of people employed to technologies in the era of digitalization (robots, artificial intelligence, etc.) the impact of political shifts on market and social status changes, climate change and environmental migration. Their resolution will be very important to predetermine precisely the possibility of increasing economic efficiency and expanding social inclusion.

In turn, the attention of the authors of purely research publications, such as[5], focuses on issues relating to partial fragmentary changes in the direction of general social progress. However, the mature need concludes in holistic coverage of fundamental shifts that determine, ultimately, the long-term directions of development of the whole society without questioning the full significance of current changes, market and others.

Consideration of the phenomenon of fundamental shifts in their integral unity in time and space may be possible based on the transformational paradigm. The recent contributions confirm this proposal[6,7]. Let us, at least in the first approximation, try to present the image of global future progress precisely by means of a transformational approach without any futurology.

The indicated task predetermined the logic of the structuration of the paper. In its initial part, the conceptual vision of social progress is justified from the standpoint of the theory of social transformation. Further, in the article the key question considers concerning the possibility of overcoming the existing global regress for the transition to a sustainable overall social transformation. The following parts of the article are devoted to the sketch presentation of a sustainable social system transformation along its main lines. In addition to this, the issue of choosing the national institutional model that is most suitable for sustainable general social transformation specially investigates in part 5. Concluding remarks present in the final part.

2. A CONCEPTUAL VISION OF OVERALL SOCIAL PROGRESS

It seems reasonable to refer to the theory of social system transformation, relying on recognized outstanding contributions[8–11]. In accordance with this theory the research paradigm, concluding in the treatment of the development of the social system as a transformation of its multidimensional structure, is legitimate. This approach assumes an integrative representation of the significant components of the development vector of a particular society as a social system in a real time-space dimension.

Transformation of the social system in its traditional (narrow) understanding encompasses the main fields of social action, economic, political and societal (status), characterized by the existence of a defined institutional design and resource provision. At the same time, it is necessary to take into account that social changes in institutionally structured fields have inevitably accompanied in large degree by non-institutionalized processes of technological, demographic and climate changes.

Thus, social system transformation occurs in a result of the interaction of endogenous institutional/resource shifts, as well as a variety of exogenous processes. Such as the invention of fundamentally new technologies, the change of cycles of solar activity, etc.

The initial premise of the system transformational concept of development-progress lies in the permanent change in production, personal and social needs, based on achievable new resource, institutional and technological capabilities, expected demographic and climate changes[12]. These requirements, in turn, predetermine the future structural / multi sector vector of the desired output in the economic space and the vector of the desired long-term shifts in other fields of social actions. They directly act as objective guidelines for the fundamental development of the social macros as an integral system, during which, while ensuring the necessary conditions, desired transformations can occur in accordance with the criterions of progress. At first place, the criteria for improving well-being in its broadest sense, including the state of the human environment, reflected by internationally recognized quality of life and human development indices, as so as in the happiness index (subjective well-being). Also, following a realistic research position, it is reasonable to judge the general social progress by the criteria of rationality and efficiency of capital movement in its various forms (including natural capital), taking into account the relationships between generations. A number of different indicators apply to represent this criterion[4].

Without resorting to obvious mathematical proofs, one can assert. Grounded on the well-known criteria of optimal inter-temporal ratio of costs and outputs, the transformation of social macros as a system on a stable and plausible long-term trajectory is preferable. Its immanent feature is not a spasmodic, but a steadily consistent movement to the achievable boundaries, based on the identified opportunities. Social transformation along such sustainable trajectory fully, it is worth noting, corresponds to the ideology of New Normal, which has been widely recognized after the crisis period 2008–2009.

Thus, in order to justify the concept of future social progress, it is logical to expose a universal idea of integrative sustainable development, moreover, as applied to the system (precisely system!) transformation of the whole society. Following this approach, an inalienable feature of the desired development of society as an all-encompassing social system refers to a sustainable transformation. It expresses in the reproduction of the promising development vectors of the overall social system, which believed to be sustainably acceptable.

At the same time, it makes sense to clarify. The desired transformation of society is not fully exhausted by the processes of sustainable change. It can include processes of more progressive changes that act as the results of initiative decisions of purely market agents and social entrepreneurs under the condition that sustainable development trajectories prevail in the main fields of social action.

Judging by the harsh contemporary realities, with respect to the national interests of individual countries the imperative of sustainability has most clearly manifested in the guarantee of maintaining an acceptable quality of life and well-being levels. This is attainable through the interaction of all public forces, including corporate and other businesses. Nevertheless, the main responsibility in the constant ensuring the sustainability of the national development results put unequivocally on the state.

This role of the state as a guarantor of sustainable development is definitely incompatible with neo-liberalism, as well as with the neo-conservative capitalist doctrine. The same concerns the ideology of modern corporatism. The effect of charitable activities, called socially responsible, of large corporations is inevitably limited.

Undoubtedly, the indicated initial approach to the design of future social progress substantially connects with the revised framework concept of Sustainable Development (SD), presented in the official memorandum "Transformation of our world: An Agenda for Sustainable Development for 2030" or simply an Agenda. As is known, this concept is integrative. Achieving the set goals in principle supposes to be equally priority and interdependent within the 15-year perspective (2016–2030).

The fundamental innovation concludes in the statement of the imperative to create effective institutions at all levels, recorded in Agenda Goal 16. Almost decisively successful integrative SD, according to the adepts of the renewed concept, acquires the phenomenon of the spread of inclusive institutions[13]. These institutions, mostly based on the principles of universality and non-discrimination, provide equal rights and opportunities for producers and consumers, as well as access to all resources and services. They are confronted by exclusive institutions that ensure the withdrawal of resources in favor of groups that have economic and political power at the expense of the rest of society[14].

As stressed in the Memorandum of the G-20 Summit in China[15], the necessary step concludes in approving a suitable institutional environment for inclusive independent business including social entrepreneurship. Exactly the inclusive business is called upon to play a key role in implementing the imperatives of future sustainable development.

However, by opinion of many researchers (the author among them), the current framework concept of SD remains selectively segmental and in fact far from the system one. It mainly focuses on environmental and humanitarian issues, the conservation of natural resources and the use of reproducible resources, overcoming the consequences of climate degradation, improving the efficiency of individual institutions. Opposite to it, the problems of fundamental institutional reforms and adaptation to fundamental technological changes have only fixed using previous traditional formulations[16]. Namely from the resolution of these problems, the possibility of achieving sustainable acceptable production, consumption and employment trajectories depends to the greatest extent, as well as achieving purely ecological, climate and humanitarian targets.

In our opinion, the treatment of inclusive institutions, represented by the adherents of the framework concept, also needs a serious adjustment. It should be borne in mind that not all effective institutions needed for sustainable development are inclusive; moreover, not all can be incorporated into the framework of contractual relations. That has been said above primarily concerns the institutions of public regulation. Many of them, in principle, are not inclusive, such as progressive taxation rules. Also, key institutions that function in corporate and other limited competition markets, a number of informal political institutions and, to a large extent, informal social norms conditioned by the specifics of national development are certainly not inclusive.

Even more significantly, the describing concept in question is not essentially a transformational in the institutional projection. The desired patterns of inclusive institutions as if have a priori fixed, although their development supposes largely due to a purposeful public policy at different fields of social action.

In line with the overall social system transformation, the time-space positioning of institutional and resource changes has a decisive value taking into account the influence of changes on the "adjacent" fields of social actions and relatively exogenous factors (technological, demographic and climate changes). Therefore, an adequate reflection of the integrative transformation of the entire vector of parameters of the social system becomes possible, proceeding from the imperatives of sustainability. Besides, we should especially note, the attainment of ecological improvements and relative climate stabilization depends on an assumed integrative consequence of all transformational outcomes.

3. TRANSITION TO GLOBAL SUSTAINABLE SOCIAL TRANSFORMATION: POSSIBLE FUNDAMENTAL SHIFTS

It is appropriate to focus attention on a number of possible fundamental shifts, the synergetic implementation of which will open the road to a sustainable transformation of the world community within the framework of the main social fields.

The first shift. Exclusive importance for improving the state of the world economy and geopolitical situation will have a successful embodiment of the idea of the implementation of the ripe "new deal", which has now become a popular expression, in the EU countries, to which Japan deserves attention. The great economic, innovative and human potential of the countries-conductors of European integration in its new capacity allows us to hope for final success, despite significant centrifugal processes[17].

The crucial point is the implementation of a new European defense program initiated by France and Germany. The EU needs to be armaments capable of curbing the potential aggressor by an adequate preventive / retaliatory strike. Large-scale developments in this direction can bring, judging by the example of China and Russia, to a practical positive result in the short term.

The second shift. The grandiose economic expansion of the Celestial in a non-Western world will be even stronger on all grounds. It manifests in the increase of economic growth and consumer welfare in many countries. As known, Chinese leaders are in favor of an early reform of the world monetary and financial system. It may become an important step towards the establishment in the future of a fair economic order at the global level.

The third shift. India, Brazil, Indonesia and a number of other post developing countries with their combined enormous potential are definitely capable of achieving significant economic and humanitarian progress in the short run perspective. At the global level, it will visibly reflect in the long-awaited reduction in poverty and the income gap.

Also in the short term, it is possible to predict the political progress in many countries of Latin America. Favorable economic, and with them, political shifts will probably occur on the African continent.

The fourth shift. The problem of adaptation of scientific and technological achievements in various economic and social sectors can be successfully resolved through a large-scale and simultaneously selective innovation policy, especially in the leading European countries, China and Japan. Then it will be difficult to reevaluate the global effect in the coming period of the diffusion of new digital and other technologies called the fourth industrial revolution, which will manifest itself in the global innovation/technological progress affecting most of the countries. The prevailing trend of inertial development of the world economy will be overstrained.

The fifth shift. Based on a broad international consensus, an adequate response to the global migration challenge can be given. A firm, justified migration policy, while taking into account humanitarian values, is asserting itself. The achieved agreement on the positions of the EU countries on migration policy issues is a convincing confirmation of this.

At the same time, intensive financial assistance to developing countries and the most active participation in the reform of their economies and social sectors by the EU, Japan, China and other industrialized countries remain extremely necessary. As a result, the number of weak, politically dependent states will drastically decrease, which will entail a radical weakening of migration anomaly.

The final shift. The joint efforts of the progressive governments of developed and other countries to stabilize the climate, predetermined by the Paris Agreement in 2016, and the improvement of the environment will crown with considerable success. Then probably there will be real world recognition of environmental and other imperatives of sustainable development, ultimately affecting the United States and Russia, as well as the entire post-developing world.

Ultimately, in the event of these transformational changes, the factors of global progress will obviously prevail over the inertial factors in the economic space and the increase in social welfare in its broad sense for the citizens of most countries will become a constant trend.

It is equally important to achieve an unsurmountable political progress. Thus, in the consequence of the creation of a powerful defensive shield of continental Europe the factor of military potential will cease to play a dominant role in the world balance of power. This balance will form depending on other significant factors of economic and political weight of different countries and their alliances. The notorious duopoly of power over the world will not take place despite the possible preservation of confrontation between the US / NATO and the military alliance Russia-China.

4. TOWARDS A SUSTAINABLE SOCIAL SYSTEM TRANSFORMATION IN THE TWENTIES

The system presentation of a sustainable transformation of society implies the coverage of all significant areas of social development in their integral unity at the national, regional and global levels. Apparently, two main criteria signs of this process can formulate in the following way. First, the formation of stable long-term trajectories of the main resource changes as well as fundamental institutional and organizational shifts in the direction of the required structural target points for the future, reflecting the entire set of environmental, special humanitarian and other parameters of sustainable development. Second, reliable adaptation to the expected technological, demographic and climate changes in so far as they act as exogenous factors with respect to the transformation of the entire social system and its main components.

At the same time, one cannot fail to take into account the existence of a huge number of processes of non-stable changes, bearing in mind at least cyclical fluctuations of the market situation, the impact of technological shocks, sporadic political perturbations and social conflicts. They can be count-progressive and have a very significant impact on economic, political and societal fundamental changes, leading to a violation of the conditions for a stable systemic transformation. Therefore, apparently, the problem of neutralizing such influence in the future will be central to the design of directly long-term strategic solutions and mechanisms for overcoming emerging risks[6].

Let us try to imagine lapidary at least a sketch vision of the future sustainable social system transformation along its three main directions - economic, political and societal.

Sustainable Economic System Transformation: The expected future changes in the twenties will lead to a rethinking of the understanding of sustainable economic development as an uninterrupted time-space transformational process. The most significant contribution to the economic output is called upon to make technological and institutional progress. He acts as the main means of ensuring the long-term competitiveness of national economies, but not the aggressive protectionist policy following the current American model.

The unfolding of new industrialization opens the way for the maximum reduction in the consumption of hydrocarbons and other renewable resources and their replacement by reproducible green technologies in the grandiose dissemination and the implementation of efficient infrastructure projects, specifically on environmental criteria. Consequently, the desired significant effect of decoupling will achieve, when economic results grow much faster than consumption of resources and the scale of their impact on the environment.

Apparently, on a global scale, there will be a long-awaited structural shift towards the prevalence of innovative and high-tech economic sectors, where reproducible resources and energy efficient, waste-free and low-waste, technologies will use. In addition, we can expect the establishment of a green economy in most of the world that meets the imperatives of environmental sustainability and climate improvement. Already there are a significant number of economically and environmentally effective green technologies ready for widespread use. This gives grounds to hope for a gradual (exactly gradual) elimination of the existing brown economy. A long-awaited consequence of a drastic reduction in the consumption of non-renewable resources will be the conservation of biodiversity and the enhancement of natural capital based on the restoration of ecosystems and spread of new one.

At the same time, it is definitely unacceptable to simplify the problem of market adaptation to new technologies in the incoming future[18,19]. As evidenced by numerous facts, the applying of a number of new technologies, including digital technologies, in principle does not meet the criterion of economic stability. Quite likely the shock effect of the development of individual markets, where these technologies implement, will take place. Thus, according to the resonance research's[20–22], the consequences of new automation accompanying the use of robots and technologies based on artificial intelligence will have a very strong impact on the labor markets. There will be a substitution of human labor in many areas of routine activity with an orderly increase in the number of highly qualified personnel of a new time, distinguished by the intellectual abilities of independent analysis, critical thinking and informal problem solving.

Soon there will be a long-term need for the creation of special regulatory mechanisms. At first place, it implies the dissemination directly in the market environment of new adaption technologies, which are beginning to be developed.

It makes sense to focus on the next collision. An inalienable imperative of sustainable system transformation will continue to be the maintenance of the maximum possible employment in market sectors in full compliance with the Agenda. To achieve this imperative, "three party" coordination of actions of the state, business and trade union organizations is required.

A cardinal shift in the structure of employment in favor of exclusive types of business and professional activity reasonably expects. These are individual medical and health services, resort services, private design services, etc. The area of flexible employment will expand, especially in the informal economy[23].

In addition, a more than significant potential for increasing qualified personnel is concentrated in a number of market segments of the green economy, whose growth will be driven by increasing environmental pressure and climate change[24].

In the context of the above, it is impossible to ignore the burning agenda of world migration. In the nearest future, the problem of reducing the relative share of the able-bodied contingent in the composition of the population of developed countries due to its aging will probably remain relevant and be resolved to a significant extent due to the regulated inflow of foreign workers on a strictly legal basis. However, this process will lose its former scale due to changes in the structure of employment during digitalization. A significant influx of low-skilled migrants will exhaust; meanwhile the selection of professional migrants, mostly highly qualified, according to their abilities will become an all-local practice[25].

The world migration situation will finally change, corresponding with a fundamental complication of relations between developed and developing countries. In our view, the way out of the situation lies in the most active participation of developed countries in economic reforming and technological modernization in problem countries, from which the main migration flows proceed. In this way, the desired increase in wages and employment in relatively efficient market sectors could be achieved.

The future SD also suppose a fair pay of labor including gender wage equality. We can assume that the achievement of this imperative will become much more plausible under the conditions of new automation and digitalization, when opportunities arise for complete information monitoring of the effectiveness of individual and collective labor.

Inequality in pay between highly skilled and other employees is likely to continue or even increase. At the same time, compulsory provision of an acceptable basic level of income for citizens of individual countries will remain an essential condition for sustainable overall social transformation. In accordance with the recognized point of view, this condition can be fulfilled in a result of the redistribution of national income through special taxation of producers using high-performance automation technologies with artificial intelligence and robots. It is fundamentally important that the new tax mechanism is intended to be implemented both at the national and international levels[26].

Positive changes in the distribution of labor incomes and social benefits are designed to correspond with favorable changes in the distribution of capital. In the observed perspective, it is most likely to expect an increasing of the relative capital and the incomes of innovators and high-tech producers, which largely intend to redistribute through the proposed new tax mechanism. Conversely, a relative reduction in the capital of financial entities and rental incomes is desirable, accompanied by the elimination of hypertrophied high-yielding components of the capital market and wide niches for financial and other speculations. If this scenario will successfully implement in developed countries, real opportunities will open up for a significant reduction in the differentiation of income and personal / family wealth.

At the same time, an essential condition concludes in maintaining financial balance with reference to individual national economies. Especially in the implementation of future long-term structural reforms [27].

In addition, proceeding from a number of forecasts, the current regime of a tight monetary stabilization policy will probably preserve. It should complement by neutralization of illegal / criminal economic activity and anti-corruption course on a recognized legal basis.

At the global, multi-regional and national levels, the assertion as dominant precisely the sustainable economic order is called for. It assumes an unhindered stable trade regime, as well as stable regimes of the international movement of capital in its various forms and labor and, besides, most importantly, acting on the base of coordinated application of global, regional and national legislation. Certainly, they are not compatible with the former liberal (of course, only in words!) international economic order of the era of American hegemony, the return of which is still pinned on by certain backstage circles.

It can be assumed that on the world stage, at least three competing groups of countries will be comparable in market potential: 1) the United States and other countries with the prevailing capitalistic institutional order; 2) China, India, Russia and a number of other non-Western countries; 3) the countries of continental Europe, apparently, in alliance with Japan and Canada. At the same time, the role of regional economic unions, which includes other countries, will remain highly significant. In conditions of such multilateral international competition, there are grounds to assume that most countries will act as equal rights members of the world economic community. In turn, the establishment of such an equal right order will serve as a prerequisite for further movement towards full-scale economic globalization.

Of course, we should not question the need to maintain a positive world economic dynamics for the sake of the well-being of the entire human society, as recorded in the G-20 memorandums in recent years. At the same time, it makes sense to pay special attention to the weighty arguments in favor of maintaining a relatively moderate rate of economic growth in the period of the twenties.

The first argument is quite understandable: the priorities of sustainable development dictate the feasibility of qualitative improvement of most of the existing markets with their limited resource growth. It becomes achievable because of a mutually complementary combination of two processes: the introduction of new technologies that minimize the cost of resources and the widespread use of reproducible resources and the spreading of non-waste production in technologically "old" sectors.

The second argument for the reproduction of the potential of the mature post-industrial economy, the maximum quantitative growth of new technologies and new machinery is not required. For example, the demand for new information digital technologies and computers will be limited, at least in terms of the number of their customers. In addition to this, one should take into account that, according to all forecasts, in the twenties the tendency of relative cheapening of technology will increase (in terms of the ratio of selling prices and useful effect). Also in this perspective, probably, there will not be a need for a very rapid growth in the physical volumes of buildings, structures and other objects of the infrastructure of the post-industrial economy. The compactness and ergonomics of most of the high-tech enterprises with the continuation of the trend of miniaturization of technological progress is a very weighty argument in favor of this assumption.

As for personal and family welfare, the direction of the transformation of its structure in the long term will most likely predetermine changes in rational consumer preferences. The value of the quality of life in the environment conditions of the 21st century comes to the forefront. It involves a rational personal consumption of resources that does not harm the environment. Comprehension of the meaningless to use for the sake of prestigious reasons a lot of cars, suburban buildings for the construction of which a huge mass of "brown" building materials is used, and other attributes of luxury life that are harmful to the environment, will become, perhaps, a fundamental feature of the future consumer ideology.

Finally, another weighty argument against the maximization of economic growth is due to the expectation of further institutional improvement in the main domestic markets in Non-Western countries. According to all projections, in the considered perspective the rate of profit in real sectors of their economies will decrease and will approach the existing level in Western countries. It will first happen in China, then in other Asian giants and, ultimately, in most of the rest post developing countries. The rapid growth of most commodity markets caused by opportunistic and, especially, speculative financial factors will not be observed.

And, probably, it is necessary to put a dot over sustainable reproduction of the future world economy of the post-industrial type in the twenties suggests it's stable and calm, absolutely non-explosive growth. At the same time, the rapid growth of individual markets, especially innovative ones, will be quite real.

However, as if in the end of the economic theme it is appropriate to make an important observation. Sustained favorable economic changes, objectively achievable in large part due to a purposeful national or supranational economic policy, should not interpret as ideal or perfectionist processes. They serve as necessary conditions for the implementation in principle of the most effective resource and institutional shifts initiated by the optimal initiatives of the market agents themselves in terms of technological innovations and a wide variety of investments, the use of productive capacity and qualified personnel.

Sustainable System Transformation on the Political Field: Let us now dwell at least briefly on the very fragmentally studied topic of sustainable transformation in the political field. It involves not only internal political stability, which usually considers as a condition for maintaining the favorable economic development of certain countries.

Undoubtedly, the position in favor of the formation at the global level of a multipolar political order is incompatible with the hegemony of one country or group of countries, as well as with a superpower duopoly (the United States and its closest allies, on the one hand, and China and Russia, on the other). Such an anti-hegemonic order can become the basis for satisfying the national interests of small countries.

It will be necessary to create flexible, time-mobile institutional mechanisms, including organizational structures, ensuring international security. Besides an obligatory condition for global political stability is the approval of the international legal regime.

Institutions providing stable internal political transformation of individual countries on the principles of democratization and competition are well known[28]. According to national studies, the effectiveness of the political institutions directly depends on the quality, that is, the results and costs of administrative management at all levels.

The positive impact of the formation of a stable economic order on transformation in the political space will first manifest itself in the long-predicted shift. The political elite will largely replenish by higher management in the innovative and high-tech corporate sectors, as well as in the sectors of the new economy of reproducible resources, while reducing the presence of leaders of financial and trade capital.

At the same time, it is worth noting that the achievement of a stable trajectory of political transformation would not mean a general transition to a perfect regime of democratic governance in civil society in accordance with traditional ideas. Especially in relation to countries that are not democratic in reality. Nevertheless, there will be grounds for hoping for an irreversible endorsement of parliamentary democracy in place of a populist, permanently primeval form of presidential rule in this large group of countries.

Sustainable Societal System Transformation: Now let us turn to the extremely multifaceted problem of sustainable transformation on the societal field. Its integrative criteria condition, following the recognized notions, considers the fair distribution of wealth in its broad sense (including consumption of natural and cultural goods, education) among all generations of citizens accompanied by a constant improvement of quality of life with reliable social balance.

Based on the current realities, in a very significant degree the forthcoming development of society will predetermine by the economic transformation. However, the results of transformation in this field of social actions are also of great importance. They, in turn, are significantly dependent on the productivity of public policy designed to carry out in accordance with the ideology of sustainable development.

This assessment can illustrate in relation to the fate problem of employment under the unfolding automation and digitalization. It is definitely insoluble on a market basis only. Alternative-free imperative for orderly employment growth in non-market services, though, of course, the necessary condition concludes to prevent work that is useless and wasteful in terms of resource costs as was the case during the era of totalitarian socialism in the countries of the Soviet bloc.

Following to forecasts[29], in the total number of employed persons the share of workers in such sectors as education, health and social work activities will tremendously increase. In our view, also there is a weighty possibility of a cardinal increase in employment, including various intellectual activities, in the social environmental sector, where a wide area will emerge for the use of technological innovations as social benefits[24]. This process intends to be comprehensive, encompassing both growing megacities and ordinary cities, as well as climate-challenging regions of the planet.

To ensure full or at least close to full employment in the market and social sectors as a whole migration policy in its broad sense should be oriented at the national level. It designs to act as an organic supplement to the economic policy concerning the employment.

The considered kind of transformation should be associated with gradual positive improvements in the status pyramide specially non-deviating strengthening of the middle class positions. Then, in the case of the parallel formation of a sustainable economic order, the composition of higher status groups (including the so-called transnational corporate class) will constantly update.

However, it is worth acknowledging that realistic design of improvements to the status pyramid of society represents a very complex problem. To solve it, it would be necessary to assess the impact on the status pyramid transformation of economic and political institutional progress, as well as the impact of technological and other exogenous off-system changes.

Crucial value, as the practical experience suggests, will be the realization of the synergetic effect of mutually complementary decisions in different areas of social policy with the inherent participation of business and public independent organizations. The expected progress in the field of combating poverty and in the educational sphere is called for to materialize in a significant improvement of the natural environment. In turn, it is extremely important to achieve the opposite effect of these improvements on the state of the entire national society. The favorable ecological conditions manifest as the weighty factors of the life stability in local communities and, consequently, of social stability in certain national borders, when the principle "to live at home, rather than to seek abroad" triumphs.

Judging by today's experience, the stimulation of various forms of voluntary participation of citizens in public activity becomes critical. It prevents social exclusion of certain groups of the population, in particular, the spread of youth drug addiction. Mass participation of migrants in the activities of public organizations is also of great importance, for which special educational and cultural programs are extremely necessary.

Ultimately, the satisfaction of the growing intellectual, moral and spiritual demands of citizens of modern countries presupposes a favorable cultural transformation while maintaining the divergence of national (subnational) cultures. Social policy along the lines of a sustainable system transformation should promote the orderly strengthening of the solidarity in society. Then, despite possible problem demographic and migration trends, the much-desired tightening of the integration of various national communities will be achievable.

It is also reasonable to count on the widest distribution of post-materialistic consciousness among representatives of educated and ensured stratums of society. Their preferences will predetermine by values expressed in freedom of expression and quality of life. Postmaterialists put personal entrepreneurial success and the accumulation of individual wealth along with professional achievements and long-term well-being within the human and natural environment. Besides, entrepreneurs who share this ideology will guide by the social recognition of their sustainably effective business.

However, it would be a mistake to succumb inshort mind manner to the illusion of a quite favorable social arrangement for the future. In the twenties, despite the likely spread of the post-materialist worldview, there is every reason to expect an expansion of routine, completely non-creative economic and other social activities in the conditions of using unoccupied digital-led technologies and robot technologies. A huge number, and possibly most of the employed, will be concentrated in low-tech and medium-tech activities in the service sector. The threat of preserving the non-creative needs in the life of these employers will become very significant.

Apparently, the way out to the decisive extent connects with the overcoming the social exclusion of those engaged in low-skilled labor[30]. The possibility of creating comfortable, physically and psychologically favorable conditions for this category of employees is quite accessible in the new post-industrial realities of the twenties.

5. CHOICE OF NATIONAL INSTITUTIONAL MODEL

The central question concerns the establishment of the root institutional envelope of the desired transformation of the social system, which primarily meets the conditions of sustainability. Achieving the desired benchmarks for a sustainable transformation of innovation and high-tech sectors, as well as sectors of the green economy, requires the effective complementarity of market and other institutions.

Therefore, we can assume. The national model of the middle development path or middle way, the initial idea of which had expressed by Henry George[31] even in the period of the formation of classical capitalism, corresponds to the condition of effective institutional complementarity in the future. This model characterizes precisely by the balancing of state, corporate and independent entrepreneurial orders with the paramount importance of the principles of socially effective activity and socially equitable distribution. In practical terms, sustainable transformation of these orders would mean a long-term stability of the economic and political course without tremendous turns to the right or left and, of course, without a radical change in the state system, as in the present period of tenth.

The approval of strong institutional mechanisms that ensure private, corporate, state and social entrepreneurial initiative fully corresponds to the character of the coming period of the expected grandiose technological changes in the twenties. Proceeding from the experience of Sweden, Norway and Singapore, the favorable adaptation to the markets of Progress technologies, including green technologies, had taken place due to the median institutional arrangement of the economic system and the overall social system.

As we know, the institutional model of the middle path of national development has been successfully adapted in the Scandinavian countries and East Asian countries - Malaysia, Taiwan and Singapore. One may believe that a gradual transition to this model in a number of developed countries in Europe and Asia will become possible in case of tremendous positive shifts on the world arena above noted.

Besides, a possible fundamental change in the current model of the bizarre symbiosis of state capitalism and market socialism in China may carry out taking the initial model of convergence of "socialism and capitalism" as the desired pattern[32,33]. In fact, it is a kind of middle path model. Such a metamorphosis becomes quite real, in favor of which the arguments given below notify (Inbox 1).

Inbox 1: *Substantial institutional changes in China, where, despite obtrusive predictions, there was no transformation to the market economy of the previously dominant Western model, dictate by the* *transition to a new stage of development. According to a widely accepted opinion, at present a shift from the earlier export oriented investment pattern to consumption-driven growth pattern has taken place*[34].

At the same time, there is a decline in the export advantages of the Chinese large corporate sector, previously based on cheap labor and economies of scale, and a concomitant slowdown in foreign investment in the face of the aging of the population. These trends are associated with the remaining reproduction of sufficient macro-structural imbalances, in particular between loans and debts[35]. *There is also a huge regional gap, especially manifested in the west of the country with its poor peasant population.*

Indicative unfavorable factors in the development of the Chinese economy are largely due to root institutional deficiencies. At first place, over the economic dominance and monopoly position of enterprises of the State-Corporate Sector (SOE) in priority sectors thanks to the active support of the CPC. The SOE sector suppresses other sectors[36]. *This is especially true for private enterprises, many of which in fact face an unfavorable credit regime*[37].

In addition, there is an adverse effect of the "overlapping" of institutions of state capitalist and market socialist orders in the main links of the Chinese economy. Thus, until recently, soft budget and credit restrictions along with social benefits, which were in force with respect to SOE, preserve out-of-date employment and low productivity by world standards, which are lagging behind wage by growth rate in a large number of industries. In turn, many provincial enterprises (TVE) are under the pressure of regional planning targets and oversight by CPC representatives in the field. Consequently, a distinctive feature of the Chinese economy concludes in a constant conflict of interests of managers in economic sectors under state control.

At present, the plan for reforming SOEs and other state-owned enterprises aimed at improving the competitive environment has actually implemented[38]. *The upcoming step concludes in the mixed-*

ownership reform in SOE sector, because the enterprises ownership in the form of "state-owned + private + foreign" are significantly more efficient than state ownership[39]. In this case, the need has intended to strengthen the special regulation of the stock and other financial markets in order to neutralize the speculative movement of capital.

A deep institutional transformation of the SME sector also implements. A targeted policy has pursued to orientate capital towards greater investment in small and micro enterprises and the introduction of long-term efficient and transparent business taxation mechanisms[40].

Along with this, there are grounds to expect the approval of new mechanisms for regulating wages and social transfers, as well as the formation of personal incomes and private wealth in a close measure to the Scandinavian model[41]. It is worth noting that currently wages and salaries in the SOE sector have regulated on a uniform basis.

It should be noted that an obvious condition for the transition to a pro-progressive distribution model in the mainstream of a sustainable middle path in China is curbing the over exploitation of migrants from rural areas. In the course of the new phase of reforming the economy, it seems that the problem of shortage and replacement of old personnel in advanced industries will be resolved precisely through a large influx of trained rural migrants.

We can assume that under favorable external circumstances, political and other, the opposing institutions of state capitalist, private capitalist and socialized property will replace by mutually complementary institutions of mixed property. In parallel, relatively equally important institutions of market coordination will dominate in the economic field: state regulation, corporate regulation and entrepreneurial self-regulation. Besides, within the framework of the entire social system mutual complementarity of the institutions of market and non-market coordination will achieve upon the condition of strictly demarcated areas of their functioning.

Consequently, the external political influence, primarily from the CCP, may dramatically weaken.

Finally, a system transformational transition will take place associated with overcoming the contradictory coexistence of the institutional orders of state capitalism and market socialism. State capitalism as an institutional order will not play an exaggeratedly dominant role and outperform other institutional orders meanwhile the existing socialist market order will gradually absorb.

A unitary structure-forming institutional structure will establish, ensuring the transformation of the national overall social system in principle in accordance with the background convergence model, which now can call the model of after socialist middle path. If the mentioned institutional / structural reforms succeed, the necessary conditions will arise for sustainable overall social progress in China in the coming twenties. In particular, there will be an ordinal reduction in the differentiation of income and wealth accompanying with a disappearance of the obstacles to the growth of green economy and green non-market sectors on the base of sustainable use of natural resources.

It makes sense to stay, at least briefly, on an important collision. Institutional arrangements characterized by the prevalence of capitalist institutions, especially corporate capitalist ones, are likely to continue in a number of countries. However, these countries will not receive the same advantages in the economic arena in terms of capital growth, income, consumption and employment. On the contrary, they can be a loser in the conditions of asserting a sustainable global economic and social transformation. At least, for two fundamental reasons. First, the reduction in the relative contribution of physical capital and labor, especially in the corporate sector, to economic output, as opposed to a relative increase in the contribution of technological and institutional-managerial progress, largely socialized. Second, the expected slowdown in many branches of the brown economy - the main foothold of past century capitalism with its well-known institutional framework.

That said does not call into question the possible growth in the future of local real estate markets, individual luxury goods, specialty medicines and medical services (such as stem cell transplantation operations). At the same time, the role of these highly profitable markets will be limited at the world and regional levels.

If the national model of the middle path of development will prevail on a global scale, there will obviously be a fundamental weakening of the factor of institutional divergence. Thus, the main obstacle to the movement towards full-scale economic globalization will eliminate.

6. CONCLUDING REMARKS

Sustainable overall social transformation in its main interconnected fields performs as an indispensable attribute of future human progress. Despite the likely weightiest costs and significant counter actions, the need for transition to this type of social development looks unambiguous.

A purposefully maintained movement along the trajectories of a sustainable social system transformation is by no means a path into a "bright future" in the spirit of communist ideology. New burning problems will arise before the planetary community. Definitely implementation of strategic plans of progressive development, at first place sustainable development, in the period of the twenties will come across serious various obstacles - sources of risks. Suffice it to say about the threats of tech-gen disasters (the uprising of robots with artificial intelligence is no longer exclusively a topic of fantasy literature), unexplored before epidemics and ethno-national conflicts. However, these obstacles, if the ideology and practice of sustainable development has established, might be overcome in an acceptable way without long crises and immense social damage, on the base of global, regional and national consensus.

In regards to individual countries, the substantiation of realistic feasible support for the main areas of the sustainable social system transformation will be an important initial step towards the development of a national development strategy. Judging by international experience, it is definitely expedient to fix the benchmarks of sustainable transformation and other transformations within the framework of the system development strategy embracing the whole society. It calls for the identification of ways to achieve the future, which the majority of the national society desires and deserves.

At the same time, it is worthwhile to remain realistic. Processes of deliberately unstable, accelerated transformational changes are called upon to account within the certain directions of the national development. For this purpose, special strategic approaches should approbate in practice.

Obviously, the implementation of overall social transformation national strategies can provide the positive impact on the current design practice and public monitoring of the selected SD targets[42,43]. Due to the integration of these strategies, the possibilities of achieving these benchmarks in time as well as in space can assess for different countries and at the global level.

REFERENCES

[1] IMF (2018). G-20 Report on strong, sustainable, balanced and inclusive growth. Available online: *https://imf.org/external/np/g20/pdf/2018/111918.pdf*

[2] OECD (2016). The Productivity-Inclusiveness Nexus, Paris. Available online: *https://oecd.org/.../the-productivity-inclusiveness-nexus-9789264292932-en.htm*

[3] OECD (2017). Update Report 2017 - Inclusive Growth. Paris. Available online: *https://oecd.org/inclusive-growth/Bridging_the_Gap.pdf*

[4] The Inclusive Growth and Development Report (2017). Geneva: World Economic Forum. Available online: *http://www3.weforum.org/docs/WEF_Forum_IncGrwth_2017.pdf*

[5] Fleurbaey, M., Bouin, O., Salles-Djelic, M.L. and Kanbur, R. (2018). *A Manifesto for Social Progress: Ideas for a Better Society*. Cambridge: Cambridge University Press.

[6] Islam, N. and Iversen, K. (2018). From "Structural Change" to "Transformative Change": Rationale and Implications. DESA Working Paper No. 155. Available online: *https://un.org/development /desa/ publications/working-paper/wp155*
[7] Transformation towards Sustainable and Resilient Societies in Asia and in the Pacific (2018). United Nations, Asian Development Bank, United Nations Development Program. Available online: *http:// sdgasiapacific.net/download/SDG_Resilience_Report.pdf*
[8] Polanyi, K. (1944). *The Great Transformation*. New York: Rinehart.
[9] Parsons, T. (1951). *The Social System*. London: Routledge.
[10] Giddens, A. (1984). *The Constitution of Society*. Cambridge: Polity.
[11] Luhmann, N. (1995). *Social Systems*. The Stanford: Stanford University Press.
[12] Martynov, A. (2016). The system transformation of economy and society: The Russian choice (in Russian). Moscow: Lenand.
[13] Global Sustainable Development Report (2016). United Nations, pp. 61–76. Available online: *http://sustainabledevelopment.un.org/ globalsdreport/2016*
[14] Acemoglu, D., Liabson, D. and List, J. (2015). Why Isn't the Whole World Developed? // Chapter 8, in Macroeconomics, Pearson. Available online: *http://pearsonhighered.com/acemoglu-econ*
[15] G-20 Action Plan on the 2030. Agenda for Sustainable Development. 2016. Geneva. Available online: *htpp://ictsd.org*
[16] Enders, J. and Remig, M. (*eds.*) 2015. *Theories of Sustainable Development* // Abingdon: Routledge.
[17] Meseberg Declaration 2018. Meseberg. *Available online: http:// archiv.bundesregiering.de>meta*
[18] Körner, K., Schattenberg, M. and Heymann, E. (2018). Digital economics. How AI and robotics are changing our work and our lives. Frankfurt am Main. Deutsche Bank Research. *Available online: http:/ /dbresearch.com/.../Digital_economics%3A_How...*
[19] World Economic and Social Survey (2018). *Frontier Technologies for Sustainable Development*. New York: United Nations. Available online: *https://un.orgÃÆdpadÃÆwess-report*
[20] Acemoglu, D. and Restrepo, P. (2017). Robots and Jobs: Evidence from US Labor Markets. NBER Working Paper 23285. Available online: *http://www.nber.org/papers/w23285*
[21] Acemoglu, D. and Restrepo, P. (2018). *Artificial Intelligence, Automation and Work. NBER Working Paper No. 24196*. Available online: *http:// www.nber.org/papers/w24196*
[22] Korinek, A. and Stiglitz, J.E. (2017). *Artificial Intelligence, Worker-Replacing Technological Change, and Income Distribution*. NBER Working Paper 24174. Available online: *https://nber.org/papers/ w24174*

[23] OECD (2018a). Achieving inclusive growth in the face of digital transformation and the future of work, Paris. Available online: *https://oecd.org/.../OECD_Achieving%20inclusive%20growth%20in%20the%20...*
[24] Greening with Jobs (2018). World employment and social outlook. Geneva: ILO. Available online: *https://ilo.org/weso-greening/documents/WESO_Greening_EN_web2.pdf*
[25] Poutvaara, P., Drometer, M., Rhode, C. and Burmann, M. (2018). A Novel Two-Track Labour Migration System for Germany 2018. *IFO DICE Report*, 16(1): 34–37. Munich: IFO. Available online: *https://www.cesifo-group.de/DocDL/dice-report-2018-1-onlineversion-may.pdf*
[26] OECD (2018b). *Tax Challenges Arising from Digitalisation – Interim Report*. Paris. Available online: *https://www.oecd-ilibrary.org/tax-challenges-arising-from-digitalisation-interim-report-2*
[27] G-20 Enhanced Structural Reform Agenda (2016). Available online: *http://mofa.go.jp/files/000185875.pdf*
[28] Mazarr, M. (2018). *Summary of the Building a Sustainable International Order Project*. RAND Corporation. Available online: *https://rand.org/pubs/research_reports/RR2397.html*
[29] World Employment and Social Outlook: Trends (2018). Geneva: ILO. Available online: *https://ilo.org/wcmsp5/groups/public/...dgreports/.../wcms_615594.pdf*
[30] Joint Employment Report (2017). Brussels. European Commission. Available online: *https://ec.europa.eu/info/sites/info/files/2017-comm-674_en.pdf*
[31] George, H. (1879). *Progress and Poverty*. San Francisco: W.M. Hinton.
[32] Schumpeter, J. (1942). *Capitalism, Socialism and Democracy*. New York; London: Harper & Brothers.
[33] Galbraith, J.K. (1967). *The New Industrial State*. Boston: Houghton Mifflin.
[34] Cai, F. and Zhang, X. (2017). *Reform Dividends to Sustain China's Economic Growth. // China's New sources of Economic Growth*. Vol.2. Canberra: ANU Press.
[35] Dieppe, A., Gilhooly, R., Han, J., Korhonen, I. and Lodge, D. (*eds.*) (2018). *The Transition of China to Sustainable Growth – Implications for the Global Economy and the Euro Area*. ECB Occasional Paper Series No 206 / January. Frankfurt am Main: ECB.
[36] Li, X., Liu, X. and Wang, Y. (2015). A Model of China's State Capitalism. HKUST IEMS Working Paper No. 2015-12. Hong Kong. Available online: *https://iems.ust.hk/assets/publications/working-papers-2015/iemswp2015–12.pdf*
[37] Johansson, A. (2015). Financial repression and China's economic imbalances. Available online: *https://researchgate.net/.../325017194_Financial_Repression_and_China's_Economic_imbalances*

[38] Song, L. (2018). State-owned enterprise reform in China: Past, present and prospects.// *China's 40 years of Reform and Development 1978–2018*. Canberra: ANU Press.

[39] Yin, Z., Liu, L., Wang, H. and Wen, F. (2018). Study on the ownership balance and the efficiency of mixed ownership enterprises from the perspective of heterogeneous shareholders. *PLoS ONE*, 13(4): e0194433. Available online: *https://www.ncbi.nlm.nih.gov/pubmed/29614126*

[40] Status of Value-added Tax Reform in the People's Republic of China (2018). OECD. Available online: *http://oecd.orgÃtaxÃcomsumption*. Available online: *https://www.oecd.org/tax/.../status-of-the-vat-reform-in-the-peoples-republic-of-china*

[41] Barth, E., Moene, K.O. and Willumsen, K. (2014). *The Scandinavian Model- An Interpretation. Journal of Public Economics,* 117: 60–72.

[42] The Sustainable Development Goals Report (2018). United Nations. Available online: *http://unstats.un.org/sdgs/files/report/2018*

[43] Global responsibilities. SDG Index and Dashboards Report 2018. Available online: *htpp://sdgindex.org/.../2018/*

14

After Socialist Institutional Transformation: China and Russia Comparison. What is in Coming Future?

ARKADY MARTYNOV[1,2*]

ABSTRACT

The comparison of fundamental institutional changes in China and Russia attributed until now to the after socialist countries – the main issue of this article. The research has based on the comprehensive institutional theory, as well as the methodology of cross-country analysis in a real space-time dimension. Proceeding from the performed analysis, the trend of the institutional divergence between China and Russia considered in the nineties changed in the further period to the opposite — the trend of convergence. A unifying feature of the economies of both countries concludes in the combination of the prevailing institutions of state capitalism with the attributes of market socialism or a socialized market. In the current moment, there are discrepancies with respect to fundamental institutional changes between two countries, which may result in the emergence of a new divergence trend. According to the author's argument, in the case of the success of further China reforms the required long-term national progress would correspond

[1]International Institute for Social Development, Moscow, Russia.
[2]Institute of Economics, Russian Academy of Sciences, Moscow, Russia.
**Corresponding author:* E-mail: socpolamv@mail.ru

to the economic and overall social transformation along the middle path institutional model. At the same time, the scenario of a desirable institutional transformational transition in relation to Russia seems doubtful.

Key words: After socialist countries, China, Russia, Economic system, Convergence, State capitalism, State-corporate sector, Socialized market, Deepening social inequality, Institutional "layering", Middle way, Heterogeneous corporate property, Harmonious combination, Authoritative establishment, Divergence.

---

1. INTRODUCTION

Institutional changes in China and Russia in the aftermath of the socialist era continue to evoke a keen interest. Selected issues related to this topic consider in a huge number of publications, which are simply impossible to list. At the same time, the phenomenon of the most fundamental transformation of root institutions remains out of sight, including the resonance publications[1–3]. Let us try at least partially to fill this gap.

First, a summary of the methodology. The initial theoretical approach to the study of the phenomenon of transformation of root institutions in the course of a comparative cross country study is quite understandable. It grounds on the recognized criterion of institutional dominance, taking into account the outstanding fundamental works[4–7]. In accordance with this criterion, the nature of the national institutional system, primarily in the economic field, may be distinguished on the base of two groups of root structure-forming institutions. The first group consists of the institutions of property: private, public and state property, corporate (group) property. The second group includes the institutions of self-regulation, public (state) regulation and corporate regulation.

Our comparative study mainly concerns the problem of transformation of root economic institutions. At the same time, the complementarity of the economic transformation by transformations on other areas of social actions — societal (status) and political — has an exceptional importance. As will be shown later, it predetermines the degree of stability of the existing trajectory of the root institutional changes.

In addition, I would like to focus on the next point. Of course, institutions do not define everything in economic and other social systems. Thus, the key role of technological innovations as a factor that initiates, ultimately, large-scale system changes associated with institutional shifts is widely recognized. Also, the processes of demographic and climate change have a significant autonomous influence on economic and overall social development. They act as special corresponding factors of the institutional transformations, which should be taken into account.

The imperative of the objectivity of a comparative study of the problem of institutional transformation in countries that attributed to the after socialist ones predetermines the logic of exposition of the manuscript in a temporary chronological sequence. In the initial part, the tendencies of fundamental institutional changes in China and Russia have compared from the moment of the collapse of the Soviet bloc in the initial period of adaptation and further in the period of zero. On this basis, in the following part the similarities and differences of institutional changes in both countries in the present period have revealed. At last, the final part discusses the prospect of further institutional transformation in the leading after socialist countries, corresponding to economic and overall social progress. A brief conclusion has presented at the end.

2. ON THE PHENOMENON THE AFTER SOCIALIST TRANSFORMATION: THE RECENT PAST

In order to understand today's collusions of institutional

transformation in above countries it is first appropriate, following a recognized theory, to turn to its starting period of the early 1990s, marked by the collapse of the Soviet Union. During the designated period, there was a definite institutional divergence of development within the former socialist world, clearly manifested in the two groups of countries - Russia and other CIS countries, on the one hand, and China and Vietnam, on the other.

As is known, in Russia and other CIS countries a transition, albeit temporary, to the neoliberal model of development had taken place, stunned many Western intellectuals. It would seem that China's experience should had been the desired model, since everyone recognized its successful market reorientation. It is appropriate to remember, that Deng Xiao Ping during the reign of Gorbachev was named the great Chinese reformer.

However, the interests of the elite and the formed bourgeois stratum (including criminal circles) in legitimizing their wealth turned out to be above all in the conditions of the prolonged dominance of informal institutions of so-called nomenclature socialism (Inbox 1). The factor of strength that the elite had in the person of the former KGB was also of great importance. Actually, elite, but by no means democratic choice occurred, contrary to official propaganda.

Inbox 1. *The phenomenon of nomenclature socialism had an obvious historical under-stitch*[8 9]*. After the constant Stalinist purges had sunk into oblivion, the order on the rights of real owners the main part of the formally public ownership passed to the highly established bureaucracy. Quite naturally, the new Soviet bourgeoisie began to replenish, at first place, at the expense of representatives of the nomenclature stratum.*

The dominant position in the society of representatives of the nomenclature directly expressed in their real incomes, received, as it were, in accordance with the communist principle by needs and tens of times higher than the incomes of ordinary citizens. This inequality decisively explained by the enormous size of "free" privileges in the form of consumption of food and other products, the use of public summer residences, high-quality medical and sanatorium-resort services and other benefits distributed through closed channels, compared to the obviously low wages of workers. In essence, the nomenclature acted as an exploiting class.

Private shadow capital, with the direct support of the authorities, has long been rooted in Moscow and the Moscow region during the Soviet era. For a long time the creation of big capital and a large personal fortune turned out to be possible only with close mutually beneficial cooperation with representatives of the Moscow authorities. In essence, the Soviet bourgeoisie nomenclature, which had enormous administrative and financial resources, was the main interested social force in the fall of the socialist state in 1991.

The system changes in Russia in the early 1990s decisively manifest in the transformation of the root institutions of ownership and coordination, affecting all fields of social action.

Corporate and personal property, as if inherited from the socialist era, occupied the largest share in the national wealth. It was this huge property that, in the course of the unprecedented Russian privatization, check and monetary, had redistributed in favor of representatives (including family members) of the old and new nomenclature. They had taken key positions in former socialist enterprises in the real sectors and in the banking sector. A particularly significant contribution to the redistribution of national wealth had enclosed by the privatization of natural monopolies within the framework of raw materials industries, coupled with the appropriation of huge super-profit owners, new and former chief managers of relevant organizations.

Institutions of coordination had also changed dramatically. Due to the one-time liberalization of prices according to the type of "shock therapy" and ultra-fast banking liberalization, the market parameters of economic activity became unconditionally dominate. At the same time, the limited potential that arose during the liberal reform of the legal field of market self-regulation had filled by the spreading of huge shadow, largely criminalized, markets. An unprecedented "piratization" of the Russian economy occurred[10].

Under the conditions of the deepest industrial recession and inflation in 1992–1995 maintaining the policy of radical liberalization itself was determined by the general interest of well-known international/domestic circles that had fostered the Soviet bourgeoisie, including the tycoon of criminal business, and the leaders of former socialist enterprises in super-profits and their profitable capitalization[11]. The full effect of the initial accumulation had manifested in this period. How not to recall the famous remark by Karl Marx that at a rate of profit 100% capital tramples all human laws, and at a rate of profit 300% there is no crime that he would not risk, even under the gallows fear[12].

The expectations for favorable changes in the social structure by the formation of an entrepreneurial stratum in the course of frontal market liberalization and privatization were not justified either. In Russia, as in most Post-Soviet States, the entrepreneurial middle class did not really have the economic and, especially, political resources sufficient for public leadership. The leading position in the status pyramid belonged to the existing integrated stratum of old and new nomenclature and shadow, largely criminal business, closely related to many representatives of a high-ranking state bureaucracy.

There was no formation of a democratic order of coordination in its traditional sense. For a long time, Russia's political life in the nineties distinguished by frank populism combined with "new" authoritarianism that violated legal and other normal conditions for business activities. The most serious authorization of state policy manifested at the level of individual regions, whose leaders gained real independent power because of the "distribution of sovereignties" as if on a democratic basis.

In contrast to Russia, the economic model reformed in China has definitely stood the test of time. Here there was a radical transformation of property relations. It reflected in the historic decision of the Assembly of People's Representatives in 2002 on the legalization of private property.

Privatization in Chinese wore the natural nature of the reform "from below". It mainly affected cooperative urban and rural enterprises (TVE), where property had taken over by internal insiders - managers and, to a lesser extent, working personnel and local administrations[13]. In parallel, a fundamental transformation of the institutions of economic coordination took place, clearly manifested in the transition to full-fledged price and tax market mechanisms.

In the course of market reforms, complex changes occurred in the stratification structure[14]. The role of the working class has weakened considerably. Simultaneously, the status of administrative and managerial personnel, as well as entrepreneurs and qualified technocrats, increased. There was also an emergence of business elite, which immediately became a partner of the party and state elite. According to the generally recognized opinion, not all these changes had a destabilizing effect on economic development, contrary to Russia.

The co-storage of absolute political power in the hands of the Communist Party of China (CPC) remained an integral feature of the life of nation. At the same time, there were signs of the spread of civil liberties and contemporary cultural values, accompanying with weakening the orthodox character of the communist ideology. Democratization had affected virtually all directions of government activity. Apparently, it most pronounced in the implementation the election of heads of local administration.

In contrast to Russia and other CIS countries, China has retained the market-oriented socialist mode as dominant, as so as the dominant socialist institutions outside the economic field of activity. It is appropriate to put the question squarely: what is the cause of the fundamental difference in the fate of late socialism at the turn of the nineties in Russia and the majority of Post-Soviet countries, on the one hand, and China, on the other?

At first place, it makes sense to focus on the following circumstance. In the former USSR, as well as the former socialist European countries, the tendency of a dead-end evolution, which continued for several decades, acquired a huge inertial mass. Perhaps most significantly, this phenomenon manifested itself in the existence of a powerful nomenclature stratum, interested in maintaining the status quo and not at all interested in system institutional changes. As a result, grandiose expenses were required to overcome the discrepancies between the command institutes and legitimate institutions of a market economy and partial political democracy.

At the same time, the period of real socialism in China was much less long. Thus, a little more than a 10-year period separates the Cultural Revolution and the implementation of system institutional reforms begun by Deng Xiao Ping and his like-minded people who had returned to power as early as 1978. Just two years after the death of Mao Tse Dong and long before the attempt to drastically reform socialism in the Soviet Union in the mid-1980s. The market reformation of socialism with Chinese characteristics took place essentially from a "clean slate", being not burdened by the presence of informal bourgeois forces, as in the period of Gorbachev ruling[15]. Speaking in a mundane language, the bureaucracy was young and simply did not have time to consolidate as a social force capable of opposing the reforms "from above". The will of the party leadership remained the supreme law, taking in a view a great fear of a new round of mass repressions as in the period of the cultural revolution.

It is impossible not to take into account and the following circumstance. China, at the eve of the collapse of the world socialist system, included largely traditionalist society. Society, where the peasant way of life with a very low population mobility played an extremely important role.

Radically different influence on the course of institutional transformation in China, on the one hand, and in Russia and other CIS countries, on the other, had a course of bankrupt neoliberal globalization, conducted by the IMF with the support of the United States and the entire western alliance[16].

China has consistently implemented a gradualist strategy of very slow market liberalization, aimed at minimally burdensome adaptation to global economic changes and attaining maximum competitiveness of national producers in foreign markets. As a result, crisis perturbations in the course of world economic development at the end of the 90s almost did not seriously touch the Chinese economy. The successful radical technological transformation in the existing "mixed" institutional environment was also quite achievable, visibly manifesting in accelerating the introduction and diffusion of advanced technological innovations in civil market sectors.

According to the generally accepted opinion, a unique demographic dividend was effectively used during the eighties and nineties[17]. The huge increase in the number of people employed in market sectors turned out to be one of the drivers of very high economic growth.

At the same time, the state of the environment has not undergone improvements in comparison with the socialist past. The negative effect of climate change had definitely seen though it had not significant influenced on the course of economic transformation.

Quite a different story - the transformation in Russia in the nineties. Here the insolvency of the institutions of liberal capitalism imported from abroad by the IMF patterns was recognized by the government with great delay only on the eve of the devastating financial crisis in August 1998, essentially resulting from the global crisis of 1997–1998. This crisis expressed in a lot of brief decline in commodity prices and a concomitant tremendous increase in loan defaults and other debt obligations, to which the Russian economy was not ready.

The result of the neoliberal stage of transformation was a dramatic decline in the resource potential of the national economy.

In a long period of radical market reform the deep crisis state of the main production sectors remained, comparable only to the state of western economies during the great depression. In parallel right up to the 1998 crisis in Russia clear erosion of high technologies and over simplification of the technological base on whole took place.

Besides, without any exaggeration, the costs usually called social were enormous. They directly manifested themselves in the expansion of the poverty zone and the increase in its absolute level, a sharp decrease in the average life expectancy and expanding the incidence of serious diseases.

The demographic failure also turn out very harmful. It had complemented by adverse environmental changes in many regions and, ultimately, a strong deterioration in the state of human capital.

The initial period after the fiasco of neoliberal globalization course in above countries characterized by a cardinal increase in state intervention in all spheres of social life, especially economic. The most widely used well-known, called Keynesian, instruments of government regulation. Among them, a special role assigned to stimulating economic activity due to state investment accompanied by spreading of a holding form of corporate ownership with state participation. It is worth noting that this practice had objectively dictated by global experience of improving corporate governance institutions on the principles of vertical and horizontal integration for the sake of enhancing market competitiveness.

In fact, a specific modern model of national state capitalism had implemented. Its distinguishing feature concludes in the direction and control of key production flows from the state precisely on capitalist principles. At the same time, the institutional area of state capitalism turned out to be limited. It complemented by other institutional areas, including the inherited socialist market.

The institutional turn to state capitalism in Russia had distinguished by two main consequences. First, the activity of oil and other raw oligopolies (monopolies) has become the object of strict external corporate control by the new government. This control expressed in the strengthening of tax discipline and the application of specific methods of state interference, accompanied by organizational and personnel changes and the tightening of internal corporate control. Second, the market power of private banks has sharply decreased, and the federal and state-owned regional banks have become dominant in the main money and credit markets. As a result, the way had opened for the long-needed large-scale investments in real sectors.

Apparently, the most positive institutional innovation was the improvement of corporate governance, which had a significant macro effect. This shift took place mainly at the initiative of corporate management due to the successful debugging of legal regulations on the base of previously adopted framework laws. In a result, it became possible to harmonize the interests of the main subjects of corporate governance.

It can state that the approval of the state-capitalist mode contributed to a rapid recovery (relative to the pre-reform level) economic growth in Russia in the middle of zero. True, according to all estimates, this phenomenon was decisively explained by the increase in the prices of oil and other raw materials, coupled with an unprecedented scale of foreign lending, including shadow, at low interest rates.

In turn, in China, the establishment of state capitalism in the period 1995–2003 was a direct consequence of the corporatization of the large-scale State-Owned Enterprises (SOE) with the involvement of private capital, but with the state control retained[18]. Later, targeted restructuring had carried out, in many cases on the ground of vertical integration, in the SOE sector accompanied by the closure and sale of property of unviable monster enterprises. Actually, the state had turned into the main capitalist - the owner/manager of countless corporate share capital with the participation of private investors, both domestic and foreign.

The giant SOEs in key industries benefit from economies of scale that reduce costs at all levels, and provide a myriad of small and medium production units with inexpensive inputs that ensure competitive manufacturing conditions in the markets. China's export success had attained largely due to the cost of inputs, provided by SOEs.

TVE's cooperative enterprises sector also became an important component of the state-capitalist structure. It should be borne in mind that in a large degree TVE had incorporated into regional industrial clusters created by means of public investment and controlled by government organizations.

The possibilities of foreign economic expansion also realized thanks to direct government support and direct participation of the state in corporate business[19]. In this way, competitive advantages had achieved, in any case temporary, of corporations with state participation in comparison with ordinary private corporations in individual markets.

Consequently, the role of the state and the CPC in the process of economic coordination dramatically increased. In fact, the concept of new authoritarianism became official, in accordance with which the development of market relations should mature gradually and under the auspices of a strong, that is, still authoritarian party-state power.

In the "after liberal" period significant shifts in the social (status) structure occurred in above countries. Thus, poverty has decreased in Russia, the share of the middle class in the population has stabilized. The number of the middle bourgeoisie had relatively reduced. This cannot be said about the rich bourgeoisie which families began to prefer living abroad, placing the capital there[20]. At the same time, China had successfully adapted itself to employment in a rapidly growing private sector. In parallel a complex stratification structure had established, characterized by the polarization of the rich and the poor[21].

The transformational turn to state capitalism in the economic field explicably accompanied by the strengthening of an authoritarian political course. It had contributed, one can recognize, to the achievement of economic stability and an acceptable climate for investors, including foreign ones. In addition, on the external political arena a shift towards opposition from both countries to the course of the United States and NATO took place finally formed after the events in Yugoslavia and Libya.

At the same time, a situation of uncertainty regarding the final choice of the economic development model of both countries persisted for a long time. The following circumstance was of critical importance. The Chinese and Russian economies had faced with the need to adapt to the global capitalist order, being highly dependent on mutually complementary global financial and commodity markets. Amid the speculative boom, the capitalization of the corporate sectors in these countries had increased dramatically, with a decisive impact on state-owned corporations and corporations with significant state participation. Their multibillion-dollar assets in the form of privatized share holdings were invested in the share capital of other corporations, even in the media. As a result, the ranks of the wealthy bourgeoisie, and, to a large extent, the wealthy bureaucracy receiving capitalized revenues, had expanded considerably.

However, all this happened before the global crisis of 2008–2009. After it, the growth trend of corporate capitalization soon weakened, as so as the dependence on the global stock market and foreign investment flows. The situation in the internal economic space had fundamentally changed in terms of the unconditional transformation of the state into the main coordinator and investor.

The result is logical: in general, the trend of institutional divergence in the considered after socialist countries has changed to the opposite - the trend of convergence[22].

3. THE PRESENT STAGE OF AFTER SOCIALIST TRANSFORMATION

First, turn to the current economic transformation of China. Some researchers, until recently, expressed the opinion that the Chinese economy would inevitably come closer to the existing economies of western countries. They proceeded from formal indicators - the share of private capital in total financial assets and the share of income of rich families. The distribution of property in key sectors, as well as the mechanisms for regulating the movement of resources, which were in the hands of the state and simultaneously the CPC, had not taken into account.

The phenomenon of the current Chinese state capitalism may be represent throw the positioning of the root institutions of ownership and coordination.

As known, the state-corporate sector of SOE still constitutes the skeleton of a multi-dimensional Chinese economy, predetermining the performance of other sectors, and primarily the TVE sector. Chinese corporations remain in the dominant part in public ownership: approximately 60% of their assets belonged to the state, 30% to private owners and 10% to foreign capital[23]. It is significant that the share of public ownership ceased to decrease after the last global crisis of 2007–2008.

Obviously economic coordination within the framework of the preeminent state-corporate sector and other sectors dependent on it has mainly carried out by means of institutions of state regulation. In the zone of their operation, a large private capital also is actually located since all well-known Chinese billionaires - the owners of private corporations work closely with the authorities[24].

Besides, an integral feature of the Chinese economic model concludes in a comprehensive government control of the banking system and financial markets. The huge Chinese state banks leading in world ratings play the extraordinary coordinating role in the main sectors of the Chinese economy. Simultaneously they serve as agents of the monetary and credit policy of the most powerful state of the East abroad.

From the previously mentioned, however, it does not follow to deny the weighty influence on the economic life of the socialist heritage. Significant arguments evident in favor of retaining the institutionalized attributes of market socialism.

Thus, public ownership of land and natural resources, which is a combination of state ownership at the national level and collective ownership at the local level, guarantees rural producers access to land[25]. In addition, the state now everywhere and tightly controls the minimum wage and remuneration of SOE managers, regulates the prices of everyday consumer products, monitors the implementation of the remaining targets for many commodity items, especially in pure regions.

To sum up, the channels of independent use of private capital and personal wealth remain limited. Based on the mentioned criterion of institutional dominance, the state-corporate order in conjunction with the socially market institutional order prevails. Therefore, there are weighty grounds for asserting that the economic transformation of China up to this day occurs to a decisive extent according to a specific model of the symbiosis of state capitalism and adapted market socialism.

How Productive is the Existing Root Institutional Structure in Terms of National Economic Progress?

According to the widely accepted opinion, a shift from the earlier export oriented investment pattern to the consumption-driven growth pattern has been taking place at this time[2]. The macro structural and financial balances have definitely improved[26]. Over the past few years, the supply-side reform has been carried out, which consists in getting rid of excess capacity and housing, maximally reducing unsecured loans, reducing production costs and overcoming resource imbalances. It becomes a prelude to the ongoing reforming of the root institutions.

In addition, China retains overall technological leadership in the global arena. High-tech Chinese corporations occupy the first places in the use of the latest information and a number of other technologies that will determine the appearance of the twenties economy. Along with this, the impressive growth of the green economy continues within the regional clusters in accordance with the imperatives of sustainable development[27]. True, the previously emerged environmental thrombus would not disappear (such as in Beijing).

At the same time, fundamental obstacles have arisen in the development of the Chinese economy. There has been a decline in the export advantages of the Chinese large corporate sector, previously based on cheap labor and economies of scale, with a concomitant slowdown in foreign investment in the face of the apparent aging of the population. There is also a huge regional gap, especially manifested in the west of the country with its poor peasant population.

The indicated factors limiting the development of the Chinese economy are largely explained by institutional flaws. At first place, over the economic dominance and monopolistic position of enterprises of the state-corporate sector in priority sectors thanks to the active support of the CPC. As a result, a depressive effect is induced on other sectors[28], especially on the private sector. Here, until recently, a discriminatory credit regime actually operated[29].

The adverse effect of the “accumulation” of institutions of the state capitalist and market socialist orders in the main links of the Chinese economy is also very significant. Thus, soft budget and credit restrictions, which still apply to most SOE coupled with special social benefits, make it possible to maintain excessive employment and low productivity in world standards. In a large number of industries, in terms of growth rate, it lags behind wages. In turn, many provincial cooperative enterprises are under the pressure of regional plan targets and oversight by CPC representatives on the ground and are not competitive, even in the domestic market. In general, a distinctive feature of the current Chinese economy remains the constant "split-up" of the interests of managers of corporations and enterprises under state control.

The results of the status transformation in China in the period of the tenths are definitely ambiguous. The tremendous reduction in poverty and the concomitant increase in social mobility have definitely contributed to economic progress and increased prosperity.

At the same time, researchers rightly emphasize the specificity of the phenomenon of the "middle income" trap of a large part of the employed, specialists and skilled workers in China manifested in their low interest in increasing productivity[30]. It adversely affects the results of economic transformation.

Besides, despite some reduction in the differentiation of current incomes, the trend of deepening social inequality in terms of disposable wealth persists[31]. It can intensify and pose a system threat in the approaching period of digitalization and the spread of labor-substituting technologies associated with the widening of the gap in earnings of the main qualified personnel and the "auxiliary" employees.

Undoubtedly, the processes of institutional reform struck with political constraints, to a decisive extent due to the imperious authoritarian power of the CPC. It is appropriate to highlight the absence of significant democratic changes over the past decade, despite serious manifestations of opposition sentiments, primarily in local elections. At the same time, the intensification of confrontation with the United States and other international conflicts in the current period dictates the desirability of maintaining rigid political leadership.

What is the Picture of the Institutional Transformation of the Economy of Today's Russia?

The structure of property distribution here in many respects similar to that existing in China. Formally, the share of private property in the main non-financial assets (funds) is very large (about 65%). However, in large part it belongs to leading corporations and their direct partners - banks, in turn, controlled by government departments and especially special services. In particular, the state acts as the holder of shares of military-industrial corporations, which are holding companies by organizational and financial form.

The ratio of the degree of significance of root institutions of coordination in the Russian economy also almost duplicates the Chinese pattern. Institutions of state coordination very strongly influence at the state of the corporate sector with its huge state / special-purpose assets — unconditionally leading in the Russian economy and the owners of a majority stake in a number of corporations - oligarchs - are completely loyal to the authorities (although some persons may be forced).

In parallel, the attributes of a socialized economy preserve. In fact, the socialization of employment in vast areas of low-paid and low-skilled labor takes place. In many ways, it is due to the need to employ a huge number of external and internal migrants in relatively prosperous regions (Moscow and several others).

Definitely, a revival of the socialist collective principle of wages occurs in certain types of non-profit activity in many regions. In addition, the resuscitation of cronyism's morals and the provision of well-paid jobs exclusively for "their" people in the tradition of the Soviet era is noticeable. The reproduction of the socialist distribution attributes in the market conditions has favored by at least three significant factors. Firstly, the unbelievably high proportion of people employed in low-skilled labor, in particular, as sellers in the most ordinary stores and auxiliary workers in construction. Secondly, the low payment of qualified personnel by world standards, especially in traditional market sectors. Thirdly, a huge number of external and especially internal migrants; due to their interest in any job, labor markets are fundamentally deformed.

Thus, there is a weighty reason to believe that the socialized market order is very significant in a mixed Russian economy. Truth, it performs as a trustworthy one, essentially fulfilling the stabilization role in conditions of an undeniable primacy of the state-corporate order.

In full analogy with China, it is safe to talk about the approval of the full market power of the largest corporations. In Russia, there is an over concentration of the largest corporate capital, unique for countries with a multi-dimensional economy. Thus, according to the results of a special survey in 2018, the share of capital of 100 largest Russian corporations in the total capitalization of the stock market was almost 90%; in previous periods it was even higher[32]. In fact, the domestic monopolies / oligopolies through their relative companies (daughters, grandchildren, etc.) own the overwhelming majority of the capital of all other enterprises. Almost all sectors of the national economy are highly dependent on the largest economic feudal lords, who, in turn, are strictly "taken care of" by the authorities.

In Russia, the number of potentially competitive companies with the average capital by modern standards turned out to be scanty: the share of employed here is below 3%[33]. The weak presence of modern medium-sized businesses is quite naturally associated with deep imbalances in the development of Russian regions, which have greatly increased over the past few years. At least, the same applies to small businesses. The individual business sector especially deforms in ordinary regions distant from the center. Here the activity of small enterprises is under the complete control of the provincial bureaucracy and organizations of the Single Russia Party. The local economy has essentially in the pen.

The consequences of institutional "layering" - the links of state-corporate and socialized market structures in Russian economic life are also quite visible.

Thus, de-commercialization of construction activities carried out at the expense of state (municipal) investments has observed. In many cases, the economic effect of this socialized activity is quite ephemeral accompanied by the reproduction of a huge number of surplus jobs and simply a waste of resources, causing ecological damage in the spirit of the socialist era.

Generally, a very unfavorable dynamics of labor productivity in most sectors of the Russian economy reproduces[34]. As numerous case studies demonstrate, this process largely explain the current resulting trends - a modest, little tangible and, to a large extent, brown economic growth and a long-term decline in the real incomes of the population.

We have to admit that the independent entrepreneurial initiative at the regional and local levels actually suppresses. For this reason, the weak development of a green economy in Russia in most of its areas is understandable. Besides, from the side of regional and local authorities there are no weighty motivations for solving environmental problems. The unsatisfactory environmental situation persists in many areas within the largest cities (including Moscow) and a large number of industrial areas.

It can be argued, that the continuing status transformation in Russia contributes to the root institutional stagnation in the economic field[11]. Indeed, the current model of social structure in Russia definitely represents an obvious pyramid. The main part of citizens is "the lower classes", which are opposed by the elite stratum and the stratum of the rich bourgeoisie with a relatively limited middle class even in its broadest sense. As a result, the semi-poverty consumption pattern prevails meanwhile the existing zones of elite consumption are very narrow.

There is a profound "proletarianization" of society, when, by the number of the sexes, the semi-poor strata prevail over other strata, including the extremely diverse social conglomerate in the middle class. Essentially, the limited material level of the needs of the majority of Russian residents, who do not expect to achieve a high level of well-being and quality of life, has conserved. This majority deeply accustoms to a strong socialization of economic life.

As in China, the purposeful maintenance of political stability seems to have a stagnating effect on fundamental institutional transformation. In Russia, as in most Post-Soviet countries, over the past decade, the authorization of power has only increased with the formal preservation of the institutions of political democracy implanted after the collapse of the communist bloc. As is known, the functioning of authorized institutions well combines with the socialization of the labor activity of ordinary citizens.

Is the question of the imminent collapse of the existing institutional framework of the Russian economy legitimate, as was the case in the period of neoliberal development?

Apparently not. The argument is obvious: in spite of all institutional flaws, up to now the positive shifts have produced that initiate the economic progress.

One can recognize achievements in the field of technological modernization of the economy that is taking place in parallel with the implementation of programs to create new weapons and military construction. Large-scale infrastructure projects have implemented on a new technological base, the full effect of which is likely to be very weighty. The state-capitalist economy of clearly Keynesian type turned out to be quite adequate for solving these ambitious tasks.

The potential for the future development of purely civilian branches of the Russian economy, estimated at the assumption that the institutional environment remains unchanged[3], is far from being exhausted. Thus, under the conditions of the Western sanctions the experts cite many examples of successful import substitution, especially with regard to investment goods. Sufficient favorable changes are also taking place in the urban economy in relatively prosperous Russian regions, which occurred largely due to the improvement of the institutional mechanism for the implementation of infrastructure programs and projects using public-private partnerships. In addition, we cannot ignore the phenomenon of the emergence of new markets, in particular, initiated by the use of robots and artificial intelligence technologies.

Partial overcoming the demographic failure inherited from the late socialism and the nineties period contributes significantly to the preservation of long-term stability in the course of the transformation of the Russian economy. In addition, in the longer term, the effect of reducing the number of able-bodied contingents due to the aging of the population will likely be neutralized by the spread of deserted and laborsaving technologies.

It should be noted that the deterioration of the climate in some periods had a strong adverse effect on economic activity, especially in the agricultural sector and in a number of regions. However, in the last period, adaptation to climate change has been observed to a large extent due to targeted state policy.

Now it is logical to ask the question: does the previously established trend of convergence of development between China and Russia persist?

We cannot give the affirmative answer, based on a comparison of economic transformation results. The common feature of both national economies concludes in the presence of a dominant state-capitalist or state-corporate order. At the same time, the Chinese economy is deeply reformed, but the Russian one is not.

Definitely, comparing the results of status transformation reveals the significant signs of divergence. In China in recent years, there has been an increase in the relative size of the middle class, with some reduction in the proportion of the big bourgeoisie[35,36]. This is definitely not the case in Russia.

At the same time, the immanent closeness of authoritarian political regimes in China and Russia remains indisputable, to which their military-political alliance contributes. By now, the military-strategic parity of these countries relative to the United States and its closest allies has definitely achieved.

4. WHAT IS NEXT?

Of extraordinary importance for fate of the after socialist world is the further institutional choice for the transformation in China. Regarding the medium-term prospects for the development of the economy of this country, the required key institutional shift concludes in liberation the corporate sector from government dictate and reduction the public sector itself while drastically expanding the space for independent entrepreneurship, especially innovation, in accordance with the global market competitiveness and adapting technological progress during the twenties. Following the objective interpretation of the official position[37], in the foreseeable future dominating the established institutions of state capitalism is not suitable for China. The threat of the loss of national competitiveness seems too great in many progressing world markets. The same concerns the threat of further increasing social inequality, casting doubt on the ruling of the CCP.

In the coming confrontational period of world development, of course, it would be wrong to ignore the possibility of implementing the scenario of the reverse movement, at least partial, to the market socialism of the nineties. It substantially connects with the inheritance of the socialist core values and the actual predisposition of poor Chinese to the socialist ideology[38]. The main political background of this alternative is completely understandable. It consists in the preservation of the social support of the CPC in the face of the employed in the state-corporate sector, which presumes the preservation of special privileges for them.

It is appropriate to assert. The idea of a "new socialism" causes skepticism relate to real implementation without a propaganda raid. According to most experts, in the event of the abandonment of the fundamental reform of economic sectors with state participation, strengthening CPC interference and directive planning while restoring the former attributes of socialist distribution, China will lose its acquired competitive positions on the world stage. They will inevitably aggravate in the conditions of continuing tough political confrontation and the unfolding trade war with the United States. Moreover, the plans to create a modern welfare society, which necessarily supposes overcoming regional imbalances and environmental clots, will postpone indefinitely.

There are prerequisites for a much more preferable scenario of transition to a new institutional model of development instead of the current controversial model of the bizarre symbiosis of state capitalism and market socialism in China. I would like to make weighty arguments in favor of this statement.

At present, mixed-ownership reforms in commercial SOEs has implemented, aimed at improving the competitive environment[1]. According to the stated intentions, these reforms will accelerate and deepen. In practical terms, this means that the strategic restructuring of SOEs is designed to be accompanied by the transformation of their property into a mixed one. In China, judging by the statements of officials, they intend to do without frontal privatization in its traditional understanding. The sale of SOE assets expects mainly to institutional investors representing already existing holding-type corporations with mixed ownership.

As a result, the necessary conditions will arise for the approval of a model of mixed heterogeneous corporate property. One should expect the preservation of wide participation of the state as an investor and shareholder, to whom considerable dividends are paid, with a parallel increase in the presence of foreign shareholders. At the same time, by all indications, the volume of investment in the activities of restructured former SOE private non-corporate capital will be deliberately limited.

In accordance with the declared plans, a deep institutional reform of the SME sector is also expected[39]. A course has been determined to ensure the viability of individual entrepreneurs and the orientation of capital towards greater investment in small and micro enterprises.

The reform of property institutions intends to be complement by targeted changes in the structure-forming institutions of coordination.

Thus, an inalienable priority in the course of further restructuring of SOE concludes in maintaining the level of production capacity and, of course, technological potential. For this reason, it is planned to strengthen the special regulation of the stock and other financial markets in order to neutralize the speculative movement of capital. The creation of the necessary framework financial and other conditions will make it possible for the institutional mechanisms of corporate regulation, exempt from state dictate, to function effectively with respect to the reformed former SOE sector, where the mixed form of ownership will establish.

In addition, the goal of implementing long-term efficient and transparent tax mechanisms for large, medium and small businesses, regardless of their form of ownership, is quite achievable. The plan concludes in expanding the coverage of small and micro enterprises with a 50% benefit in calculating income tax with the additional provision of credit benefits. If such stimulating innovations succeed, significant expectations of steady high growth of independent entrepreneurship based on the mechanisms of self-regulation with equal coexistence with the reformed state-corporate and ordinary corporate structures will arise.

There are no less weighty reasons for the speedy adoption of new mechanisms for regulating wages and social transfers, as well as the formation of personal incomes and private wealth on a strictly legal basis. At present, as is known, wages and salaries in the SOE sector have become to regulate in a uniform manner. Probably, taxes on high incomes on a progressive scale will soon be implanted.

In the course of the new phase of reforming the Chinese economy, seemingly it will be possible to resolve the problem of shortage and replace old cadres in advanced industries through a wide influx of trained rural migrants. Therefore, the transition to a progressive distribution model will be associated with overcoming over exploitation and low earnings of migrants from rural areas.

We can assume that under favorable external circumstances, political and other, institutional reform in the indicated areas will express in fundamental system changes. The opposing institutions of state-capitalist, private capitalist and socialized property will replace by mutually complementary institutions of state, corporate and individual-group (entrepreneurial) property. In parallel, relatively equally important institutions of coordination will dominate in the economic field: state market regulation, corporate regulation, and entrepreneurial self-regulation. At the same time, the external power impact on economic life will drastically weaken, primarily from the side of the CPC.

As a result, a system transformational transition will occur, connected with overcoming the contradictory coexistence of the institutional orders of state capitalism and market socialism. A uniform root institutional order will establish, ensuring further progressive transformation of the national economy.

Within the entire social system, mutual complementing will be achieved - the complementarity of market coordination institutions and institutions of public regulation instead of their opposition. This kind of complementarity can be sustainably reproducible, subject to the full and unambiguous demarcation of the action areas of the relevant institutions. Of all the real-life models, the middle (in relation to recognizing capitalist and socialist) development paths models - the Scandinavian and Malaysian/Singapore- correspond to this condition to the greatest extent[40–42]. They distinguish by a harmonious combination of purely market institutions and welfare society institutions for all.

The necessary conditions will arise for sustainable overall social progress in China in the coming twenties period. At first place, there will be an ordinal reduction in the differentiation of income and wealth in relation to various social strata, taking into account the expected demographic dynamics. Besides, opportunities for the growth of green economy and green non-market sectors, providing a favorable social climate, and neutralizing adverse climate change based on the rational use of natural resources will improve.

In the case of overall social transformation in China towards the middle way, we can expect the emergence of a new generation of entrepreneurs with modern education and, more importantly, the approval of a powerful strata of technocrats, including managers, in the conditions of the expected technological boom in the twenties. It is reasonable to predict the dissemination of post-materialistic consciousness and post-material values, expressed in freedom of expression and quality of life within the existing society and the natural environment, among representatives of educated and wealthy strata of society.

It is impossible not to draw attention to the fact that the notion Xiaokang society, that is, "harmonious society", is a product of traditional Chinese philosophy and culture. By the middle of the century, the Chinese model is designed to become adequate, namely, the Xiaokang society, quite differentiated, on the one hand, but lacking the sharpest political, social and economic contradictions, on the other. This suggests that further substantial polarization of wealth, leading to destructive social conflicts, is unacceptable for Chinese society.

In the future, although not close, the fulfillment of the forecast of the further democratization of society, in the course of which the CCP will eventually give up its monopoly on power, seems likely. The transition to a pluralistic political regime will dramatically expand the possibilities of harmonizing the interests of various social groups, primarily the elite, middle and low-income strata.

In a result of the designated economic, status, and political transformational changes the necessary conditions will arise for the sustainable overall social development of China. The implementation of the principle of balancing the structure-forming institutional orders obviously fully meets the currently recognized imperatives of the sustainable development of society in its main directions.

In the unanimous opinion of experts, the choice of China will very seriously influence the further root institutional transformation in Russia and other Post-Soviet countries. Definitely, a rejection of the wasteful state participating in the economy and inefficient employment in the spirit of Soviet socialism, which has officially proclaimed, would contribute to a departure from the current development model of Russia. The requirement to increase the efficiency of market activity and especially investment dictates the expediency of forming a truly independent corporate sector. This outcome clearly stipulates by a reduction in the weight of the state-corporate sector in Russia due to a fundamental change in relative world oil / raw material prices.

As in China, the forming of the prevailing sector with a heterogeneous mixed share capital structure is quite realistic. The presence of the state will remain significant, but it will not interfere with corporate business initiatives.

Also in relation to the Russian economy, the need for a cardinal increase in the role of small and especially medium-sized businesses and achieving its equal position with other sectors in all regions is increasing. Without such a shift, the desired accelerated economic development of backward Russian regions and especially the resolution of their purely social and environmental problems, seem impossible.

According to all forecasts, in the event of successful restructuring of the economy in the period of digitalization of the early twenties, an ordinal increase in the number of well-paid professionals may occur. It will entail a long-awaited shift in the social structure in favor of the middle class - the most important prerequisite for a gradual transition, following China, to a more preferable institutional model of national development. Besides, many representatives of the younger generation will join the ranks of highly skilled professionals, technocrats and managers. They do not suffer from the inveterate miserableness of the older generation and are likely to be susceptible to the experience of progressive institutional transformations.

At the same time, the scenario of the desired institutional transformational transition with respect to Russia and other Post-Soviet countries that depend on it evokes great doubts. First of all, for quite a transparent reason. The current (exactly the current) authoritative establishment in Russia, represented by the chiefs of the ex-KGB and the highest federal / regional bureaucracy and the business elite allied with them, is quite satisfied with the status quo in terms of the distribution of capital and income. This establishment does not attract by the cardinal overcoming of the standard of semi-poverty, as well as the low level of quality of life in most of the Russian regions as inherited attributes of Soviet socialism, that probably would result in a consolidated public demand for democratization of state ruling.

It is reasonable to take into account also the phenomenon of the immanent conservatism of the provincial Russian bureaucracy, which continues to remain corrupt according to the old "Soviet" pattern and budget-socialized. She is quite satisfied with the preservation of the current state policy and its institutional setting in the form of bizarre state capitalism with socialist seasoning.

Semi-poor society is easier to manage; moreover, the methods of such management have long tested. Especially successful practice concerns targeted deafening of the poor, especially young people, with the help of mass media, which virtually monopolized by the authorities.

It would be wrong to completely exclude the possibility of the new privatization of the corporate sector in accordance with the private interests of its management, the remaining super-rich bourgeoisie and, of course, the power establishment. Then there will be a fundamental turn to capitalist development of a neoconservative type according to the current American model.

The implementation of such a scenario of institutional transformation in Russia, even to a partial extent, will be clear confirmation of the well-known collision. The factor of power, taking into account the presence of military-political ability to prevent "external" intervention, can suppress the factors of appropriate institutional changes, based on the criteria of economic and social progress towards sustainable development.

5. RESUME

It is appropriate to formulate the three main conclusions that follow from our research.

The first conclusion. In the period after the global crisis of 2008–2009, which questioned the viability of modern capitalism, the trend of institutional divergence largely after the socialist world changed to the opposite — the trend of institutional convergence.

The second one. Institutional transformation in China and Russia, as the after socialist countries, continues according to the symbiosis model of state capitalism and the socialized market, adapted to the external environment as a whole.

The third one, which should treat hypothetical. The required long-term progress in the countries under consideration would correspond to the transformational transition to the middle path institutional model. In the future, it seems feasible in China. At the same time in Russia, such an institutional metamorphosis seems doubtful because of the "above economic" fundamental factors.

The last maxim. The author does not seek to impose his point of view on other researchers. A relative scientific consensus concerning after socialist institutional transformation will become available in the course of further fruitful discussions.

REFERENCES

[1] China's 40 years of reform and development (1978–2018). Canberra: ANU Press.

[2] China Systematic Country Diagnostic (2017). Wash., DC: World Bank.
[3] Russia's Economy: Preserving Stability; Doubling Growth; Halving poverty. How? 2018. Russia Economic Report #40.Wash., DC: World Bank.
[4] Sombart, V. (1902). Der modern Capitalismus. Leipzig: Erste Aufl.
[5] Eucken, W. (1940). *Die Grundlagen der NatioallØkonomie*. Berlin: Springer-Verlag.
[6] Schumpeter, J. (1942). *Capitalism, Socialism and Democracy*. Floyd, Virginia: Impact Books.
[7] Kornai, J. (1992). *The Socialist System: The Political Economy of Communism*. Princeton: Princeton University Press.
[8] Voslensky, M. (1984). *Nomenclature: Anatomy of the Soviet Ruling Class*. London: The Bodley Head Ltd.
[9] Shlapentoch, V. (1989). *Public and Private Life of the Soviet People*. New York: Oxford University Press.
[10] Goldman, M. (2003). *The Piratization of Russia: Russian Reform Goes Awry*. Abingdon: Routledge.
[11] Martynov, A. (2016). System transformation of economics and society: The Russian choice (in Russian). Moscow: Lenand.
[12] Marx, K. (1990). *Capital. Volume I*. London: Penguin.
[13] Naughton, B. (2007). *The Chinese Economy. Transitions and Growth*. Cambridge, Mass. The MIT Press.
[14] Bian, Y. (2002). *Chinese Social Stratification and Social Mobility*. *Annual Reviews of Sociology*, 28: 91–116.
[15] Chow, G. (1985). *Chinese Economy*. New York: Harper & Row.
[16] Wallerstein, I. (1996). *After Liberalism*. New York: Free Press.
[17] Cai, F. and Wang, D. (2005). China's Demographic Transition: Implications for Growth. *In*: Garnaut and Song (*eds.*). *The China Boom and Its Discontents*. Canberra: Asia Pacific Press.
[18] Chavance, B. (2017). Ownership Transformation and System Change in China. Revue de la Régulation - Capitalisme, Institutions, Pouvoirs, Association Recherche et Régulation, Vol. 21.
[19] Kurlantzick, J. (2016). *State Capitalism: How the Return of Statism is Transforming the World*. New York: Oxford. University Press.
[20] Novokmet, F., Piketty, T. and Zucman, G. (2017). *From Soviets to Oligarchs: Inequality and Property in Russia, 1995–2016*. NBER working paper 23712.
[21] Lin, T. and Wu, X. (2009). The Transformation of the Chinese Class Structure, 1978–2005. *Social Transformations in Chinese Societies,* 5: 81–116.
[22] Carlsson, M., Oxenstierna, S. and Weissmann, M. (2015). *Russia and China –Study on Cooperation, Competition and Distrust.* FOI-R—4087—SE. Available online: *https://foi.se>FOI-R—4087—SE*

[23] Piketty, T., Li, Y. and Zucman, G. (2017). *Capital Accumulation, Private Property and Rising Inequality in China, 1978–2015*. NBER Working Paper No. 23368.

[24] Cendrowski Scott (2016). China's Global 500 companies are bigger than ever - and mostly state-owned. Fortune, July 22.

[25] Long, Z., Herrera, R. and Andréani, T. (2018). On the Nature of the Chinese Economic System. *Monthly Review*. New York.

[26] Zhang, L. (2016). *Rebalancing in China—Progress and Prospects*. IMF Working Paper 16/183. Wash.: IMF. Available online: *https://imf.org> issues > 2016/12/31*

[27] Weng, Q., Xu, H. and Ji, Y. (2018). Growing a green economy in China, *In: IOP Conference Series: Earth and Environmental Science,* 121(5): 052082.

[28] Batson, A. (2016). The state sector's new clothes. *China Economic Quarterly*, 20(2).

[29] China's Financial Repression: Symptoms, Consequences and Causes. *CBS Open Journals*. Available on*line: https://rauli.cbs.dk/index.php/cjas/article/viewFile/.../6152*

[30] Zhang, D. (2014). *The Mechanism of the Middle-Income Trap and Potential Factors Influencing China's Economic Growth. In Frontiers of Economics in China*, 9(3): 499–528.

[31] World Inequality Report 2018. Paris. World inequality lab. Available online: *https://wir2018.wid.world*

[32] Russia's Largest Companies by Capitalization – Results of 2018 (in Russian) 2018. Moscow. RIA rating. Available online: *https://riarating.ru> 20180130*

[33] Sector of small and medium entrepreneurship: Russia and World (in Russian) 2018. Moscow. Institute of economic growth. Available online: *http://stolypin.institute/wp-content/uploads/2018/07/issledovanie-ier-msp-27.07.18.pdf*

[34] Russian Statistical Yearbook. 2017; 2018. Moscow. Rosstat. P. 115. Available online: *http://gks.ru> doc-2017 > year > year17; http://gks.ru> doc-2018 > year > year18*

[35] Wu, X. (2018). Inequality and Social Stratification in Post-socialist China. *Annual Review of Sociology*, 3(1): 3–31.

[36] Martin, W. (2019). These are richest billionaires. Business insider. March. Available online: *https://businessinsider.com*

[37] Jinping, X. (2017). Secure a Decisive Victory in Building a Moderately Prosperous Society in All Respects and Strive for the Great Success of Socialism with Chinese Characteristics for a New Era. Beijing. The 19th National Congress of the Communist Party of China. Available online: *https://chinadaily/com.cn> China*

[38] Naughton, B. (2017). Is China Socialist? *Journal of Economic Perspectives*, 31(1): 3–24.

[39] Tax Reforms Will Strengthen Support for SME's in 2018: Ministry of Finance. 2018. China Banking News. March 7.
[40] Barth, E., Moene, K.O. and Willumsen, K. (2014). The Scandinavian model-An interpretation. *Journal of Public Economics,* 117: 60–72.
[41] New economic model for Malaysia 2010. Putrajaya. Prime's Minister's Office of Malaysia. Available online: *http: / /pmo.gov.my >NEM_Report_I*
[42] Tan, K.S. and Bhaskaran, M. (2015). The role of the state in Singapore: Pragmatism in pursuit of growth. *Singapore Economic Review*, 60(3): 1–30. Research Collection School of Economics. Available online: *http:/ /ink.library.smu.edu.sg/soe_research/1876*

15

The Best Ways to Reward Employees

ALMAS SABIR[1]*

ABSTRACT

Every company needs a strategic reward system for employees that address these four areas: compensation, benefits, recognition and appreciation. The problem with reward systems in many businesses today is twofold: They're missing one or more of these elements (usually recognition and / or appreciation), and the elements that are addressed aren't properly aligned with the company's other corporate strategies. A winning system should recognize and reward two types of employee activity-performance and behavior.In a competitive business climate, many businessmen are looking at improvements in quality while reducing costs. Meanwhile, a strong economy has resulted in a strict job market. So while small businesses need to get more from their employees, their employees are looking for more out of them. Employee reward and recognition programs are one method of motivating employees to change work habits and key behaviors to benefit a small business. This paper will highlight the outstanding performance of entrepreneurs by providing an edge to competitive corporate climate. In this paper we will also discuss how to improve, develop and implement reward program that will encourage communication between employees

[1] College of Business Administration, University of Hail, Hail, Kingdom of Saudi Arabia.
**Corresponding author:* E-mail:almas.sabir083@gmail.com

and management. When the reward is changed frequently, employees will be more surprised and the process will be more exciting. When employees are excited about rewards, they will work harder to achieve them.

Key words: Rewards, Recognition, Employees, Communication, Corporate climate, Management, Recognition and appreciation.

INTRODUCTION

Every individual is motivated by different things. Money, awards or even just public praise are all parts of motivation. In this study, I would like to dig a little deeper and look at the forms of incentive and rewards programs. Over the years that has obviously changed and companies have come up with many new ways to motivate individuals.

Sometimes, simply receiving a paycheck is not enough of an incentive to keep employees dedicated and focused. Managers must think of new ways to hold an employee's attention and interest on a project, or the company as a whole. Many companies employ motivational tactics and rewards systems, both of which have advantages and disadvantages. One of the most common ways that companies put motivation programs into action is by putting together some type of incentive system like:

- Companies use both positive reinforcement and negative reinforcement to motivate employees.
- Many managers believe that using positive motivation techniques encourages employees to produce more and better quality work.
- Companies reward their employees with both tangible goods, as well as praise.

For Example

- A sales department may offer a monthly bonus to the highest earner. Not all tangible rewards come in the form of money.
- Some companies host free lunches, or give away company gear to good workers. Many managers choose to reward their best employees by simply praising them for a job well done, or by recognizing the hardwork they put in to a project.

The most important asset to any company is its people. Keeping employees happy in the workplace can make company a stronger, unwavering force within your industry. We took a look at what companies ranked in "Fortune's annual 100 Best Companies to Work for List" are doing to retain their employees and found several fantastic ideas. While some of these examples are a little extreme and might not fit into budget, I want you to be inspired and remember that every individual wants to be recognized for their good work.

Incentives go beyond the standard benefits program. We're talking about creating the best atmosphere or employee retention. We need more than just financial rewards. "Pay raises are generally effective for three months," says Richard Bead, Vice-President of Human Resources for TELUS Corp; without further incentives, the motivation fizzles. While rewarding an employee with money is effective; money, once spent, can be forgotten. And not everyone is motivated by money, so non-financial rewards can be important alternatives.

Successful organizations understand the importance of developing a recognition and reward program to recognize the accomplishments and validate the work of their employees. These programs may be formal, offering material incentives for employees who achieve predetermined goals, or informal, providing positive feedback in the form of verbal praise. Perhaps, the most effective program is that which encompasses a range of recognition activities that reflects the unique culture of the organization.

Organizations hope to achieve a number of results through recognition and reward programs, including

- Creating a positive work environment
- Attracting and retaining employees
- Creating a culture of recognition
- Motivating and reinforcing high performance
- Increasing employee morale
- Supporting the organization's mission and values
- Encouraging loyalty.

Many employers are resistant to adopting recognition and reward programs. They tend to dismiss these programs as high-cost, "feel-good" activities with few tangible benefits to the organization and its employees. However, research suggests that recognition, ranging from verbal praise to small non-cash awards, can be a cost-effective tool to raise employee morale and lower stress, absenteeism, and turnover. Furthermore, while employees benefit from recognition programs, the organization's adopting them also tend to see increased worker productivity and performance, improved profitability, higher retention rates, and decreased costs associated with turnover. Rewarding specific behaviors that made a difference to your company is more challenging than rewarding performance, but you can overcome that obstacle by asking, "What am I compensating my employees for?" and "What are the behaviors I want to reward?" For example, are you compensating employees for coming in as early as possible and staying late, or for coming up with new ideas on how to complete their work more efficiently and effectively?

Analysis-Employee Recognition

This study has uncovered compelling evidence that there are clear differences between how men and women give and respond to recognition. While employers are currently developing schemes to appeal to all, it appears they should in fact be catering for the differing demands of men and women.

In general, women give and receive more recognition while men are more likely to give recognition in the form of a higher monetary value. Men become more engaged when there is a monetary reward involved whereas women tend to be better at just saying thank you. A total reward approach is holistic; reliance is not placed on one or two reward mechanisms operating in isolation, account is taken of every way in which people can be rewarded and obtain satisfaction through their work. The aim is to maximize the combined impact of a wide range of reward initiatives on motivation, commitment and job engagement. As Sandra O'Neal (1998) has explained: 'Total reward embraces everything that employee's value in the employment relationship'.

An equally wide definition of total reward is offered by World at Work (2000) who state that total rewards are 'all of the employer's available tools that may be used to attract, retain, motivate and satisfy employees.

Total reward, defined by Thompson (2002)
Definitions of total reward typically encompass not only traditional, quantifiable elements like salary, variable pay and benefit its, but also more intangible non-cash elements such as scope to achieve and exercise responsibility, career opportunities, learning and development, the intrinsic motivation provided by the work itself and the quality of working life provided by the organization'.

The conceptual basis of total rewards is that of configuration or 'bundling', so that different reward processes are interrelated, complementary and mutually reinforcing. Total reward 744 Rewarding People strategies are vertically integrated with business strategies, but they are also horizontally integrated with other HR strategies to achieve internal consistency.

P&MM has conducted an analysis of recognition generated and received by 30,857 employees within two large, nationwide recognition programmes in the financial services, and manufacturing sectors.

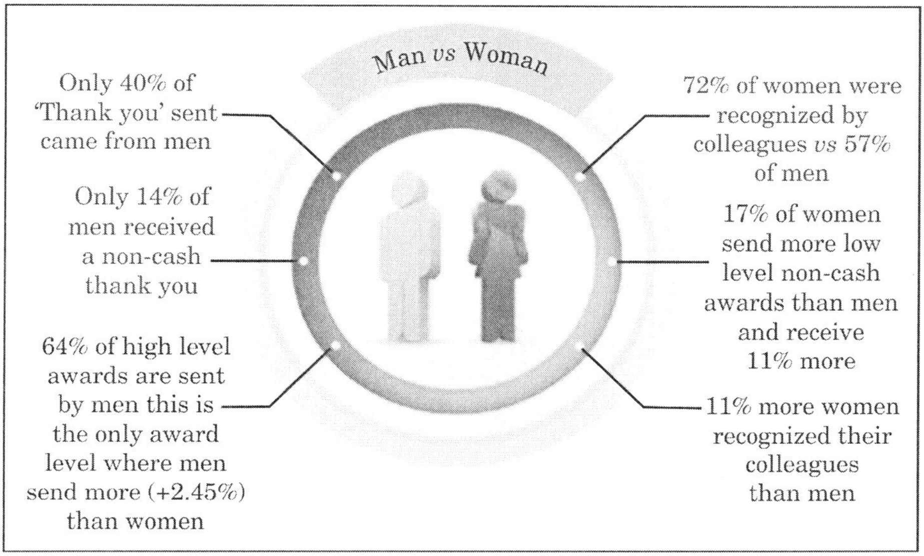

Analysis-Compensation and Incentive

With compensation contributing to the largest share of total expenses, it is imperative to ensure that total rewards programs are competitive, yet also aligned with business goals. These are the following important points that needs to be discussed:

1. Understand the rate at which direct compensation costs are increasing and how this reflects the FTE (Full-Time Equivalent) count in the business—if your costs are higher and rising faster than your competition, then you are at a cost disadvantage, which will impact profitability.
2. Identify effective cost management options by analyzing where people costs can be flexed to reduce expenses or speed up revenue creation. For example, overtime spending, budgeted salary for open hiring requisitions, forecasted bonus expenses, and costs of contingent workers are all variables that can be analyzed.
3. Understand how entries to and exits from an organization impact the total compensation expenses.

4. Move beyond total rewards and consider your total cost of workforce—including taxes, long-term incentives, facilities, contingent labor, and other costs—to accurately plan for the future.
5. Improve productivity by implementing employee incentive programs that recognize and reward top performers.

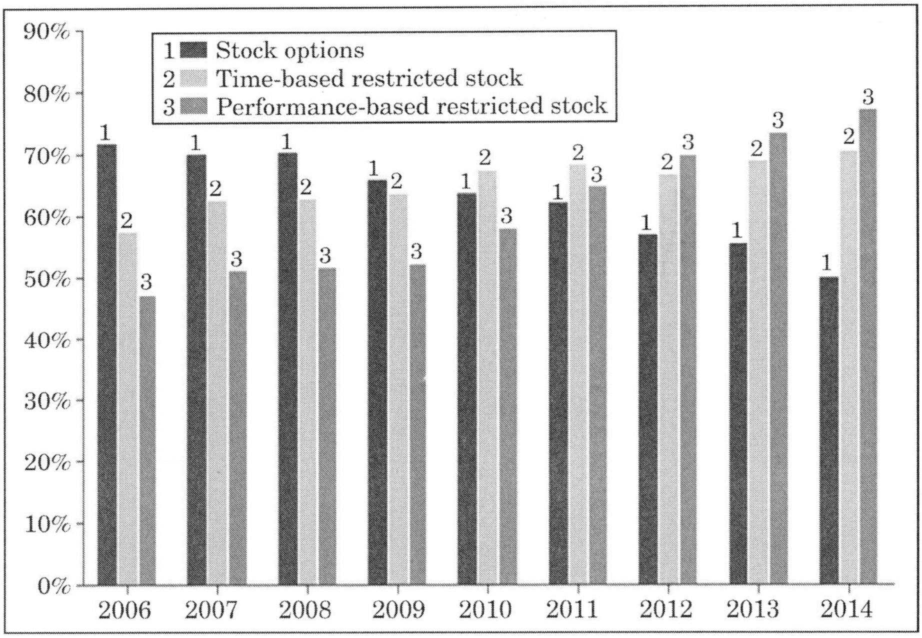

Percentage of companies offering each type of incentive, 2006–14.

The percentage of companies offering stock options to top executives has declined from 72 percent to 50 percent since 2006, while the share offering performance-based restricted stock has grown from 48 percent to77 percent. The share of companies offering time-based restricted stock grew from 58 percent to 70 percent.

But Fried says a problem with options and restricted stock is that CEOs will be rewarded—or penalized—for factors beyond their control. For example, falling or rising oil prices will have a big effect on an oil company's stock price. "I would like to see something that corrects for industry effects, and some companies do that," Fried says. One way is to have options and restricted stock vest only if the company's stock price improves more than those of competitors or if it beats the S&P 500.

Others say equity-based pay encourages CEOs to manipulate the stock price. "Stock buybacks are the critical way of manipulating the market and getting your stock price up fast and cashing in on it," says William Lazonick, Co-director of the Center for Industrial Competitiveness at the University of Massachusetts, Lowell. When a company buys stock back from shareholders that reduces the number of shares on the market, automatically increasing the percentage of the company represented by each share, and thus usually hiking the price per share. Such repurchases drain money from a company's treasury that could be spent investing in its workforce, Lazonick says. "Buybacks should be illegal".

But when a firm has more cash than it can use in its current operations, buybacks are a wise move, says Murphy of the University of Southern California. "Managers have a tendency to waste that cash, and giving it back to shareholders who can invest it more productively elsewhere is a good thing.

After analyzing, I think an effective employee recognition system should be simple, immediate, and powerfully reinforcing.

We need to establish criteria for what performance or contribution constitutes reward able behavior or actions.

The five most important tips for effective recognition.

- You need to make all employees eligible for the recognition.
- The recognition must supply the employer and employee with specific information about what behaviors or actions are being rewarded and recognized.
- Anyone who then performs at the level or standard stated in the criteria receives the reward.

- The recognition should occur as close to the performance of the actions as possible, so the recognition reinforces behavior the employer wants to encourage.
- You don't want to design a process in which managers select the people to receive recognition. Employees will see this type of process forever as managerial favoritism. Or, they will talk about it in words such as, "Oh, it's your turn to get recognized this month". This is why processes that single out an individual, such as Employee of the Month, are rarely effective.

RECOMMENDATIONS

In many organizations recognition and financial reward are joined at the hip. An employee does something above and beyond and receives a gift card or a lunch with the boss; a team achieves a goal and is rewarded with a party. These rewards, however, can backfire; they tell the employee that he or she is worth *n dollars* to the organization for some level of effort. In my opinion this approach misses the point of recognition: people are motivated by more than money. People crave positive feedback, recognition they put in extra effort, acknowledgement of leaders and peers, the glow that comes with knowing an achievement has been seen, appreciated and celebrated. I love this place. But I'm also realistic as I look at ways leaders can recruit and truly nurture current and future talent.

Financial reward is a great thing, don't get me wrong, but it's not the equivalent of recognition. Let's not kid ourselves. It's a short term solution. Neither is constant praise for average work. Recognition is a key tool in employee retention programs for a reason: people need more than constructive feedback and positive affirmation. They need recognition of extra effort. They need to "feel" it. This will never go away as a basic human need.

An Effective Approach to Employee Recognition Encompasses These Key Points

***In the moment*:** As much as possible, be timely. Catch people doing exemplary work and acknowledge their efforts. Don't be knee-jerk – showing up for work on time does not count in most cases. Be specific, descriptive and measured.

***In context*:** Recognition is most effective when it's given in the context of a larger goal or business-results-focused activity.

***Random affirmations*:** Are much less meaningful than those tied to a business goal. An employee who lands a big contract by putting in the extra effort needs to know you noticed, and understands the employee's effort to ensure business success. This matters a lot.

***Appropriate in volume/scale*:** Think back to the mom in the market. Was the praise she doled out appropriate in scale and volume? Not really. Here again randomness is not your ally. Recognition should match effort and results, or it loses meaning. This is where the complexity lives.

***Authentic, not automatic*:** You have to mean it when you give employees recognition. This is my chief worry about automated recognition systems – they remove the human touch so important to effective recognition. Can we find a smart balance? Can we make social HR Tech software work?

***Tied to the employee's perception of value*:** People know when they're valued, and they should have a good idea of their value to the organization. Monetary rewards can skew this notion of value, linking it to cash when it should be linked to appreciation of extra effort and smarts. Money is appropriate much of the time, but it's not the only – or even the most effective – motivator. Treat employees as valued team members, not as numbers. Most of the time it's the best way to really recognize a valued player.

There is HR Technology that's super sexy and relevant for engagement. I'm over thinking it at the moment. This is typical as we find the most meaningful ways to innovate the future of work. I'm excited about software and social applications for rock star leaders and workplace culture. It's all good. Now we seek to connect the most relevant, human and inspiring dots.

I have many thoughts about how we, as a society and a global social leadership community, handle recognition, but I'd like to hear what's on your mind. Please weigh in and tell me what recognition means to you, and how you've successfully recognized your employees and co-workers. Leaders jump in here too. Lead the revolution. You Rock.

CONCLUSIONS

The results and discussion indicated the relevance of individual and organizational factors in influencing the value that an individual associates with recognition. This present study summarizes the major learning of the study, recommends a basic framework of recognition for organizations and indicates the implications for practice. Suggestions for future research endeavors are also made.

To conclude this study I would like to highlight certain points which is necessary to take for consideration.

1. The results of the study indicated insignificant role of individual demographic (age, sex) and functional factors (years of work experience, career stage and functional area) in determining the value of recognition for employees. That is, the value associated to recognition by employees is independent of their demographic or functional factors.
2. The employee choices as regards the delivery of recognition involved a formal setting, public forum, written form, monetary token, conferred by the senior and delivered after achievement of target. These choices were independent of individual characteristics; no differences were found across

sector and across organizations in case of employee choices as regards delivery of recognition.

3. Offering praise and recognition costs nothing, but studies indicate that it can even be as effective as giving employees a financial reward. In 2008, strategy consultancy White Water Strategies reported that being praised can have the same impact on job satisfaction as being awarded a one percent pay rise. Meanwhile, the Japanese National Institute for Psychological Sciences has investigated the neurological impact of praise, discovering that being paid a compliment activates the same part of our brain as receiving cash!

   There's little doubt that praising and recognizing the efforts and achievements of others can bring about some very positive results in the workplace. Being praised makes the recipient feel good about them and this can help to boost their performance. Praise provides the kind of positive experience or 'uplift' that can increase employees' morale, motivation and engagement, and renew their commitment to their manager and the organization. For praise to have this kind of impact, however, it needs to be delivered effectively. Only genuine achievements should be praised, and managers should ensure their feedback is constructive and specific.

The Benefits of a Total Reward Approach Are:

- ***Greater impact*:** The combined effect of the different types of rewards will make a deeper and longer-lasting impact on the motivation and commitment of people.
- ***Enhancing the employment relationship*:** The employment relationship created by a total rewards approach makes the maximum use of relational as well as transactional rewards and will therefore appeal more to individuals.
- ***Flexibility to meet individual needs*:** As pointed out by Milkovich and Bloom (1998): 'Relational rewards may bind

individuals more strongly to the organization because they can answer those special individual needs'.

- ***Talent management*:** Relational rewards help to deliver a positive psychological contract and this can serve as a differentiator in the recruitment market which is much more difficult to replicate than individual pay practices. The organization can become an 'employer of choice' and 'a great place to work' thus attracting and retaining the talented people it needs.

REFERENCES

[1] *http://www.inc.com/encyclopedia/employee-reward-and-recognition-systems.html*
[2] 20 Ways to Increase Employee Motivation Using Rewards, *www.talkdesk.com/blog*
[3] AboutEmployeeMotivationandRewardSystemsbyAmeliaJenkins, studio, *http://smallbusiness.chron.com/*
[4] Rewarding Your Employees: 15 Examples of Successful Incentives in The Corporate World.
[5] Daniel, T. and Metcalf, G. (2005). *The fundamentals of employee recognition.*
[6] *http://staffmotivationmatters.co.uk/employee-recognition-analysis*
[7] *www.experfy.com/workforce-analytics/compensation-and-incentive-analysis*
[8] *http://businessresearcher.sagepub.com/*
[9] 5 Ways Leaders Rock Employee Recognition, *http://www.forbes.com/*
[10] *http://shodhganga.inflibnet.ac.in/bitstream/10603/3354/17/17_chapter%207.pdf*
[11] *https://www.entrepreneur.com/article/75340*
[12] *https://nscpolteksby.ac.id/ebook/files/Ebook/Business%20 Administration/ARMSTRONGS%20HANDBOOK*

Subject Index

T

U

V

W

Y